BOLD
BRAVE
and
Breathless

**Reveling in Childhood's
Splendiferous Glories**

**While Facing
Disability and Loss.**

MARGARET ANNE MARY MOORE

BOLD
BRAVE
and
Breathless

**Reveling in Childhood's Splendiferous Glories
While Facing Disability and Loss**

MARGARET ANNE MARY MOORE

woodhall press

Woodhall Press | Norwalk, CT

Woodhall Press, 81 Old Saugatuck Road, Norwalk, CT 06855
WoodhallPress.com

Cover design: Jessica Dionne
Layout artist: L.J. Mucci

Library of Congress Cataloging-in-Publication Data available

ISBN 978-1-954907-95-9   (paper: alk paper)
ISBN 978-1-954907-96-6   (electronic)

First Edition
Distributed by Independent Publishers Group
(800) 888-4741

Printed in the United States of America

This is a work of creative nonfiction. All of the events in this memoir are true to the best of the author's memory. Some names and identifying features have been changed to protect the identity of certain parties. The author in no way represents any company, corporation, or brand, mentioned herein.

This book is dedicated in memory of Terrence M. Moore, my incredible father, who was taken too soon but who continues to inspire me every day by his indomitable spirit of determination and perseverance.

This book is also dedicated to my beyond-phenomenal mother, Anne Mulville Moore. I have always believed my mother to be amazing, but in writing this book, I have had the opportunity to ask her, in a more in-depth manner than I would have thought to otherwise, to tell me about the fine details of her experiences as our mother. Mom, I am astounded at the obstacles you have overcome and how you have done so with such a positive attitude. Thank you for working so hard to give me, Brian, and Sean unbelievably remarkable lives. I don't take any of it for granted.

To my brothers, Sean and Brian. Thank you for treating me as a typical little sister who needed extra help but who could still get involved in sports, games, and an endless supply of pranks.

Finally, this book is dedicated to the administration, faculty, and staff of Long Meadow Elementary School. In writing about my wonderful LMES memories as an adult, I now see the remarkable devotion you had in creating an atmosphere of acceptance and inclusion and in seeking and implementing the most effective teaching strategies and assistive technology for me. Your efforts enabled me to flourish and achieve success beyond my wildest expectations. I am so grateful for you and so proud to be a Long Meadow alumnus!

The Meaning of Life

The meaning of life is a beautiful thing!

It kind of hits you with a ping.

But what is the meaning of life?

It comes with every husband and wife and every child in the world.

The meaning of life is God put us on this planet for a reason,

To love, to learn from our mistakes, to learn about our history.

I'm so glad he put us on this planet, and you should be too!

And every night when I go to bed, I thank him,

Because things happen for a reason,

Like people dying and people crying.

And that is the meaning of life.

—Meg Moore, Long Meadow Elementary School fourth grader, 2006–07

Chapter 1

Life, Death, and the Light That Shines In Between

Open your eyes, take a deep breath, and marvel at the wonders of the world around you.

This wide-eyed, open-mouthed splendor occurs at the beginning of one's life and often at its conclusion too. It happens in the seconds, moments, and years that span between birth and death. Both consciously and subconsciously, it happens in both the minor and monumental moments throughout life. To breathe is to live. All individuals get a chance to breathe and to live, even if it is for a brief tick of the clock.

"Congratulations, Mr. and Mrs. Moore! It's a girl!"

No one really had time to celebrate this news. There was no cry erupting from my newborn body—I remained hushed as everybody around me began to shuffle into a panic.

"She's not breathing! Let's move NOW!"

I had arrived and was technically alive, but there wasn't a breath to be found in me.

When a baby is born with complications, the maternity ward staff is trained to conceal the magnitude of the crisis from the parents. They are instructed to hide their own emotions under their crisp, white surgical masks; to keep them locked away under their scrubs, in the crack of their breaking hearts. They work fast and furiously to try to save the child's life, but they do not let on that their rapid efforts have a very slim chance of success. They put on a brave demeanor for the parents, but the level of crisis is easily detected through the instructions they shout to one another.

"We need assistance in here," the staff members screamed into the sterile hospital corridor. "Assistance! Now!"

I was born at Saint Mary's Hospital in Waterbury, Connecticut, on February 16, 1997, at 2:58 in the afternoon, just as the next shift of medical staff was preparing to clock in. They quickly jumped into action, assisting the original staff with what had begun as a normal birth now transformed into a Code Red situation. As my delivery was taking place, my umbilical cord prolapsed. I lost a critical five minutes of oxygen as a result, and the chances of my survival were increasingly slimming.

There was no time for my parents, Anne and Terrence ("Terry")—Mom and Da—to cradle me in their loving arms for the first time. My parents didn't even have a chance to register reactions. Everything was moving so fast as staff hustled to get the flow of manufactured oxygen to rush through my airways before it was too late—if it wasn't already too late. The doctors whisked me past my parents, purposely passing my mom's bedside to give her a glimpse of me, and into an incubator.

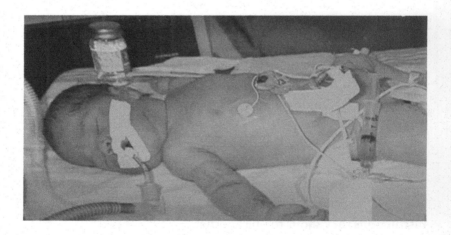

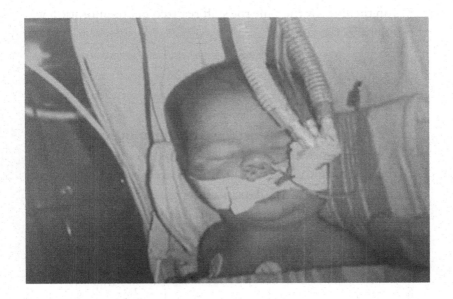

My mother had always had an impeccable sense of intuition. She could feel it within her heart when loved ones were going to have significant health complications, even before a diagnosis was given. It was as if an alarm blared inside her, rattling her soul, sending her thoughts about the loved one she later found out was in distress.

In the moments before giving birth, she had a feeling the pregnancy had taken an unexpected turn. She knew something potentially dire was going to impact her baby and maybe even herself. Where was the doctor? Had he seriously left the hospital to travel across the city to the other hospital? The other medical personnel assured her that everything looked good, but her instincts were telling her they were wrong. Just as they had when the doctors had listened to my heartbeat in her womb and predicted, without confirming on the ultrasound per her desire to leave my gender a surprise, that she was carrying a little boy and not a girl. But what was now occurring was more critical than debating a baby's gender—this was about my life being on the line. By the time the staff realized her premonition was correct, it was too late.

⌒◯⌒

When the Saint Mary's staff had done everything they possibly could to save my life, a priest arrived to give me last rites.

Baptism, though, must come before last rites, even when the clock is running low on minutes. Baptism should be a joyous occasion for all present. It is the child's initiation into faith, the seed enabling him or her to one day grow in and with their spirituality, the gateway to the sacraments, and the moment when he or she is blessed with one of life's most beautiful gifts. It typically takes place in a church before family and friends, beaming as they shift themselves to catch a glimpse of the baby in a crisp, white gown releasing a squeal as the holy water cascades over the little bald head. In normal circumstances, the family gazes at the baby with warmth and delight.

Around the time I was baptized and given last rites, a staff member snapped a picture of my parents and me. This person thought it would be a nice keepsake for my family—something for them to remember what I looked like. No matter what happened, this picture would live on.

This picture is nothing like the typical photos taken at a child's birth. There are no smiles, balloons, or cute little blankets. I am not in the comfort of my parents' arms; my mother is not looking down at me with delighted eyes. Instead, I am lying down on some sort of hospital bed. White and clear tubes are protruding from the white mask on my mouth, and they are connected to two thick tubes—one is white, the other a shade darker than my father's robin's egg–blue collared shirt. Behind me, the tubes intertwine with thinner, clear tubes, and all are connected to a gray machine behind the right side of my body.

Aside from my tangle of tubes, the most striking feature is my mother's appearance. Her pale arm and hand, accessorized by the gold ring on her finger, are extended to hold my hand, her fingers completely enveloping it. Thick, black eyelashes frame the whites of her eyes, which have reddened to practically match the color of an emergency room sign—it is rare to see eyes so red and raw. The tears have caused her ordinarily fair-skinned face to burn into a vibrant shade brighter than the auburn curls that frame her face.

In the space between us is my father, looking straight into the camera. At first glance, he looks to be putting on a brave face; his tan face, framed by nothing but his chemo-induced baldness, holds a simply serious expression. A closer look reveals the raw reality. His eyebrows are peaked above the thin brown rims of the glasses he wears, and one can see the pool of tears welled up in his eyes.

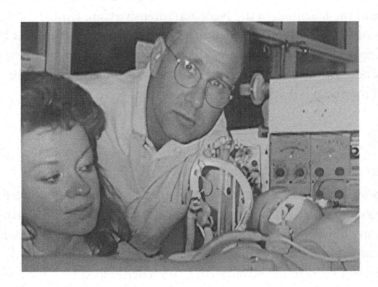

⤬

This was the only time my parents had with me that day. When the staff had exhausted all their efforts, a doctor who had connections at Yale-New Haven Hospital recommended that I be transported there.

⤬

"I've phoned the Mother House," Sister Rita Corley, Saint Mary's head of pastoral care, told my parents after I was sent to Yale. "She's been put on the prayer line."

As prayers started to rise throughout my family, on my grandmothers' prayer lines, among the nuns in Waterbury, at the Mother House—the heart of spiritual headquarters in Montreal, Canada—and in many more locations, I was being hooked up to countless breathing machines in the Neonatal Intensive Care Unit.

My parents were informed that I wouldn't survive the night but weren't allowed to spend any of those precious last moments with me because the doctors were still hard at work on my newborn body. All they could do was wait, hope, and pray.

⤬

My mom was graced with the presence of almost all the nuns in Saint Mary's Hospital, who did their best to comfort her after my departure. As my mother knew many of them personally from Notre Dame Academy, her Catholic high school alma mater, and from my dad's frequent visits to the hospital, their presence helped tremendously.

Of course they couldn't stay with her all night. My mother found herself in a room in Saint Mary's maternity ward, trying to cope with the stabbing pain of heartache slicing through her entire being every time she heard a newborn's first cry from down the hall. She knew what it was like to experience the sheer joy of holding one's own child for the first time—a feeling that had captured her heart in 1992 with my brother Sean and again in 1993 with my brother Brian. As she lay in the hospital without her newborn daughter on that February night, all she could feel was the thousand-pound burden of not knowing whether she would be bringing me home or planning a funeral.

"I couldn't even tell the boys she might not make it," my dad told her over the phone that night. "I just couldn't."

"Sure, give *me* the dirty work," she replied with a hint of somber laughter.

She understood, though. Da was coping with his stomach cancer diagnosis so bravely, but she knew that his health and my situation were taking their toll on him in more ways than one. She just didn't know how either of them would give my brothers the news when and if it came to that.

Mom knew there was a good chance she would have to formulate those words, though; the doctors were almost certain of it because of my complete dependence on ventilators. Some staff members seemed to already be mourning, looking down at me and thinking about all the joys in life that I would miss out on.

I would never know the outside world—the closest I had and would ever come was transferring between hospitals and the ambulance. I would never know what it was like to have my lungs inflate with the world's sweet air. I would never know what it was like to be held by my parents or play and laugh with my brothers—I would most likely not even meet my brothers. I would never see relationships with family and friends bud and blossom. I would miss my opportunity to live life to the full.

My parents had not yet learned that they should expect the unexpected from me. They did not know that my prolapsed cord was only the first of many surprises I would bring, but they caught on when they received the phone call the next morning.

"We have no explanation for this," medical personnel told them, "but she seems to have made a miraculous recovery! We'll need to set up a meeting to make plans for her discharge."

No medical or scientific explanation accounts for my sudden capacity to breathe independently. Some might find this unsettling, even annoying, but I find it comforting, as it affirms the beliefs I inherited from my family. I had entered the world without a breath in my body; I had shown signs of a failed battle and, by the grace of God, had lived.

Chapter 2

The Shoes of Hercules

I remained in Yale–New Haven Hospital for about two more weeks as staff scrutinized me to confirm my good health.

Later in my life, I realized how this had impacted my family. Mom and Da were very hands-on, wanting, like most parents, to be with their children at every stage of life. They both managed to be by my side at Yale–New Haven. It was not easy for them to visit me, though. With our family life, it took some creativity.

Just over a year before my birth, Da had been diagnosed with a rare form of stomach cancer. While he was receiving most of his care at home, there were periods when the illness stormed his body at full force, sending him for a stay at Saint Mary's for days on end. He and Mom believed in the importance of being there for their children, though; they couldn't stand the thought of the boys proceeding through the stages of childhood without access to either of our parents, even when medical conditions were at their worst.

This inspired our mother to carefully craft her routine so that she could be there for us all. Having been laid off from her project management job when her company was bought out in the early stages of her pregnancy with me, she had become a stay-at-home mom, concluding that it might be better to leave herself available for the family and the medical needs. When Da was hospitalized, she rose with each day's sun to get the boys fed, dressed, and off to school. She then drove to visit me, finding me among the room full of premature babies in Yale's NICU.

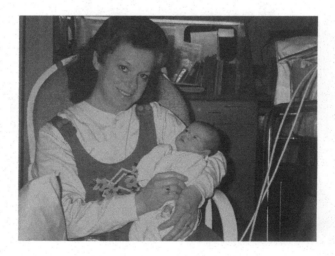

"You looked so big in there—like a giant," she told me later in my life. "The other babies were *so* little, and then there you were—full-term and full-sized."

She had named me Margaret Anne, blurting my first and middle name out on the day of my birth, despite the shock that enveloped her as I was whisked past her bedside. Margaret was for my great-great-grandmother; Anne was my mom's first name. Hearing the medical staff call me Margaret, my parents decided that name was too formal for a baby, so they nicknamed me Meg.

After getting her Meg-fix for the day, she headed back to Waterbury to pick up the boys, stopping by Saint Mary's if Da was well enough for a visit with the three of them. She then brought my brothers home so she could make them dinner, help with homework, and put them to bed herself. Believing they would drift off to sleep better, she never wanted my brothers to be tucked in by someone other than her or Da.

By the time my brothers had fallen asleep, Mom's cousin Shirley would arrive, offering greetings in hushed tones before Mom returned to Saint Mary's. Visiting hours would be over, but my mother knew the staff well enough to get special permission to spend a few extra hours with Da.

Mom was doing the impossible—she had found a way to be there for us all. Later on, she made it sound effortless. Of course she was home by midnight to relieve Shirley. Of course she turned in after a long day and was back up with the sun to do it all over again. This was the only way to see all of us, and that was what she wanted most.

❧

Mom also knew this routine had an expiration date. When I was deemed well enough, I was transported back to Saint Mary's, about two miles from our family home, and examined by local doctors. Scans showed a dark area on my brain—a permanent scar from the deprivation of oxygen—indicating a disability. It wasn't yet determined how severe it would be, how much it would impact my life, or even what it was. As I was otherwise healthy, I was free to go home to build a life with my family.

"I think you have an angel with you," Sister Rita Corley, the head of pastoral care, told my parents when she saw me return to Saint Mary's alive and well.

My parents smiled, agreeing that I had been revived by an act of God.

❧

At Saint Mary's, my parents eagerly awaited my arrival with my older brothers, Sean and Brian. Sean, four years old, brunette with chocolate brown eyes and a naturally tan complexion, and Brian, three years old, brunette with bright hazel eyes like Mom's and fair skin stippled with freckles, were excited to meet their new sister. With "Welcome to the World" gifts—stuffed animals—in hand, they finally took their first look at me.

After my birth and recovery, my parents had simply told them that I had to stay in the hospital longer than expected. Mom and Da were not trying to protect them from the reality of my disability. There was not a diagnosis to explain at this point. I'm sure Sean and Brian didn't know what to think. I was their new baby sister, and with the muscle stiffness that left my right arm rigid as a board at my side and my floppy posture among other symptoms, it was clear that I had some sort of disability. This was not in the package description, but our parents immediately began to teach them that I should be treated with respect, just like everybody else.

We later met other families who had children with disabilities. Some parents kept the able-bodied siblings at a distance from the child with the disability. Telling us about the experience as adults, these children grew up wanting, but not having an opportunity, to get to know each other. They were practically acquaintances, brought together by blood but having no close relationship. Mom and Da saw no value in this. With Da's cancer already threatening to put an expiration date on quality time with him, they valued togetherness. They began to show my brothers that while I needed extra support in my endeavors, I could interact with them like an average kid. While this was the gateway to a life of being subjected to my brothers' pranks (luckily, I was quick to learn that there was a little thing called payback), fostering this bond between us was one of the greatest gifts our parents gave me.

The truth was, though, my parents had no idea what to say or expect. Mom had thrown the baby book straight into the trash when she learned of my homecoming. *What to Expect the First Year* was now useless to her, its pages narrating a story of stages I may never meet. My mother was not hopeless, though—there were no tears streaming down as she watched the voluminous book sink to the bottom of the pail with a *thunk*.

Later in my life, I observed new parents cradling their babies and noticed how they seemed to glow with love while peering down at the child. In my early adulthood, I witnessed from a distance two new parents cradling their first baby. It was hard to overlook the way their joy was muted like rain falling from sunny skies.

"Didn't you hear?" a friend asked my mother and me. "Down syndrome. They had no idea. They're devastated."

Hours later, I remarked privately to my mother how it seemed they had already assigned a death sentence to the little girl. Her heart was beating, but it appeared that the parents were already mourning the loss of a normal life for her.

"She could be high functioning," I said.

"I know; it's sad," my mother sighed. "Parents have this thought in their heads that the child is going to come and everything is going to be perfect; then, when it's not, they are too disappointed to see the potential."

Yes, my mother had thrown out the baby book upon learning that I would be coming home with battle scars from the war that God and I had just won over death. She had not, however, done this out of mourning of what my life could have been. She knew she should expect the unexpected—she had gleaned this from my life's first minutes. She knew I would write my own book—that I would exceed expectations.

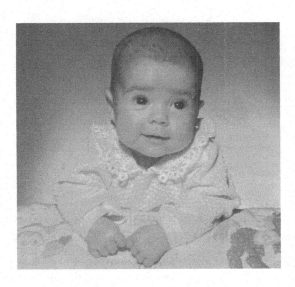

There's a story about my father and me, told to me as an adult by a family friend, Sister Pat McCarthy. Visiting us at home shortly after my birth, she sat by my father as he cradled me in his arms, perhaps gently rocking me.

Photo Credit: Anne Mulville Moore

"She's not going to have an easy life," Sister Pat remarked softly.

"Whatever the obstacle," Da replied without hesitation, "we will overcome it."

This is likely the best depiction of the philosophy that both my parents adopted in coping with my disability.

16

I don't know how I was this blessed, to have two parents who approached the obstacles of my life with such a spirit of perseverance and optimism. They were determined to raise me as a normal kid, embracing my challenges without letting them bar my enjoyment of life's pleasures.

Perhaps it was my mother's father, James Mulville ("Grampy"), who had inspired her. He had passed away when my oldest brother, Sean, was an infant. My grandfather had to take a permanent leave of disability from work when Mom was two years old, and she grew up watching him continue to lead a normal life despite a nasty fall on icy concrete steps on his way to church slowing him up.

Perhaps my father was inspired by his own life. He had been a magnet for childhood disease in his early years, had been given last rites due to complications with colitis at twenty, and, about two decades later, was facing a rare form of stomach cancer. He refused to succumb to the threat of the disease. He rose each day with the sun, carried on with his career, and continued to enjoy fatherhood. My parents never gave up—a common quality they shared and passed on to me. This is perhaps the greatest gift they could have given.

∼✑〜

My brothers and I soon became close. They seemed to enjoy helping take care of me, even taking turns feeding me my bottle. They both sat by my side, and whoever wasn't feeding me eagerly reminded the other that it was almost his turn.

"Okay, dude," Sean would say. "One more minute, and then it's my turn."

"How about five?" Brian asked, removing the bottle from my mouth to turn to him.

"One," Sean insisted.

17

Once I was old enough to speak, I interjected like the referee of a sports game. My days of being bottle-fed had faded into the past by then, but I still needed—and would always need—help bringing a cup to my mouth.

"Can I have my drink now?" I asked. "I'm thirsty."

Our eyes met one another's before our laughter began, rumbling through our bodies. This sort of easy laughter meandered through the normal childhood our parents worked so hard to give us.

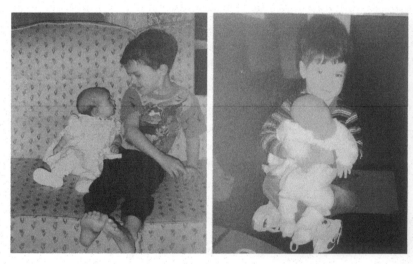

Photo Credit: Anne Mulville Moore

As normal as our parents made our childhood seem, we had to face the reality that medical conditions played a big part in our lives. Each weekday brought house calls, starting with my therapists around 7:00 a.m. and followed by Da's visiting nurses about an hour later. Holy Cross High School students also came regularly. Mom had heard that Da's alma mater was seeking community service opportunities for students and had called to inquire.

"Some people say they have a lot on their plate. I have the full banquet table—a husband with cancer, two toddlers, and a newborn with a disability," she told the school administration.

Even decades later, my mother still talked about the kind and helpful demeanor of the girls whose community service projects focused on lending a hand to our family. They helped with basic tasks—grocery shopping, playing with my brothers and me, and being the extra set of hands for outings—but their support was instrumental in easing the chaos of our medical-centered household.

Before I even arrived home for the very first time about three weeks after my birth, a therapist was at the house, preparing to give me my first therapy session immediately upon my entry. Home therapy continued through to my third year; after that, my parents had to bring me to outpatient clinics each week. Although nobody was yet sure what disability I had, it was certain that therapeutic treatment was necessary, as my muscles were significantly weaker than those of an average newborn. The stiffness of my right arm, amidst other weaknesses and tightness of muscles throughout my body, had the potential of improvement through exercises and stretches. Therapy would increase the functionality of my muscles, helping me complete simple, everyday tasks.

At six months, I was diagnosed with cerebral palsy. CP is a motor disability caused by prolapsed umbilical cords, lack of oxygen at birth, and abnormal brain development. It causes muscle weakness and affects speech; the ability to walk, stand, and sit independently; and sometimes impairs cognition. Cases can be severe, moderate, or hardly noticeable.

Cerebral palsy serves as an umbrella term for many smaller diagnoses specific to certain muscle groups. I had athetoid cerebral palsy with dystonia and chorea, which explain the rigidity of my movements. I also had dysarthria and dysphasia, which describe the weakness of the muscles in my mouth and the reason my speech would be significantly unintelligible.

Although it couldn't be determined how severe my case would be (my parents were clued in that the CP did not affect my cognitive state when I began to attempt to roll over, to go through all the typical baby stages, though), it was certain that I needed assistance with feeding, dressing, bathing, and transferring to and from equipment and furniture. I would always need both physical and occupational therapy.

Having begun at just a few weeks old, physical, occupational, and speech therapies are in my memory without a start date; they seem to have always been normal and part of my life. While we all have days when we lack energy for our life's routine, I never disliked therapy. My family members enjoyed staying physically active, and this was one of the most effective means for me to do so.

Physical therapy (PT) focuses more on stretching and strengthening the core and lower body, working on standing, walking, balance, sitting, and more. I grew up working with physical therapists and knowing the meaning of the phrase "it hurts so good." Pain is not what I experienced in PT. It was the burning sensation of stretching that best describes it.

My hamstrings were my biggest problem; the bands running down the back of my legs to my ankles were too tight to allow me to fully extend my legs. Their tightness prevented me from walking and standing on my own, but their elasticity presented the hope of gaining flexibility with stretching. The physical therapists—and my family at times—placed one hand on my knee and the other behind my ankle. Gently pushing my knee down and pulling my ankle up, they ignited a burning sensation that ran down the back of my leg.

I squirmed for the duration of the stretch. It made me slide out of my comfort zone just a little, yet it relieved me of the stiffness that came from sitting for longer periods of time than able-bodied people.

My PTs used various pieces of equipment. Beginning when I was just a few weeks old, they sat me on a padded bench, probably no more than a foot high, to correct my posture, nudging my side to center my position as they encouraged me to hold my trunk muscles tight to keep my otherwise floppy posture upright. They would smile at me, encouraging me to use my muscles just a little longer.

"Come on, just five more seconds. You've got this! Keep holding it!"

The turquoise padded top was always cool to the touch as I pushed my fists into it. Just as fatigue began to shake my strength, burning a fire in my muscles, the PTs would tell me to relax and would catch me as my body lost its position, slightly resembling a ragdoll.

"Nice job, Meg! Let's relax for a moment."

PTs and occupational therapists (OTs) often put me on a huge therapy ball to strengthen my core muscles and increase my ability to balance myself. Sitting me on top of the ball, they would gently bounce and roll it beneath me, encouraging me to tighten my abdominal muscles to stay upright. My hands fell to my sides, pushing into the ball's squishy surface as I fought against gravity to keep myself upright. My hands would lie on the grooved rubber surface, walking down the grooves as the therapists had me push myself up on my elbows. As a child, pushing myself up was hard. To distract myself from the burning sensation in my biceps, I studied the ball—how it always had a scent of plastic and how it made a soft *ping* sound if I slapped my hand down just hard enough.

Some exercises and stretching had to be repeated every few hours for substantial results. Trained by my therapists, my mother and father (when he was well enough and home from the hospital) guided me through range-of-motion exercises—rotating and lifting my arm from my side, straight up, and back down, gradually increasing my

21

flexibility. They even took turns stepping out of bed, walking across their bedroom to my crib in the middle of the night to do this with me—a total labor of love. When my therapists came, they continued with this and other routines.

My father often sat me on our living room floor and planted himself next to me, holding my torso in an upright position. Still maintaining a secure hold on me, he gently reduced his grasp to try to encourage me to hold myself up. I smiled as an adult hearing these stories from my mother, and I can imagine my father beaming down at me as he did this. Perhaps he made a silly face, giving a little gasp and feigning surprise when he caught my torso as it swayed and toppled into him. Perhaps he caught me as my balance gave way, enveloping me in his arms and gently easing us backward so he could bounce and play with me as I sat on his lap. I imagine us both giggling—an incredible sense of humor was his claim to fame among family and friends—and as a bubbly character who from an early age often couldn't stop laughing at simple humor, I'm sure I found my dad hilarious, even in his efforts to train my balance.

Photo Credit: Anne Mulville Moore

It wasn't all lighthearted play and laughter of course. While conventional occupational therapy focuses on the upper body and everyday actions—dressing and undressing oneself, handwriting, and more—my OT during my early childhood focused less on those activities of daily life that my parents would take care of and more on developing the basic movements I would eventually need to be able to accomplish these actions myself.

OTs would place a foam board in front of me and have me pull plastic pegs of all colors—purple, blue, green, red, yellow, and orange—out of the holes that pierced its surface. For the first few years of my life, I was ambidextrous and could do this easily with both hands, pulling on the wide, almost fist-size top of the peg until it came free, making a *thunk* sound as it exited the hole. The therapists commended me, bending to pick up the stray pegs that rolled off the table as I added more to the pile of loose pegs. Rolling them toward me, they instructed me to put them back in the board, stabilizing my hand as I pushed the pegs into the holes.

They colored with me to strengthen my fine motor skills, hand-over-hand or having me scribble across the paper on my own as they held the page down. While still pleasurable, coloring was at first exhausting; my hand burned with fatigue as I dragged the crayon across the page repeatedly in my early childhood. My movements always brought the crayon to the wrong side of the picture outline, making jagged spikes of color outside the lines. This lessened over time.

Though I noticed that my coloring pages didn't resemble the carefully filled in, not-a-bit-of-crayon-outside-the-lines masterpieces my peers created growing up, I don't think it bothered me. My parents always fostered an environment in which even the smallest acts—making a new craft with a particularly creative appearance, completing or moving toward completing a project without anybody assisting me—were celebrated enthusiastically as meritorious achievements. Just as my family praised it, I always found a reason to take pride in my work. I did find, though, that seeing those jagged spikes of color made me want to better my fine motor skills so that my pictures could resemble the designs I had envisioned in my mind.

OTs often collaborated with speech therapists to develop the best strategies for feeding me. The OTs made sure I was seated in correct posture, with my head straight and level on the black padded headrest of my bubblegum-pink manual wheelchair, my elbows at right angles on my clear plastic tray and my legs straight on the black metal footrest.

My speech therapist showed my parents how to feed me—how to help me learn to activate the muscles in my mouth to be able to process my food. My weak muscles did not permit my tongue to easily move from side to side. Therapists taught my parents how to train my tongue, bringing food from one side of my mouth to the other to entice my tongue to move more normally.

Speech therapists increased their range of services for me as I grew older. When I was around twelve months old, I tried to verbalize. Because of my weak muscles, my words sounded garbled, almost unintelligible. Later in life, I was introduced to technology that helped me articulate my words clearly for all the world to hear. It changed my life and set me on a path leading to great success. However, my family and therapists didn't want to wait that long to learn my thoughts. When my first words emerged, they learned to hear the coherent thoughts that hid behind the unintelligible tones emerging from my mouth. They grew accustomed to the way my body formed language. After a while of spending time with me, their ears learned to decipher my sounds, translating them into the bright thoughts that flashed across my unimpaired mind.

Speech therapists asked me questions during sessions to elicit verbal responses.

"If you didn't know me, how might you say hi?" they inquired, smiling.

"Hi," I pushed out of my mouth, struggling to coordinate my breathing with my speech and to make my lips shape to form consonants. "I—m-my name is M-m-ah-eg . . . Eg . . . M . . . Meg."

"Good job," they exclaimed. "Can you try to put your lips together more when you make the 'M' sound? Watch me. *Meg. Meg.*"

❦

My family learned to compensate for sounds I couldn't make, developing our own little language. I could not coordinate my lips to make *B, Br, S,* or *Sh* sounds, so I unintentionally renamed Sean and Brian "aw" and "eye-yuh."

"If you hear her call Brian 'eye-*yen*' or Sean 'aw-*n*,'" Mom often told people throughout my childhood, her voice shaking with laughter, "you know they have done something to bug her."

My family had me spell words they didn't understand, having me say the letters or reciting the alphabet themselves and asking me to stop them at the appropriate letters.

"I'm not getting it. Spell it. What does it start with? A? B? C? D? E? F?"

"Yeah, F," I would say as they prepared to restart the alphabet to get the next letters.

They were incredibly patient with this process, urging me to go on even when frustration diminished my desire to articulate my sentence.

"Just forget it," I said in these occasional moments. "It was nothing anyway."

"No, Meg," family members always replied. "I want to know what you were trying to say. Come on, what's the next letter?"

These moments would occur later in my childhood. At the time of my homecoming, though, there were plenty of other challenges to conquer.

For the most part, I really enjoyed my therapies. I loved trying new ways to be active. I was born into a family in which each member enjoyed physical activity, and I had inherited these genes. It was almost a game for me to use my theraball; I even began asking to use it during my leisure time as I grew older. Going from a kneeling position and gently lunging forward to land my stomach on the ball's squishy rubber surface as the ball slowly rolled was like having a playground ride in the comfort of my own home. My brothers and I made little games involving the theraballs and other equipment, laughing as we took turns bouncing and rolling on it. I think our parents loved the fact that I was eager to explore and exercise with my equipment.

Other parts of my therapy did not play out as pleasantly or as planned, though. I vaguely recall visits from a therapist with strategies too rough for a baby. My eyes flooded with tears as she pushed my kneecaps down too roughly and rapidly, sending the sudden, intense burn of a stretch down the back of my leg.

"This is clearly a sign of behavioral issues," the therapist told my parents.

"No, it is absolutely not," my mother replied, first to the therapist and then to the management of the therapy agency. "Meg is a happy baby and loves being with her therapists and all she meets. What is being done in PT now is too rough for her. It's to the point where she starts crying when she sees this particular PT coming. I watch her getting stretched, and it's way too much too fast. She's a baby—she needs to be handled gently."

Eventually I was removed from this therapist's caseload and placed with somebody who could improve the flexibility of my muscles while maintaining the smile on my face.

⁓

My mother also had to fight not only to get me infant-appropriate care but also to make sure the therapy itself actually happened. We endured a period in which the therapist stood us up week after week, providing less-than-legitimate reasons for last-minute cancellations.

"I was going to come," she once told my mother over the phone, "but I've decided to stay home and make my son breakfast."

Each week brought a new excuse, leaving my mother annoyed and in disbelief. She knew how vital receiving therapeutic treatment was at an early age and cringed to think of all I was missing. She also couldn't help but think about the schedule of our one-disability–one-cancer-battle–three-young-children household. She set time aside to remain available and attentive during my sessions and could have scheduled other appointments during that slot had she known the therapy was not going to happen on those days.

"What do you mean she hasn't been at your house in weeks?" the agency's management replied when my mother called to ask what was going on. "We receive her time sheet every week, and every week your daughter's treatment is listed."

❧

"I need to use your phone," the therapist said when she arrived at the house for the next appointment.

"Sure," Mom replied, letting her into the house. "Having trouble with your cell phone?"

"No," she snapped. "I now have to call the office when I get to each patient's house, and I have to do it from the patient's home phone so they can verify I'm here."

Mom remembers how strained the relationship between us and the therapist was after that, but it was all worth it to her. She knew that getting me the treatment I needed was of the utmost importance, and she hoped her complaint had stopped the therapist from doing this to other families.

Looking at this situation through adult eyes, it amazes me that people go out of their way not to do their jobs and then are angry and surprised when there are consequences. As a patient, I always wished that medical personnel better understood how much their actions impacted their patients. When they do not keep their appointments, it inhibits patients' ability to progress. In some cases, therapy appointments are the only relief from pain and stiffness, so patients really count the days to their next appointments. Fortunately, I was never a victim of chronic pain. But throughout my life, I sometimes experienced pain because of my equipment becoming out of alignment due to my growth or because of some new tightness in my muscles. Therapy really was the only relief in those situations, and when appointments were canceled, my discomfort was prolonged.

As an adult, I also realize that it must have been time-consuming for my mom to track down my therapist. This was only one part of her plate full of mothering, taking care of my father, leaving herself time to relax, and working to find the best services and assistive equipment for me.

Assistive equipment had a heavy presence in my life almost immediately after my hospital discharge, aiding me in and sometimes even enabling my ordinary as well as extraordinary endeavors.

I relied on a wheelchair to support my posture, putting me in the proper position to sit in the correct formation; to stabilize me as I ate, played, and, later, spoke and completed basic activities of life. I recall how my first wheelchair, delivered a few months after my birth, hugged my body, its pink seat back gently supporting my spine behind me and its matching seat cushion keeping my hips straight. There was a large black foam block between my thighs designed to keep my posture from slipping, and a black seat belt with a turquoise button secured me at my waist. A black headrest, shaped kind of like a mustache, supported the back of my head. A semitransparent rectangular metal plate supported my feet. Bordered on three sides by black bars, a clear plastic tray sat on my black leather armrests. Behind me, a long black handle, shaped like a golf club, protruded from underneath the chair and was the height of most people's waists. I always loved my wheels—two smoky gray tires outlined with black bars. These tires sat with their tops just below the armrests. By the footrest, two smaller black wheels rolled in all directions. I grew up seeing the value of my wheels—they helped me navigate to adventures indoors and out.

Photo Credit: Anne Mulville Moore

I was very fond of my walker early on too. My first walker was metallic silver, its metal frame surrounding three of the four sides of my body. Red plastic handles, grooved to allow a comfortable grasp, were fixed on the front ends of the frame. Pads and straps wrapped around my torso, keeping me upright and secure. My legs were free to take strides, making the small black wheels fixed to the bottom four metal bars propel as fast as I could move. I was free to run alongside my brothers just like any other kid. The walker practically gave me wings, letting me defy the stationary life that my disability tried desperately to impose on me.

I needed to wear ankle foot orthotics (AFOs), also called braces. Shaped like little booties that fit inside regular shoes, the custom-made plastic orthotics stabilized my feet and corrected the tendency for me to turn one of my feet inward and the other outward when weight-bearing. Except for times of extreme temperature, when the plastic mimicked the heat or cold outside and the times, usually at the end of the day, when my feet were tired and needed to flex freely, I hardly noticed them. They became part of my normal attire.

My first braces were a simple white plastic mold, resembling the exact shape of each of my calves and feet. Velcro straps secured them on my legs—one at the calf and another across the top of the foot. One might say they looked like Egyptian-inspired footwear.

Bringing them home from a local orthotics and prosthetics clinic, Mom put them on our dining room table and left the room. The 1997 calendars were halfway in the past by then, and Disney had released the movie *Hercules*—an animated film in which the young Greek demigod has lost his place in Mount Olympus and must earn it back. He eventually rescues and falls in love with a mortal woman named Megara, nicknamed Meg. In one scene, Meg claims that a great weakness of hers is having weak ankles.

At the time, my parents were still mulling over the best way to explain my disability and assistive equipment to Sean and Brian. Having therapists come had been no big deal—the boys were used to medical personnel coming and going because of our father. My equipment, though, was more complicated. How could our parents teach them not to be afraid to touch it and to interact with me as I used it, but also that it must be handled carefully?

Brian was already a step ahead of them. When Mom returned to the dining room, my braces were nowhere to be seen. Stunned, she looked around, certain that she had left them on the table. A soft noise under the table clued her in, and she peered beneath the tabletop.

There was Brian, attempting to try on my braces.

"Mommy," Brian began. "Why does Meg get Hercules shoes and I don't?"

This gave my mom a great laugh, and suddenly my parents weren't worried about how the boys would take my disability. They would learn by exploring my equipment, turning it over in their hands to see how it looked up-close and even what it was like to try it. Mom and Da taught them to explore with careful fingers, balancing their curiosity with the delicacy of the equipment. Little by little, they came to understand my disability and assistive technology.

As for why I get "Hercules shoes," I *am* Meg. I was in the movie—I even have the weak ankles to prove it.

❧

Medical conditions were a big part of our life, but in many ways, my baby years mirrored an average child's and were filled with the typical joys of childhood. My maternal grandmother, Frances Mary Mulville—"Grammy"—gifted me my baby blanket. She crocheted it with room for growth, the alternating rose-pink and snow-white stripes as wide as shawls. I always cherished it, a symbol of her love and faith.

Grammy offered wisdom that soothed Mom as she watched me begin a life of obstacles.

"First cancer and now a disability," Mom said to her once in a moment of emotional and physical exhaustion. "What else is going to come our way? How are we gonna do all this?"

"Count your blessings," Grammy replied.

"What?"

My mother relied on her faith to get through the best and worst of times. In my teenage years, she detailed her commitment to faith on a form requesting approval to accompany me to a youth group camp. I watched her put the pen to the page then lift it up again, her mind searching for adequate words to illustrate the intricate relationship.

"I've got it! Listen to this," she finally exclaimed. "'I *live* my faith every day.'"

Even as a teenager, I was astonished at the power of that sentence. In just a few words, my mother had provided such a comprehensive view of her spirituality. She leaned on it in hard times, letting it give her hope and inspiration to keep moving forward. She let it guide her, taking action however it called her to.

Faith was a huge part of her life, but at the time she was talking to my grandmother shortly after my birth, counting her blessings seemed like a peculiar way to deal with her stress. She wasn't quite sure what her mother meant at first.

"*Count your blessings,*" Grammy insisted again—this time more adamantly.

Mom began to see Grammy's perspective. Before my mother was born, Grammy and Grampy lost two babies. Grammy attempted to articulate what it was like to lose their son Bobby and their daughter Mary Frances. They had slipped away without much warning—technology was not yet able to detect medical complications in babies far enough in advance to save lives. My grandparents went on and had a healthy four sons and my mom, but the ache remained in their hearts. Hearing the stories again, now as a mother who had almost lost a child, renewed my mom's strength, giving her a fresh perspective.

Knowing how fortunate we were that I had survived and that Da had lived long enough to father three children, Mom took Grammy's advice to heart, often reminding my brothers and me of her words as we grew up. Because of those words, Mom always strived to make the most of our lives.

When reflecting on the first years of my life, I do not associate our home on Waterbury's Cooke Street with the health conditions. The first thoughts to come to mind are not related to the nurses and therapists who visited or the equipment inside the pastel-yellow–shingled house with the orange roof. Instead, they are about the time spent playing with my brothers in the playroom beyond the large front picture window. I recall being rolled under the archway to enter the rectangular room and peering into the toy chest—each side of hard plastic a different color: blue, green, red, and yellow. I recall sitting for hours in that cream-colored room playing with dolls, blocks, puzzles, and board games.

Among the toys with "don't leave the room or house without" status was an inflatable Jiminy Cricket. Though technically a bath toy, I insisted on practically always having it in my company.

"It was a toy we just randomly picked up for you, thinking you might like it," my mother told me later in my life. "Never did I expect this little bath pillow would become your favorite."

To this day, Jiminy's famous ballad, "When You Wish Upon a Star," remains one of my favorite songs.

Also almost always nestled in my arms was a baby doll whose plush body was covered in a taffy-pink onesie featuring illustrations of yellow ducks and white clouds. Lavender scalloped cuffs framed the apricot-colored plastic hands and face. I named her Meg and took her almost everywhere I went.

❧

I came to associate the open plan of our second floor with games of hide-and-go-seek, the dining room's oriental rug—burgundy and flowered—muffling footsteps as my family ran with me, the crystal chandelier shedding light in the corners of the dining room, the coral-red walls of the living room becoming a blur as I was carried away from the person covering their eyes as they counted to 10. I alternated between teams—joining forces with my brothers or my parents. My infant size was key—I was easy to pick up and run with. I was easy to conceal.

"They've gotta be in here," Brian said as he and Sean entered the bathroom one day.

From my spot in the laundry basket, with a soft, white bath towel draped over my head, I could see my mother tucked between the back of the door and the wall. As our eyes met, I began to come down with my classic case of the giggles, shaking as my volume grew louder and as Mom, beginning to laugh herself, placed an index finger to her mouth—an effort that was no use.

"Gotcha," Sean exclaimed as he pulled off the towel and lifted me out of the basket, joining in on the laughter as we began to leave the room.

Warm evenings were spent out on the second-floor porch that my father had screened in to make it all-season. I always remember this as a fun play space, with my dollhouse and the boys' Hot Wheels racetrack lined up along the forest-green turf our parents had used to carpet the floor. In the center hung a toddler swing made of cherry-red plastic. It was a favorite activity of mine, grasping the two ropes—two white-and-blue braids, gritty with the material's fibers, suspended from the ceiling—and laughing and feeling my stomach flip as Mom, Da, and my brothers took turns pushing me. As I grew older and reached two or three years old, the boys and I made a game out of seeing whether I could touch the tips of my sneakers to the wall of lemon-colored siding several feet in front of me. That porch hosted innumerable bouts of giggles during our childhood.

Later in my life, I heard of parents of children with disabilities sheltering their families, keeping the fun limited to the home or to settings made for accessibility. Some never ventured out without their whole extended families. Others simply wrote off outside adventures, explaining to the kids that it would be too hard to make accommodations.

Mom and Da never hesitated to take us beyond the walls of the house by themselves, walking us down the street to Fulton Park carrying partial loaves of bread. Reaching the grassy area in front of the Aegean-colored pond and opening the bags of bread, we broke the spongy white slices into small pieces and tossed them to the ducks. Stationing ourselves there, we would look out at the fountain in the pond's center, mesmerized by the water that rose and elegantly cascaded back down. This was our little oasis—a soothing setting where we could go after long days of appointments, school, and treatments to soak up the sunlight and fresh air.

Photo Credit: Terrence M. Moore

Photo Credit: Anne Mulville Moore

My father's cancer was like a tether at times, though, allowing him to remain active yet limiting his endeavors. He and Mom wanted to take us on vacation, but it was often too much of a risk—with his rare cancer, he needed quick access to his specialists if a complication arose.

They found the perfect solution, and most of our summer days were spent at the Lake Quassy Outing Club in Middlebury—a small town that neighbored Waterbury. My parents would sit behind me on the beach, supporting my back as I constructed castles out of the sunbaked sand, scooping it into pails first with a shovel and then, tossing the shovel aside and grasping handfuls of the tan grains, letting them rain into the bucket before my family flipped it over. Supported by my family, I would rise and run into the cool water, splashing in the waves.

Photo Credit: Anne Mulville Moore

Da liked to stand me with his arms under mine and wade into the waves, dipping my toes into their cool surface. As my mother retold these stories to me as an adult, a beautiful image came to my mind. I imagine my dad holding my arms tight enough to support my posture but loose enough to be flexible and allow me to swoop down into the water and back up again. Laughter undoubtedly filled my body as it always did throughout life when I suddenly encountered the sensation of being lifted or put down to meet the cold shock of water or other unique textures and conditions. I'm sure my dad chuckled with me, watching how the lake never lost its novelty no matter how many times my feet plunged into it.

My parents would lay me down on a blanket in the grass next to my friend Sydney, who was a month younger. Though it is natural for babies to nap in public, it became a unique scene when grown men followed our lead. When his cancer symptoms made him feel slightly sick, Da laid down next to me. Sydney's dad, simply tired, would come nap next to her.

"I don't know what it is about that area," Fran McDonald, a regular at the lake, always laughed. "But everybody who goes over there falls asleep. Watch out if you're going by."

Laughing, Mom and our friends made light of Da's condition. For a little while, he was simply the goofy dad napping with his baby. For a little while, the cancer was not the focus.

The cancer was sometimes tame enough for us to leave the city and get away to Da's favorite vacation spot, where he had spent summers of his youth with his parents, Edwin and Bernice—Pop and Nanna—and his three sisters and four brothers. Watch Hill, Rhode Island, was the go-to spot and quickly became the favorite place for Mom, my brothers, and me.

Our days were spent in The Village, window-shopping as we passed the two strips of little shops lining the narrow street. Running from ceiling to floor, the windows housed collages of souvenir T-shirts and sweatshirts folded in squares to show only Watch Hill's name.

We always stopped in the center of the strip at the ice-cream shop, St. Clair Annex, waiting in the line that coiled in front of the walk-up window and became more like a pod of people. The rich chocolate ice cream would defy the heat outside, freezing our throats in the most satisfying way as we sat on the sidewalk around a petite black-wire table.

Strolling to the end of the road, we visited Watch Hill's famous carousel. As a child, the stone hut and hand-painted horses always seemed so huge. With adult eyes, I would see that the hut was no bigger than a gazebo and that each horse was a bit larger than a dog.

I loved the carousel—the cool breeze blowing as the platform spun, my stomach flipping as the horse rose and fell, the mane of real horsehair gently dancing in the breeze, the coolness of the twisted gold bar, and the bell clanging loudly. My parents had permission to walk alongside my cream-colored horse, holding me up as it elevated and lowered me. I was like any other child, reaching out to try to catch the golden metal ring—almost wide enough to be a toddler's bracelet—which the attendant held out toward the riders using a long-handled dispenser. The dispenser contained one golden ring and many silver rings. A golden ring meant a free second ride.

The best rides, though, were not from any of Watch Hill's attractions. The best rides were those led by my father. He had bought a small sailboat before he met my mother. Da gifted me my love of the ocean, how the navy-blue bow of his boat would rock softly as it dipped and rose with the swell of each wave, how the salty sea breeze inflated the white sail on the chestnut-colored mast that practically scraped the baby-blue sky. He led us through the water, always driving the boat as a strong sailor.

He would need this strength as the wind blew him into choppy waters during the first year of my life.

Chapter 3

Anchors Away

Gone From My Sight

I am standing upon the seashore. A ship, at my side,

spreads her white sails to the moving breeze and starts

for the blue ocean. She is an object of beauty and strength.

I stand and watch her until, at length, she hangs like a speck

of white cloud just where the sea and sky come to mingle with each other.

Then, someone at my side says, "There, she is gone."

Gone where?

Gone from my sight. That is all. She is just as large in mast,

hull and spar as she was when she left my side.

And, she is just as able to bear her load of living freight to her destined port.

—Henry Van Dyke

They say I cried practically straight for two weeks, a scream echoing throughout my baby body during most of my waking hours. We lost him three weeks before my second birthday.

I didn't understand. He was with us one day and gone the next. There were all these people coming in and out, crying, smiling at me, but through their tears. Mom was the only one who really got it. She didn't walk away like the others. She sat and cradled me as I cried. I just couldn't wrap my head around it. Where did he go? Where was Da?

"This is just too much grief," friends said as they rose to leave after only a short visit.

"Welcome to my world," my mother replied with a somber smirk as she rocked me gently in her arms.

She understood, though—she knew that I missed my father just like everyone else. Da was often home, too sick to work for lengthy periods of time. For the almost two years of my life, he had been right there with me, caring for me, playing with me, and his presence was imprinted in my mind. I noticed his absence when he was gone. I noticed that he no longer appeared above my crib, grinning as he scooped me up. I noticed that he did not settle onto the couch at night with a book in his hand, leaning so that my mom, my brothers, and I could see the pictures as he read us our bedtime story. I noticed that one of the most important figures in my life was gone, and I was reacting accordingly.

Photo Credit: Anne Mulville Moore

Her eyes popped open on the morning of January 22, 1999, and rolled over the numbers on the clock near her bedside. It was between 6:00 and 6:30—right around, they believe, the time his heart stopped.

My mother's timing was always impeccable like that—her intuition would alert her when a loved one was experiencing a dire or out-of-the-ordinary situation. She sometimes picked right up on it and sensed that something was happening. Other times, she began to think of the specific individual or would arouse in some way without knowing why. In those cases—in cases like this one—it wouldn't occur to her that she felt a signal until the event had been revealed.

"We overslept," she said groggily. "Come on. We have to get moving."

He seemed to still be deep in his slumber. As if he hadn't heard her, he didn't budge. It was then that she noticed his color was already paling into a lifeless shade of white, and that his hand—the hand that would appear in her dreams for several weeks after—was hanging limply over the edge of the mattress. Stunned, my mother leaped out of bed.

She quietly walked into our sunroom, finding my brothers sitting contently engrossed in cartoons, and managed to conceal her grief for our sake.

"Okay guys," she said with a smile as if everything was normal; "time to get dressed."

As she watched them begin to stand, a thought tumbled into her head: *They always go into our bedroom to bounce on the bed and say good morning—they'll see him.*

"You know what?" she asked. "Why don't you take a few more minutes to watch cartoons?"

"Really? Okay!"

They beamed as they turned back to the TV while, under her mask of smiles, our mother tried to hold the pieces of her heart together.

47

✦

"Frank?" she urgently projected into the phone when she was out of earshot.

"Ah, well, hello Mrs. Moore. Calling awfully early this morning, aren't we?"

My father's friend, who had offered to be on call to help bring my father to appointments and hospital visits, had not yet picked up on the fact that my mom had not addressed him as "Mr. Hartnett" in her jokingly sophisticated tone as she usually did.

"Frank," she said frantically. "Frank! I–I think Terry died."

There was a momentary silence. When the shock had settled, he simply stated, "I'll be right over."

✦

Years later, Mom made light of this conversation. Here she was telling Frank that one of his best friends had just passed away and, rather than gently easing him into the news, she had blurted it out. She had also used the wording "I think" when there was no question about whether my father was living.

In the moment, though, there was no room for laughter or even time to shed the first of many tears. My mother was occupied with giving instructions to the rapidly growing crowd passing through the door—friends, including Frank, Ralph and Chris, Lew and Lois.

"I don't want the kids to see him being taken out in a body bag," she explained to the group, remembering how, even as an adult, seeing her own father being removed from her parents' home had left her scarred. "I need time to start making the arrangements too before I tell them—I want to be able to focus on helping the kids through it.

Pick a kid, get them dressed, and get them out of the house—and please don't say anything. I need to be the one to tell them."

I was scooped up by a couple who knew my parents from church. Lew and Lois Carrington had stepped forward during an early stage of my father's cancer and offered to take care of me while my parents were tied up at the hospital and appointments. Many of my days had been spent with Lois coloring, playing games, and going on outings—trips to the local library and to swimming pools in nice weather. I'm sure she never let a visit go by without giving me some of her delicious homemade chocolate pudding. Some of my earliest memories were of me smiling up at Lois, mirroring the grin that spread across her fair-skinned face framed by short golden hair. I never remember a bad day at their house or expressing a lack of desire for the visit while my mother got me ready to go. I came to view them as surrogate grandparents and maintained this feeling through adulthood. It didn't surprise me when my mother told me later in life that they were among the first people to show up at the house on the day of my father's death. Of course they were. They were always there for us.

Photo Credit: Anne Mulville Moore

Mom was relieved when they arrived—she knew I was in responsible hands and that I would be spoiled by Lew and Lois all day. Now it was just a matter of finding care for the boys.

"I'll take Brian to breakfast and drop him off at school," Ralph volunteered.

"Hey," Sean interjected, appearing in the doorway. "What about me? Don't I get to go?"

With a sad chuckle rippling through the room, Sean was invited, and the three of them soon departed, our parents' friend left to struggle with keeping his own grief at bay.

Amid the day's chaos, Mom called both boys' schools, notifying the staff of Da's passing and asking them to leave the news for her to share with the boys. Sean's teacher at Saint Mary's School later told Mom that she struggled to look at him that day and had to leave the room multiple times to drain her eyes when they could no longer hold back her tears. It broke her heart to know the reality awaiting his six-year-old self at home.

Brian's teacher at Wee Care Nursery & Daycare actually prepared my five-year-old brother to receive and cope with the news. Subtly incorporating it into her lesson, she presented the class with a metaphorical story of a goldfish (I'm sure Da would appreciate being likened to a goldfish). She told of how the fish had lived a fantastic life but one day became very sick, passed away, and was buried by his family. His family was sad for a little while but later learned that they could remember him while still enjoying life. Brian would remember this as he faced his grief at home.

In the hours between our departure and arrival back home, Mom continued to push through her grief to organize our father's arrangements—calling the funeral home; notifying family, friends, and doctors; even setting up a phone tree so the news could trickle down to abundant loved ones more efficiently.

At one point her grief began to cloud her mind. Even the strongest people have to humble themselves sometimes and give into their emotions. She wandered into our small, pastel-yellow kitchen and began to open and close our wooden cabinets, her eyes not seeing what she was looking for, not really seeing anything at all.

"Uh," her friend Chris began from the doorway. "What are you doing?"

"I have to, uh," my mother began to stammer, "make the kids lunch."

"Go sit down," Chris replied, a gentle sigh accompanying her words. "I'll get it."

My mother has faced tough situations when taking care of family and has had to develop a skin that is equally as tough. She is always the one to lend a shoulder to cry on and to pick other people up when they stumble and fall in the wake of a crisis. It is good that my mother was reminded to take some time for herself. After all, she had just lost the great love of her life.

Da was originally diagnosed with a rare form of stomach cancer in 1995, experiencing flu-like symptoms at its onset. The doctors thought he simply had the flu or a gastrointestinal bug. It was my mother who insisted that they run tests to see if there was anything else going on.

"Just humor me. Order some bloodwork—we can stop at the hospital on the way home," she pleaded with the doctor as the appointment was coming to its conclusion. "He just doesn't look right to me. Look at his coloring—he's gray."

Following his blood draw, my parents went home, only to receive a call that Da needed to return immediately for admission due to the irregularity of his lab work. His stay lasted for months, with a discharge finally emerging after the new year. When evaluating him and his unbearable stomach pains, medical personnel thought adhesions from past operations were the root of the problem and scheduled a surgery to remove them.

During her daily visits to see my father in the hospital after this operation in November 1995, my mother noticed that his complexion was still an unusual gray hue.

"It's just the aftermath of the surgery," his doctors told her. "It's nothing to worry about."

"I'd feel better if he went through further evaluation just to make sure," she replied.

The hospital called in renowned surgeon Dr. Stanley Dudrick, who performed an exploratory surgery the following month. For seven hours, he and his team—which included anesthesiologist Chris Bottino, who knew my mother from Irish step dancing and who regaled everyone with stories of performances as they operated—combed through the depths of his stomach, hunting for the source of his agonizing pain. For nearly seven hours they found absolutely nothing. Just as they were preparing to sew him back up, Dr. Dudrick decided to lift the flap covering the lining of his stomach. Discovering an operable tumor, he scheduled a second surgery to remove it along with 80 percent of my father's stomach in December 1995. Though his second with Dr. Dudrick, this was my father's third major operation in five weeks.

After this procedure, my father was able to come home, but not without new challenges. Along with receiving daily treatment through house calls from the Visiting Nurses Association, Da had to learn how to eat again, as he could no longer consume food through the normal digestive tract. Fortunately, Dr. Dudrick was the renowned inventor of total parenteral nutrition—a solution to the problem that had previously taken the lives of too many patients who had lost the ability to digest food naturally. Total parenteral nutrition (TPN) is a method of feeding used when nutrients are unable to be obtained and absorbed through the normal digestive tract. Administered through an IV, it comes as liquid in a clear plastic pouch. My father was put on TPN after the surgery and had these pouches delivered to the house weekly.

"Where do you store these?" Grammy once asked as she watched Mom accept a delivery.

"In the fridge," Mom replied.

"But where do you keep your food?" Grammy asked, stunned at the size and quantity of the pouches, thick in width and huge in length.

"We have a separate fridge in the apartment downstairs just for them. The apartment is locked, and the fridge is locked so the kids can't get them."

Grammy marveled at this unique arrangement that had become a monumental part of her daughter's adult life.

Before she went ahead with the wedding, my mother was asked by a friend if she really knew what she was getting into by marrying my father. Cancer had not yet invaded his body, but he had dealt with epilepsy since third grade and had contracted practically every childhood illness. My mother's friend must have feared that Mom's life would be filled with medical complications and stress instead of romance and happiness.

"I'm marrying the person," Mom replied, "not the medical conditions. I'm marrying Terry because I love him."

Mom always said my father was different from his family members and from other people. He had a unique perspective on life, probably because, she reasoned, his life had been threatened by illness in his youth. Having last rites when he was twenty years old due to complications with ulcerative colitis seemed to have made him see what was truly important in life. He did not get tangled in webs of gossip or politics. Instead, he saw the beauty of life and tried to build a positive relationship with all who crossed his path.

She fell in love with his sense of humor—a characteristic he was famed for among his friends and family. It amused her to observe him watching TV at night, to see him rush from his recliner to the phone after seeing an ad for Rogaine, a men's hair-loss treatment. She shook her head, laughing, because she knew there was no stopping him from prank-calling his brothers or his friends. At a time prior to caller ID, he disguised his voice and pretended to be a persistent telemarketer, insisting that they desperately needed the product. She laughed as she watched him dial the number on the screen and arrange to have free samples shipped to his brother's and his friends' houses.

She came to know to expect the unexpected from my father—to have pranks and jokes emerge at any moment of the day. She grew accustomed to being shocked by the scenes she would walk into and to releasing a sigh when she realized it was merely a prank. On three separate occasions—shortly after each of my brothers' and my births—she entered our home with arms full of groceries and stopped short in the kitchen when she saw Da sitting in a wooden chair in the center of the pastel-yellow room, holding their newest baby on his lap with one arm while holding up a chocolate chip cookie with the other hand, acting as if he was about to feed it to a child too young to tolerate normal foods.

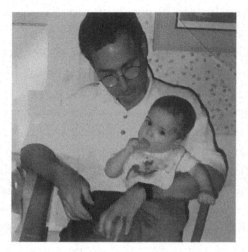

Photo Credit: Anne Mulville Moore

"Can we at least try regular solid food first?" Mom asked him the day she came home to find me in his arms and a cookie in front of me.

"I did this with the boys," he replied. "I couldn't leave Meg out."

My mom loved my dad for the person he was. This feeling in her heart outweighed the stress caused by diagnoses and medical conditions. In sickness and in health, she had promised to be by his side, though I'm sure she didn't realize how literal that part of the wedding vows would become.

My father became a frequent flyer at Saint Mary's Hospital, spending weeks or even months there for post-op recovery or particularly harsh spells with symptoms. My mother continued to bring the boys and me to visit him, trying to maximize the quality time we had together.

56

"I was always amazed at how you figured things out," Sister Rita Corley, manager of Saint Mary's Hospital Pastoral Care at the time of Da's illness, once remarked to my mother. "The boys would situate themselves by Terry's bedside, and you would lay Meg down on the gurney with him so he could hold her. You all found ways to be together."

"Yeah, and Sister Pat Corcoran always showed up with new toys for the kids to play with," Mom smiled. "I can't tell you how much we appreciated that."

Da's hospital stays escape the grip of my memory, but I imagine my father sitting me in front of him so that I faced him. Perhaps he bounced me lightly, making both of us laugh. I'll bet I reached for his glasses, trying to pull them off—I was the type of kid who couldn't resist doing that to people, too curious not to take my hand and explore what they were wearing over their eyes, what shiny loops were strung around their ears, fingers, and necks. Somehow, it brought me comfort as an adult to know that I had this time with my father, these special moments even in the most dismal of places.

For just under a year, Da celebrated a cancer-free period. Everybody really thought it was gone, although the medical staff had warned us that the cancer could return, and that if it did, it could be terminal. Just ahead of Thanksgiving in 1996—three months before my birth—severe pain interrupted his day at work. An ambulance screamed as it flew down the streets from his Southern New England

Telecommunications office, rushing him to Saint Mary's Hospital. My mother dropped everything to hasten to his side as soon as she received the phone call.

Not only had the cancer returned, but it had also invaded the stomach lining and was inoperable. I imagine my parents huddled together in the hospital, their fingers intertwined, tears coating their eyes as the news settled uncomfortably on them. Cancer in the stomach lining meant the cancer cells had become a permanent fixture in his body. Cancer in the stomach lining meant that it dictated the time remaining in his life.

From stories told by family and friends, I know my father worried about leaving us in a good place, easing the burden imposed on my mother to find the resources we needed to live a healthy and sustainable life. My mother always describes the amazing quality of their marriage and the joy Da found in his fatherhood. I imagine it was heartbreaking for him as well as my mother to know he didn't have much time left to enjoy these gifts. To prolong his time, he underwent chemotherapy from the end of 1996 through 1997.

Despite the challenges that came after his diagnosis, Da still had to work. It was a necessity—not going back would mean losing his health benefits and our source of income. My mother remembers his stories of how he made it to the end of the workday; he was feeling okay enough to work, but he often felt exhausted as his energy hadn't yet returned. He learned to create a balance, making sure to fulfill his responsibilities within work hours—but putting his head down on his desk to rest several times a day.

I imagine my father's eyelids feeling like they weighed a ton—almost impossible to keep open at times. Having his body endure so much trauma from the cancer, the procedures, and the treatments must have made each movement feel like a marathon, tiring and seemingly endless. Our church had run some fundraisers to help with our astronomical medical bills—initiatives my family appreciated beyond the sentiments that can be expressed through words—but I'm sure his worry about making ends meet and his desire to provide for the family were both immense, driving him to press on. Considering his perseverance has always inspired me to push relentlessly against obstacles until reaching my goals.

Moments my father had between hospital visits and the workday were spent intentionally, designed by my parents to cherish as many of life's gems as possible. Our summer days were largely lake days, lounging in the sun until it slipped beneath the waves. My parents maintained an open-door policy at home, welcoming friends to stop by for frequent visits.

My parents' friends were a tremendous support system throughout Da's cancer journey. Judge Jim Lawlor made himself available for my parents' questions and concerns whenever called upon. He was instrumental in navigating Da's medical paperwork, helping to look into potential schools for my brothers and me, and providing my parents with general guidance for their various obligations.

Other close friends—Frank Hartnett, Tom McCarthy, Mike Brennan, Dave Dillon, and Kenny McKeeman—took turns being on call to bring Da to appointments. Mom always reflects on how, especially when Da's need to see a doctor emerged suddenly, this was an incredible help that allowed her to get my brothers and me settled with a babysitter before joining my father at the appointment. She later realized that this must have been a gift for his friends as much as it was to us—it was an opportunity, an increasingly frequent one, for them to stay close to Da during his final days. Even decades later, some of them, like Frank, still talk about the jokes made en route that helped relieve the tension of anticipating what might happen when they passed through the hospital's entrance.

⌇

In September 1998, Da's symptoms worsened, signaling the beginning of his final decline. Mom remembers how immensely his health fluctuated toward the end, moving from an okay state to one that was intensely more severe and returning to the more manageable status frequently and rapidly. My mother has always been open about how stressful it was never to know when the next round of complications would send him to the hospital and how tough it was to watch him decline, although I'm sure words cannot fully express the rigor of the experience. Both of my parents must have been physically and emotionally exhausted during those last months. The way they pressed on and continued to show their dedication to each other, to my brothers and me, and to getting through the challenges until the end has always amazed and inspired me.

⌇

Although they did not explicitly say so, the medical staff indicated that Da had four months to live. They were spot on. Even though everyone knew the terminal prognosis, the day he died was a shock to all.

They say patients with terminal cancer experience something called "The Last Good Day" just before they pass away. The Last Good Day slips into the patient's life subtly—no one wakes up in the morning and realizes it is about to take place. The patient's symptoms appear to be at bay, and it is almost as if they have been restored to their pre-cancerous self.

This is exactly what happened with my father. He arose from his slumber on January 21, 1999 with a spring in his step and joy in his heart. He spent a great portion of his day enjoying time with our family of five and playing with my brothers and me. He even felt well enough to cook dinner out on the grill and to walk down the street to get a few groceries at Hart's Market.

"Hey, Terry," friends and neighbors called as he strode along the sidewalk in front of the line of two-family homes.

"Hey," he smiled. "How are you? How've you been?"

"Good. Wow, you look great!"

Less than twenty-four hours later, these friends recounted these exchanges through a fog of disbelief.

"But I just saw him out walking yesterday," they replied after learning of his death. "He looked great."

While sharing the news with grown family and friends was extremely difficult, my mother had an even worse task ahead. Like a boulder, it weighed heavily on her mind throughout the day and dropped into her conversation with the Saint Mary's grief counselor as they sat on our couch.

"How am I going to tell the kids?" she asked. "I have to tell them when they get home."

"Kids, in general, are selfish," the counselor explained. "They'll want to know how this is going to impact their lives. You have to get them to understand that it's okay to grieve and miss him, but that life has to go on."

These words were running through her mind when my brothers and I returned home later that day. She opened the door each time her friends rang the bell to signify our arrival. Each time she swung the door open, the adults on the other side essentially dropped us off and ran—perhaps a very somber adult version of Ding Dong Ditch. Likewise, the crowd gathered inside quickly thinned to nothing.

"We can't be here for this," they all explained apologetically. "We just can't watch."

"Gee thanks," Mom almost laughed. "Think about how I feel."

With just the four of us in the house now, we nestled in close on the couch. I imagine my mother's throat getting tight as she took a breath and began to speak to us. Perhaps she was fighting back her own tears as she prepared for the falling of ours.

"You guys know how Da's been sick for a while?"

"Yeah," my brothers each replied.

"Well, the doctors did everything they could to help him," she sighed, "but he died today."

Brian's entire being erupted into sobs, the tears streaming down thick and heavy. For years after, he awoke from his slumber, sobbing as he sat up and wiped tears from his eyes.

"Hey," Mom would say, running into his room when she heard him. "What's wrong, Bri? Are you okay? What's the matter?"

"I miss Da."

His words rang true for all of us—they always would. Grief doesn't just end when the dirt covers the casket; it is an ongoing process. You miss the person every day. You long for their presence. You always do. As strong as we are, we all have moments when the wave of grief sweeps us off solid shore.

∞

After hearing of our father's death, Sean stared at our mother for a few moments before his own tears fell, his disbelief showing in his utterances.

"But, no, he was just—but yesterday he was—no, where is he?" Sean babbled. "Yesterday he—no, he can't be . . ."

∞

Both of my brothers grew up very quickly, learning to jump in and help with the upkeep of the household, but being the elder, Sean stepped up the fastest. He found a way to be there for all of us. He often walked through the door after school, dropped his backpack off to the side, and, without even being asked, came to help me or Mom with whatever we were doing. Throughout life, he watched out for Brian and me, making sure we were happy and treated with respect by everyone who crossed our paths.

Of course he still had time to be a kid and for his own needs to be tended to. Mom found a way to balance this and, meeting her in the middle, Sean quickly found one too. When Brian and I had slipped into slumber for the night, Sean often tiptoed out of bed and into the kitchen, taking a seat next to Mom.

"Hey," Mom would laugh as she noticed his presence. "What are you still doing up?"

"I'm thirsty. Can I have a drink?"

With this repeated occurrence, Mom knew it was not just a glass of milk he was looking for. He had figured out that her attention was undivided in the quiet hours of the night. He loved being with his siblings, but he needed his one-on-one time with her. They both cherished this intimate time together—a peaceful treat in the juggling act of a single-parent household.

These were the moments that would make up our new reality in the future—the moments that, on the night of January 22, 1999, seemed like weak strains of light in the shadows of our sorrows. Down the road, the boys and I would learn from our mother how to rise above our grief, but for the moment we remained in our little huddle of tears, wondering how we would endure our fatherless future.

Throughout life, people beyond my immediate family have adamantly told me that Da was not in my memory—that I simply remembered him from the stories told.

"No, you don't remember him, Meg," they reply when I say that I do in response to their irritating "I know you don't remember him, but" sentiment preceding a story, or to their questions about whether I remember. "You just think you do."

"Oh, no, I remember him," I always reply, smiling as my most vivid memory with Da—a scene of him and me on the boat—sails across my mind. "I actually do."

"No," they sigh, a little perturbed. "You don't."

I could always feel the heat rising in my face as I listened to the classic rationale: "You were way too little."

To them, it is impossible for someone to remember life during infancy. Psychological research explains that, and it cannot be debated—it is factual knowledge, they insist, not a mere opinion. These people do not take into account, however, that research, while insightful, does not describe how life unfolds for every single person on the planet—that some of us have experiences that fall outside the normative patterns because of our circumstances.

"I do remember him, though," I explain.

"No, Meg, you think you do, but you don't."

If only you could see what I see, I say to myself.

"You know what I hate?" I ask my mom and my brothers after leaving the company of those people.

"What?" Their eyes begin to dance with curiosity. "Hate" is a strong word.

"When people tell me I don't remember Da."

"I always see people doing that to you," Sean often says. "It drives me nuts."

"Me too," Mom agrees. "*We* know you remember. They just don't get it."

"Yeah," I sigh. "It's like, how would they know what I remember?"

While in this case the psychology is wrong about my ability to remember the dad who died about three weeks before my second birthday, another psychological concept fuels my confidence in my memory. False memories form when people adopt stories they have heard and blend them into their minds as if they are their own memories.

My memory is not false. It is not attached to a particular story of the boat—it is simply a moment I shared with my father. The clarity and detail of the scene is too vivid for it to have been recounted by a bystander. I just don't have a way to show them what I see. My mind is not a movie theater open to the public—I cannot invite them to physically come inside and watch the memory that plays in my head like the beloved feature film it has become for me. All I can do is speak and write about it, sharing an account of a moment I actually witnessed.

It is what they cannot see that makes me so sure I remember him. They, of course, cannot see the ocean I do in my mind's eye, or the deck of his sailboat that lay beneath his tan topsiders, which seemed to be miles below me. They cannot feel his solid arms cradling me, tilting me forward so that he could show me the turquoise waves swelling in an endless blanket before us. They cannot feel the warmth of the sun's rays on the top of my head or the soft fabric of his shirt and the solid build of his chest as the back of my head rests against it, but I still do.

Da may have set sail on another boat on that January morning, but we were still watching him from the shore. We would not take our eyes off him, even when he had blended in with the sun behind him. Mom would make sure of that.

My father Terrence sailing on his boat.

Chapter 4

Nevertheless, She Persisted

She chose to rise.

She chose to do so immediately.

Life, she knew, was too short to remain in a veil of grief for too long, and our childhoods would go by in a flash. Seeing Da's life cut short at forty-four years had reminded her of the fragility of life. She knew she needed to balance supporting three grieving children with moving the family forward, but she knew the onward momentum was critical.

My mother had begun to prepare for this before Da passed, planning for the necessities required to maintain a sustainable lifestyle: finances, good health-care providers, the certainty of needing a more accessible house to accommodate the bigger assistive equipment I'd receive upon hitting my growth spurts. My parents had prioritized this list together before my father fully declined. They pushed to find the best health-care and financial planning options, leaving the rest for my mother to tend to later.

"Don't worry about it," Mom had told Da when he became too sick to continue. "I'll figure it out. We just need to focus on you and on enjoying your time with us."

Da seemed to know that Mom would figure out how to handle the juggling act of single parenthood. Perhaps he knew that her genuine devotion and desire to give the boys and me the best life possible would motivate her. He worried, though, that she would immerse herself in her single-mom routine to such an extent that she would not leave space to put her own needs first on occasion. She has often told the story of how, unbeknownst to her, he had mapped out a plan to guarantee that she would take time for herself.

"Terry told me to call you after he passed," Patty K., my mother's Irish step dancing instructor, explained over the phone shortly after he died. "Said to have you sign up for class."

Since Grammy had enrolled her at four years old, Mom had been a passionate and talented Irish step dancer. Considered a professional dancer by the time she reached adulthood, she performed all over Connecticut, the United States, Ireland, and even at Carnegie Hall with her troupe. In spare time between her project management career at GTE and motherhood, she had joined Patty K.'s weekly adult céilí class but had stopped attending when life began to take off with the demands of motherhood and Da's cancer and final decline.

"So he's still having his stunts pulled even after he's gone," Mom chuckled. "I'll come back soon—I just have a lot on my plate right now."

"He made me promise I wouldn't let you hang up until you signed up."

"Okay," Mom laughed. "I guess I'll see you the first Tuesday then."

❦

Each Tuesday, she carved out time to attend class, either having a babysitter come to the house or bringing us with her. Later in life, she always told of one of the first times she brought us. Sitting cross-legged on the polished hardwood floor of the studio—me between the boys as they kept close to spot me while I sat independently—we watched her dance among the lines of women before the wall-length mirror. Her legs moved gracefully, crossing themselves, kicking outwards, bending to bring one foot up to the opposite knee to tap it three times before she hopped, stepped twice, and repeated.

"Knee, knee, hop two three! Knee, knee, hop two three! Hop one two three four five six seven," Patty K. shouted from the front, clapping her hands rhythmically. "Good! Keep going."

As we sat on the floor, our eyes were glued to our mother. A smile glistened on her face, growing wider with each turn, with each hop that made her auburn curls bounce on her shoulders. I always felt my own smile broaden as her body moved through each step with elegance and grace. Passion sparkled in her eyes as she twirled to the music's Celtic rhythm.

"You have the most well-behaved kids I've seen here," Patty K. exclaimed. "They just sit and watch you. Most kids run around the place like crazy."

"Yeah, they're great kids," she smiled. "They've always loved watching me dance."

Being so young, I don't think I realized what I was really watching. I was seeing my mother look at herself in the mirror and, despite all the tragedy and pain that now made up the snapshot of our lives, choose to pick herself up and rediscover and bask in the joy in life. I could also see my own reflection in the mirror. Perhaps I was seeing my own reaction to my mother's moves and how I delighted in them, how I was taking this lesson—this dance of picking oneself up after the hardest of times—and learning how it could apply to our lives then and beyond.

I imagine my mother's grief for my father and her transition to single parenthood was tougher than my brothers and I ever realized. Under all the positivity, love, and encouragement she perpetually provided, there was most likely still the heavy weight of bereavement and uncertainty of how she would make everything work. Dancing seemed to rejuvenate her, helping her tap into her passion and refreshing her so that she could take on all our obstacles.

❦

Da had only been gone a day or two when she took the first step of helping us rise from our grief. Our first floor was packed with my parents' friends, and our front door had become a revolving one, with people arriving as others departed. The shock of his death had not yet settled among family and friends. Even with the time for gradual farewells that terminal cancer permits, loved ones are never totally prepared for the loss. It quiets the chaos of daily routines, making them realize what a precious gift the person had been and what the world will now be missing. It inspires reflection—thoughts of the last interactions with the person as the heart and mind work to commit each detail to memory. It acts as ground zero, a place to examine the devastation of the event and ponder how to begin to rebuild life.

The smoke and rubble left by my father's death had not cleared the area that day. All were still dazed, trying to find their way through the cloud of grief.

"If there's anything I can do to help with the kids," Mike Brennan, a close friend of Da's, said to my mother, "let me know."

"You're in charge of sports. You can be the boys' baseball coach."

Mom could feel the shock on her face as the words fell from her mouth. It matched the stunned expression on Mike's fair face, framed by short, russet hair, as he stammered.

"I can—I can do that. I'll coach Annie's T-ball team this year and have them on it."

❦

Years later, Mom still marveled at her directive to Mike. She had not intended to say it—at least not that soon after losing my father. The words had simply slipped out of her mouth, as easily and automatically as the air that left her body with each breath. I suppose the thought had been lying beneath all her somber emotions during that period. My father's death had not only left her grieving. It had presented her with the greatest concerns of her motherhood: How would she make life work? For her, it was not a question of *if* she could accomplish it—it was a question of *how* she would. My mother knew that for us to reach our full potential, we needed to have the life she and Da had envisioned for us, and she had a tremendous faith that she would find the right people to help her achieve her goals.

Mike was good to his word. When the bitter winter melted away into a warmer season, the doorbell rang each week and Mom opened our door to find Mike and his daughter Annie, who was Sean's age, standing there in pine-green hats and jerseys identical to my brothers'. Eager to play, Brian, age five, and Sean, age six, jogged to the door, the white numbers on their shirts blurring as they moved, each hugging Mom and me on the way out.

"Alright," Mike always said, bending to plant a kiss on my forehead. "We'll be back."

❧

Beginning at age two, some of my favorite memories were game days. When the boys left, Mom scooped me up and gathered the cooler, sunscreen, toys—ingredients for a good day out.

"Ready?" Mom would ask, holding me close as my arms looped around her neck and my legs straddled her hip. "Who do you think will win today?"

"Sean and Brian's team!" A smile always came to my face when voicing this.

"Me too!"

She would bring me to the van, securing me in my car seat before driving to the park.

Even into my adulthood, my mind replayed memories of sitting in the gentle heat of the spring and summer, looking out over the green grass of the field and the contrasting tawny dirt of the baseball diamond. I loved seeing Sean and Brian each step up to home plate, the toes of their black cleats just in front of the white surface speckled with dirt—so much so that the base almost looked bronze. They took their stances, bending their knees, leaning forward. With a twist of their hips, they took their swing, knocking the ball off its tee—a black stand that came to the boys' waist in height.

Crack!

The ball launched into the air as the hitter flung the bat to the side and dashed to first base. I could see the smile under the hard brim of the black batting helmet as my brother ran.

"Yeah," Mom always shouted. "Go Sean! Come on, Brian!"

"Go, go, go, go," I remember chanting as my brother ran the bases, feeling myself scoot to the edge of my chair or Mom's lap—whichever seat we had decided was best for me that day.

Beyond the pitcher's mound, boys from the other team hustled to try to catch the ball, narrowly avoiding careening into their teammates as they lifted their tan baseball mitts. All around me, players' families cheered.

"Alright, boys, nice one! Let's keep it going. Finish strong, finish strong!"

I always remembered the sights of Sean and Brian crossing home plate, running over the base and onto the dirt on the other side as they slowed to a stop, Brian placing a palm on the top of his helmet as he leapt over the base, Sean's head held high as his chest heaved from the sprint.

"Safe," the umpire would call from behind home plate.

It was as if my voice became one with a chorus of screams, blending with the crowd's to create a roar of celebration, a wall of sound, on our side of the field. It almost felt like the world was vibrating. I could see my brother's smile spreading beneath his helmet. It was contagious, and my own smile broadened. I loved the determination in both boys' eyes as they stepped up to home plate. I loved their smiles when they sent the ball sailing into the balmy air.

The toddler mind works in eccentric ways, though, often going in multiple directions simultaneously. When the boys were batting or about to make a catch on the field, my eyes were glued to the game. When they were in the dugout or in the outfield during calm innings, my mind drifted between the field and whatever toy or activity had traveled with me from home. I raised my head to look at the field every few moments before turning my eyes back to the craft or toy my hands were shakily manipulating.

Sometimes friends joined me in my playtime, coming by Mom's invitation or because they were related to someone on the team. On one hot summer day, a small group of us sat in front of our parents, painting with watercolors. Our heads were down as we each dragged a plastic paintbrush over a page. While the piece I crafted is not in my memory, I imagine it looked like—or perhaps even was—one that Mom saved from my childhood. I imagine I spent most of my time spreading my favorite color, purple, across the page, moving my hand across the paper's length in long, wobbly strokes until the paint and water disappeared from the brush's bristles. Perhaps I speckled the remaining blank areas with my other favorite colors, pink, green, and blue, or perhaps all the colors to create a rainbow—a scene that always pleased my eyes.

Mom stood behind us, holding a plastic cup of water that had turned a murky green with the collision of everybody's color schemes. Her eyes moved between the field and the artists, bending toward us each time someone needed to dip a brush.

She stood in just the right place as a ball was sent swirling through the air. She watched it shift directions, noticing how it was curving toward our heads as if drawn by a magnetic force. A gasp left her body as she thrust the cup into the air. The ball landed in the cup with such force that the water splashed in all directions, raining down on our heads.

"I don't even think you guys noticed the ball coming," Mom remarked when retelling the story later in life. "You were so engrossed in painting. You all just started giggling when you got splashed. It probably felt good too—it was hot that day."

The coach from the opposing team couldn't believe his eyes.

"Get that mom a jersey," the coach shouted. "She's on the team!"

The opposing team's coach didn't know my mother, though. He didn't know that she was not just a team player—that she was the one writing the playbook for this next inning of our lives. Having

Mike coach Brian and Sean was only the beginning of her plan. Three weeks after loved ones had gathered in our home to mourn our loss, they returned to celebrate my second birthday. My mother says they were all stunned when she informed our friends that the party would still be happening. They thought for sure it would be too soon for us to celebrate, that she would not be adjusted enough to her single parenthood to host a party. Perhaps, too, they thought she would be focused on our grieving, waiting many turns of a calendar's pages before initiating any joyous event. My mother knew that life, as Da's short time with us had demonstrated, was too brief to skip any stage.

Yes, the party went on in full force. Somehow it was the first birthday party to stick in my memory. The odd tricks of time have blurred the images, but as an adult I can still picture that Winnie the Pooh–themed tea party. I can see a vague image of my legs stretched out in front of me on the floor as I sat in my plush Pooh chair—my favorite seat to be in when I was not in my wheelchair. I can almost still feel the soft gold fabric of the seat supporting my back, the gold bolster armrests under my forearms, the red seat beneath my thighs. Behind my back, Pooh's face sits as a one-dimensional black imprint. All around me are blurred figures of my friends sitting on the floor. Above us, blurred figures of adults stand like giants, watching us and helping Mom serve us small, plastic teacups—white with purple, blue, and pink flowers—filled with water. That was one of my all-time favorite birthday parties.

This period in my family's life, though, was largely bittersweet. People had come together to grieve with and support us when Da passed. We were all in the same boat I suppose, trying to come to terms with the loss of a man who was loved so deeply and widely. After the funeral, though, the dynamic changed. Da's best friends—Frank, Roger, and Tommy, among others—stayed by our sides through my adulthood, being on call when we needed anything, whether a laugh over crazy pranks Da had pulled or another loved one to be there as we reached life's milestones.

Many years beyond that early birthday, Frank turned to me and said, "Your father would be *so* proud of you today."

We were outside a banquet hall, The Aqua Turf, watching fountains cascade into the pond surrounding the white, window-filled building. We waited beside the bridge leading to the building—Frank, Sean, and Brian in suits; Mom in her black pantsuit and turquoise button-down; and me in my silky purple floral blouse, purple blazer, and black slacks—among other friends in our company. I was to accept a small, one-year scholarship, and, in a matter of months, I would start my college education at Fairfield University.

"*So* proud," he continued, raising his eyes and his fair face, framed by a white goatee and short white hair, to the turquoise sky. "Just look at this day—he's smiling down."

I grinned broadly. These reminders of my father, often given by Mom as well as Da's friends, were always welcome and loved.

In the weeks after Da's passing, we were surrounded by family and friends, enjoying their company at birthday parties, sports games, Home Depot kids' workshops where the boys (and sometimes I, hand over hand with a family member) spent a weekend morning every few weeks assembling wooden birdhouses or other structures as employees gave tutorials. Gradually, though, these loved ones decreased their presence, some of them practically vanishing from our lives altogether.

"It's just too hard without him there," they told Mom. "There's just too much of a reminder that he's gone."

"Okay," she sighed, disappointed that they were not seeing the bigger picture. "But I've got three grieving kids that need all the support they can get right now. We don't get to choose whether we face our home life without him."

I imagine she was craving support for herself too. She was trying to foster a loving environment for two young boys and a baby as she also balanced my disability and medical care as well as her own grief. She must have been looking for all the moral support she could get and must have been disappointed that some loved ones couldn't muster the strength to be there.

Others grew angry, dwelling on life's greatest injustice and expressing it in their words and deeds. It wasn't fair that some of us got to live while others had to die young. It wasn't fair that they were watching his family keep moving forward despite their grief.

Even as an adult, I could never quite understand their distance and aggression. My family and I have had many discussions about how people grieve differently and how they grieved through their anger. Still, I always wondered what went through their minds.

I gained a sliver of understanding in college. I don't recall how it came up. I just remember sitting in my Fairfield University dorm apartment, listening as Mom told the story. This was one of my favorite aspects about her—she always kept my father's memory present in our lives, sharing pictures and stories every chance she got. The stories ranged from the best of times to the greatest challenges she faced as his caregiver. I never tired of listening to them. They kept his spirit and my own memories alive and gave me a clearer picture of the person he was, of their marriage, and of our sometimes-turbulent reality.

Leaning against the stone-gray kitchen counter and white cabinets, my mother told of a walk she took us on weeks after my father's death. I could envision what we must have looked like as we looped around the green in front of our house, Mom pushing me in my forest-green umbrella stroller with the canopy above me and my brothers walking alongside, almost bouncing with each step as they chatted and joked, making us all laugh.

"Someone saw you walking with the kids," a friend later told my mother. "They thought it was very inappropriate for you to have the children outside after their father just died."

"I was taking my children for a *nice, healthy* walk," she replied in disbelief.

⌒◈⌒

"And what was I supposed to do?" she asked as I sat across from her in the apartment. "Keep you guys in for the rest of your lives? You were kids—you needed fresh air and exercise. We needed to keep moving forward. Da *wanted* us to keep moving forward."

"Mom, that's *ridiculous*," I exclaimed, the absurdity boggling my mind. "That's *literally ridiculous*. Someone criticized you for taking us for a walk? That's just—oh my gosh."

"Yeah, well, that's why I just kept raising you guys how Da and I had wanted. You are *my* kids—who cares what they think? I was giving you the life you needed to have to succeed."

⌒◈⌒

In two years' time, my mother had adjusted well to the routine of juggling the single-parent household. She had visions of us thriving in new, more adequate spaces, though. It was just a matter of whether we, as kids, were emotionally ready. A grief counselor had told her to wait two years before making any drastic change to our lives. Had two years been sufficient? How could she know if enough time had passed?

"Can we move?" Sean asked out of the blue one day.

"What?" Had she heard him right?

"I don't know, just—can we? When are we moving?"

Incredulously, she looked at my brother. He had just answered her questions with his own.

Chapter 5

Ready, Fire, Aim

My mother's account of how my preschool teacher tried to erase me sticks in my mind.

Volunteering on Picture Day and greeting me in the gym, Mom escorted me to the backdrop as my teacher hurried ahead with the class, getting each student seated for the class picture.

"Okay," Miss Treet called to the photographer. "We're all set—go ahead."

"Hey!" Mom called as we approached. "What are you doing? Meg isn't over there yet."

"We'll take another one with her," Miss Treet replied.

"But *why*? We're right here. I'll just scoot her in now."

"No, we'll take another one. Okay, everyone! Smile!"

I imagine my mother wheeling me into the second picture, seething while also putting on a good face, stepping behind the photographer and making funny faces to make me smile. She came over to say goodbye afterward, watching my aide wheel me away before she went to file a complaint with Marianne Daukus, the director of Special Education.

❧

Mom and I both had a great relationship with Ms. Daukus. I had an ongoing joke with her, sticking out my tongue each time her face came into view. She feigned shock, letting her jaw drop for a moment before she stuck her own tongue out and laughed. She was somebody Mom could count on to investigate concerns about my well-being at school.

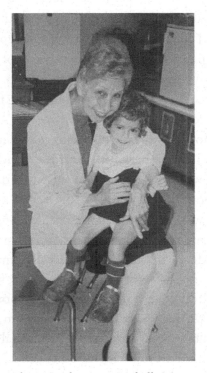

Photo Credit: Anne Mulville Moore

Despite being spoken to by Ms. Daukus, Miss Treet posted the picture that I was not in.

I was too young to understand what this meant and why it was happening. I just remember doing a double take when I first noticed the photo on the door. How could this be possible when I had posed with the class? Why was that photo used to represent the class if everyone but me was in it?

She left the photo up for the remainder of the year. I can't recall asking my mom about it—I don't think I knew that she should be made aware of it. I could sense it was wrong, but I couldn't put it into words—"discrimination" and "exclusion" were not in my conscious vocabulary yet. My eyes learned to evade the photo, looking above or below it as I passed. I avoided seeing it and letting fresh disappointment and confusion settle in.

I couldn't ignore the way my teacher regarded me daily, though. Even years later, I remembered the confusion and pain that came from interacting with Miss Treet. One particular day has engrained itself in my memory.

That day's sky was a periwinkle dome decorated only by the golden sun. The air had warmed enough for my Waterbury pre-K teachers to bring us outside for playtime. My aide rolled me next to a silver bench where my friends were playing, parking my wheelchair at the edge of the blacktop just before the sea of tan woodchips. The girls had brought out the toy tea set from the classroom and were setting up a tea party. I put my hand down on the bench, stabilizing my upper body as I manipulated the toys with my other hand. My body rumbled with laughter as the other girls lifted their cups, their pinkies up, and spoke about the imagined tea in sophisticated fake-English accents: "Would you like more tea, Miss?" "Oh, yes, please do fill my cup . . ."

Suddenly, a sharp pain sliced across the back of the hand resting on the bench.

The weight of the plastic tea set bowl pressed down harder, the protruding bottom rim imprinting onto my skin. With eyes full of cool tears, I turned to see a girl in my class with long dirty-blonde hair sitting beside me, her eyes locking with mine as she pushed the bowl harder into my hand. I couldn't slide my hand out—it was pinned underneath. Sobs emerged from me almost as quickly as the tears fell. Our teacher was already on her way over when my aide removed the girl's hand and the bowl. A long, curved crease ran from one side of the back of my hand to the other as pain raged across the surface.

∽◌◠

I remember her eyes.

I remember the eyes of my preschool teacher. They were mud brown. I don't recall ever seeing them shining joyfully—at least not when they fell on me.

Instead, I remember the flames in her eyes that day. The brown irises were alight with something that was neither joy nor love. They were angry, wild with emotions unmistakable and memorable, even to my three- or four-year-old mind. Her brown curly hair fell chaotically around her face as she screamed loudly, although she was right in front of me, looking me in the eyes as my tears fell.

My hand was still throbbing. She didn't care, though. It didn't seem like any adult did.

"*Time out!*" she shouted at me, her shrill voice piercing my ears.

I waited for the girl who had hurt me to turn and walk off the playground. She did not move, though. She was sent back to the playground as if she had done nothing wrong. It was I who was moved, my aide clicking off the brakes of my wheelchair and pushing me inside. She rolled me to the corner of the classroom, plopping a blue plastic ice pack onto my lap on her way to sit in a different part of the room while I did my time. I grabbed the ice pack from my knee and put it on my hand myself.

I was supposed to sit in the corner, with small wooden cubbies standing alone like a bookcase on my right and the larger, built-in cubbies on the wall behind me, and think about what I had done. What had I done, though? Why had the girl even done that when

I was just sitting there playing? There had been no hard feelings or friction between us. We had played together all the time and often shared a laugh. I didn't have a good way to communicate with others back then. The school provided an antiquated box, literally digging it out of the closet and dusting it off. It allowed me to choose from three buttons and initiate it to speak the words "hi," "yes," and "no" through its synthesized voice. I could laugh at others' jokes, though, and I could move my body and make funny faces in response. We always ended up having fun and giggling together. I didn't understand what had changed.

Years later, someone asked if perhaps my teacher's behavior influenced the way this peer treated me. I of course cannot say for sure, but I imagine it is possible. My teacher always berated me in front of the class and staff. Perhaps those my age began to think this was the acceptable way to treat me.

❧

I remember being yelled at a lot by Miss Treet and never understanding why. My mother had enrolled me in regular classes because she saw how intelligent I was and my potential to thrive through my schooling. I was the only physically disabled student in the class. I had no cognitive impairments, so the teacher did not have to change the way she taught. The only addition to the room was my equipment and the one-on-one aide who fed me and helped me transfer between equipment and manipulate classroom materials.

While I had that inadequate speech device that only verbalized the words "hi," "yes," and "no," I still tried to show how much I knew, pushing the buttons whenever I knew the answer to a yes-or-no question the teacher asked the class. I watched my classmates answer questions all the time, raising their hands or, when permitted, shouting out answers. I tried to do the same, but I was always sent to "Time Out" because Miss Treet said I spoke at the wrong time, although everyone else was calling out answers too.

"I wasn't trying to make her mad," I often told my mother after school, asking if she knew why I had been punished. "If I did, I didn't mean to. I really don't know what I did, Mom."

꩜

Miss Treet's class was my second experience in preschool. After my third birthday in February 2000, I attended Gilmartin School and had the most wonderful teacher, Mrs. Carmel Sierra, from February to June.

"Where's my hug?" she asked each student in the morning as we all welcomed her bear hugs. "Good morning! Ready for another fun day today?"

Photo Credit: Anne Mulville Moore

She commended each student for their efforts, celebrating right answers and gently guiding us using positive words when correction was needed. I never recall a bad day in that class. I loved my teacher, as did my mother, and I was amazed at the power of learning. My eyes and ears fixed themselves on the lessons Mrs. Sierra taught each day—numbers, letters, and days of the week.

I assumed school would always be like this, so I was confused when I met Miss Treet.

୬୬

"No, I know it wasn't you. You've done nothing wrong," Mom always said when I told her about my punishment. "It's Miss Treet. She just can't look past the CP to see that you should be treated like everybody else."

"What do you mean?"

I didn't know what discrimination was—it was simply beyond the comprehension of my child mind—but my mother tried to explain it as gently as possible in kid-friendly terms.

"You're the only one in your class with a disability. You are just like everybody else, but she doesn't see that. She thinks she can treat you differently because you have a disability."

What my mother was describing, I would learn in college, is the backbone of scholar Stuart Hall's concept of "Otherness" in his book chapter "The Spectacle of the Other." Hall argues that people take the one characteristic that makes someone differ from the rest of the group and use it as justification to treat them as inferior.

"I'm working on getting you out of there," my mother often remarked during these discussions.

Knowing we would need a more accessible home when I hit my growth spurts and required bigger equipment, my parents had considered moving before Da died but stopped when he began to decline. It was not a growth spurt that reignited Mom's interest in moving, nor—although it opened her eyes to the boys' readiness—was it Sean asking when we were moving. It was my schooling.

Mom often found me waiting for her after school, my body tensed, my bladder full, words rapidly stumbling out of my mouth as she approached.

"Can you take me pee? I've gotta go so bad I can't wait. No one took me today."

"What?" she asked, horrified. "What do you mean? You haven't gone all day?"

"No, all the other girls got to go to the bathroom, and they didn't let me go."

She raced me to the bathroom before calling Ms. Daukus.

My mother often remarks how easy it was to transfer me in the bathroom, especially at three years old, when I was so little. For her, it was a one-person job, although later, schools chose to enlist two sets of hands as an added safety precaution when staff members lifted me. Unbuckling my seatbelt, she helped me stand on the floor beneath my footrest, supporting me under my arms as she turned and walked me over to the toilet. As I held onto the metal grab bar, she pulled down my clothes while keeping one hand under my arm. Gently easing my body down into a sitting position, she secured me into the

87

adaptive commode—a seat with a backrest put over the toilet. After I was done, the reverse steps were taken, with the added need to help me clean my hands and body. The process took a matter of minutes.

⁂

Ms. Daukus was appalled that my bathroom break had been skipped, but even she couldn't guarantee school personnel would take me to the bathroom each day. She stopped into my classroom every day to check on me, but she couldn't be there every minute and could not guarantee that Miss Treet and my aide would give me the appropriate care.

"What if you take her into the bathroom when you drop her off?" she asked Mom after investigating. "That way you have peace of mind knowing she went. Just go to the classroom first to make sure she gets marked present."

My mother agreed. Each morning, she took me to the bathroom both at home and at school. Reflecting on this as an adult, it seems ridiculous and sad that no adult in the classroom cared enough to tend to my basic needs and that staff could not be trusted to do the right thing.

Mom didn't mind adding my extra bathroom trip or calls to Ms. Daukus to her already packed single-parent schedule. Her priority each day was to do whatever it took to ensure the well-being of her kids.

What did concern her were the sights she saw in the building. She noticed how the doors were never locked, leaving people free to enter the school as they pleased.

She noticed the bottle of bleach on the changing table in the girls' room and how it remained there day after day, even with her complaints to the school.

"I remember sending you into school one day in a new pink sweater," she told me later in life. "You came home with bleach spots on the back of the sweater—I couldn't figure out how they could have gotten there. When I saw that bottle in there day after day, I was concerned—what about the kids who went in unaccompanied? That bottle was *right within their reach*."

Mom called an advocate, expressing her concerns about these safety hazards and the discrimination that continued despite her infinite reporting and following up.

My mother had connected with a special needs advocate through a friend before I started school. Mom had no experience with navigating a school system with a disabled child, so she consulted with the advocate to get a sense of the services—physical, occupational, and speech therapy—that I was entitled to and what equipment and accommodations the school should provide.

The advocate agreed to observe how I was treated during a school day. I imagine my mom told me the advocate would be visiting my class—she was always open with me about happenings in my medical care and schooling, even when I was a child—but I don't remember the advocate.

My mother never forgot the advocate or her words, though.

"You need to get her out of there. Not only is she not getting what she needs, your daughter is in danger."

Those words made Mom jump into action, like lighting the wick of a firecracker before the course was fully set. The advocate told my mom what she already knew: The school was unsafe. I was not being cared for. I needed to be in a safer environment with access to the equipment and services that would enable me to thrive both physically and cognitively.

"She really didn't do too much advocating for things to change for you in the school—nothing at all actually." Mom gave a disappointed sigh as she told me this in my adulthood. "But what she said was enough for me to know I wasn't sending you back the following year."

⁕

Mom resumed the search she and Da had begun in 1994. They sought a better school system after Sean's preschool teacher excluded him from activities because he was the youngest student. They searched in towns nearby—Middlebury, Southbury, and Woodbury. When the cancer came in 1995, Da became too sick to continue and endured frequent hospitalizations and operations. Mom was also called back to work full-time—a request she had to fulfill, since she was then our sole source of income and medical benefits. Our parents' friend Betty Nejaime owned Wee Care Day Care & Nursery in Waterbury and offered to take Sean and, later, Brian. Raised with no nannies or day care, Mom hated the idea of putting her kids in day care, but the schedule set by Da's cancer and the demands of her job left no other choice. Wee Care, she later realized, was the best decision. Along with putting them ahead of the Saint Mary's School first-grade curriculum, Betty took the boys under her wing when Da was hospitalized, letting them come in early and stay after hours until Mom got Da settled.

They still had visions of better education after Wee Care, though, and resumed the search during Da's second cancer diagnosis. Although his energy seemed to be lacking, he insisted he was up to looking again. Da and Mom had their eyes on Middlebury because of its proximity to Saint Mary's Hospital for Da. Mom took a second look in the same three towns before Da began his final decline. Finding nothing and wanting to focus on cherishing Da's time with us, she stopped the search until my experience in preschool.

After Da's passing, the three towns were fair game. The options turned over in her mind repeatedly without a clear choice standing out. It finally hit her one day as a heat wave washed over Waterbury. Our house didn't have air-conditioning, so we meandered through our small backyard, trying to find relief in the shade under the trees. We tried sitting on the back porch and on the backyard swings, hoping to catch a slight breeze.

"You guys up to going for a ride?" Mom finally asked. "How about we go to the park in Middlebury? There's more shade there; it might be cooler."

We agreed, and she drove us to Ledgewood Memorial Park. I don't recall that day, but I imagine the four of us strolling along the curved concrete path to the playground—a wall of leafy trees on one side, distant views of the sprawling grass soccer fields and the rectangular gravel track on the other. I can almost picture, too, the excitement that sprang across Brian's face when he saw that Edward Garrity, his best friend from Wee Care, was also there with his family.

"Hey," Mom exclaimed as we approached them. "What good timing this is!"

"We actually live not too far from here," Ed's dad, Greg, replied, a smile spread across his fair, gray-bearded face.

"Oh, I didn't realize that," Mom said. "I'm trying to move here—I need to get Meg into a better school system."

☙❧

I can imagine Mom's surprise when she saw her friend Lisa, a high school classmate at Waterbury's Notre Dame Academy, walk by with her baby in a jogging stroller. Mom had not seen Lisa in years, but immediately upon spotting her, she flagged her down.

Something clicked that afternoon. It dawned on Mom that we had friends in Middlebury and how much time we already spent there. She and Da had been taking us to Ledgewood for years. Many summer days found us at the Lake Quassy Outing Club, splashing in the shimmering turquoise waves and building sandcastles. Summer heat drew us to Johnny's Dairy Bar, parking in front of the brick shack and letting our eyes linger on the white dome atop the building; the dome was decorated with brown paint to look like hot fudge was drizzling down a scoop of vanilla ice cream, appearing almost as good as the treats we indulged there.

"It was like we had already moved our lives to Middlebury," she remarked later in life. "All we needed was the house."

❧

"You should try my neighborhood," Lisa said that day at Ledgewood when Mom told her about her house hunting. "There are a few houses on the market near me."

Our summer soon turned into a series of house tours. At first, seeing so many houses and imagining what it might be like to live there was thrilling. During every tour, though, the boys and I grew bored—a feeling that kicked in increasingly earlier as we looked at more and more homes. We didn't care what "potential" the real estate agent said each room had. We didn't care how a uniquely shaped room could be utilized.

"Can we go home?" Sean, Brian, and I took turns quietly asking our mother.

She always nodded, raising a gentle hand to stroke the hand, cheek, or hair of whomever had asked but not moving her eyes from the agent who continued talking.

"Soon," she'd whisper. "We're almost done. We can do something fun after."

My brothers and I would eye one another and sigh. I remember fatigue settling in on top of the boredom. The houses we were looking at did not come with accessible entrances—if she bought the house, Mom would have to put them in after. My family took turns wrapping their arms around my torso and supporting me as my legs stepped through the houses. The burn of fatigue spread through my muscles shortly after the tour began, and my legs tried to fold as I fought to stay standing. My body didn't like being away from my wheelchair or walker for too long. While it is okay, even beneficial for balance and core muscle strengthening, my Cerebral palsy makes my body protest, initiating fatigue and discomfort. I tried to shift my weight from one leg to the other, attempting to relieve the sensation and stay strong in my stance.

"*Psst*," I recall Brian whispering during at least one tour. "Piggyback ride?"

My family had a knack for reading my body language. I eagerly agreed and watched as he walked over to where Mom and I stood. Squatting in front of me, he quietly asked Mom and Sean to help hoist me onto his back. Between walking with each of my family members, being carried by Mom, Brian's piggyback rides, and Sean's shoulder rides, I made it through the tours.

Mom grew tired of the search too—every tour seemed to lead to nothing. Some houses were simply too expensive. Others seemed promising, and she placed bids, only to find out that the house had issues, like termites. Exhausted, she decided to take a break from looking.

The ring of the phone threw her back into the search much sooner than she had anticipated. It was Lisa, who, since the day at the park, had made it her mission to help Mom find a house.

"I found another one for you," she exclaimed. "You've *got* to go look at it."

It was in a neighborhood my parents had already checked, but it was new on the market.

"I don't know," Mom sighed. "I think we're done for now—we're all tired of looking."

"Just one more," Lisa pleaded. "This one is perfect for you."

When Mom pulled up to the house, none of us knew, other than to humor Lisa, why we were bothering to take yet another tour that might lead to another version of nowhere.

"I don't know," Brian remarked. "It looks kinda small."

The home—half olive-green siding and half stone of various shades of ivory, sand color, gray, and taupe—sat on sprawling land. A one-level ranch, a picture window framed in white occupied most of the front.

"Yeah, it does look small," Mom sighed. "Let's just take a quick look."

When the Realtor opened the door and welcomed us in, our jaws dropped.

"I take that back," Brian whispered. "It's *huge*."

As we walked into the foyer, with its charcoal-colored slate floor, wood-paneled walls, and high white ceiling, Mom had an incredible feeling in her gut. *This is it*.

The sense only intensified as we were shown the open floor plan. The living room and dining room flowed into each other without borders, forming an "L," with the dining room running along the vertical length and the living room the horizontal, sitting between the picture window and the fireplace that matched the home's exterior stonework.

She loved the kitchen with its wood cabinets, stacked lime-green ovens, and sink, all tapering along two adjacent walls; a fridge stood in an alcove surrounded by more cabinets.

She noticed how quickly the boys and I found the sunroom—a small den facing the backyard. Sitting on a couch watching TV was an elderly woman with a bob of gray curls and wide-lensed glasses. Her pearly smile spread broadly across her face when she saw us.

"Hi! I'm Angela," she said. "And who might you three be?"

"I'm Sean."

"I'm Brian, and this is our sister, Meg."

"Nice to meet you," she exclaimed. "Make yourselves at home. Sit down if you'd like."

As the boys lifted me onto the couch and settled in, Mom appeared in the doorway, smiling, amused at how quickly we nestled in as if we were home.

"Hi," Angela exclaimed, noticing Mom. "I'm Angela."

"Hi! I'm Anne. Nice to meet you," Mom replied, her voice turning to light laughter as she continued. "I see you've already met these guys—I hope we're not interrupting you."

"No, not at all. I enjoy the company."

They began a conversation about the path that had led us to look at the house. Mom told her about losing Da and needing a better school system and a more accessible home.

"I raised two boys and a girl too," Angela said. "And my husband died a few years ago."

They noted how uncanny the similarities were, finding an increasing number as the conversation progressed. Angela was born on February 16th like I was. Her favorite color, like mine, was purple.

"Wow," Mom shook her head in amazement. "It's like we were meant to meet."

"Yeah, really," Angela agreed.

"Well, we should get back to the tour. You guys ready?" Mom watched us nod before turning back to Angela. "We'll stop in and say goodbye before we leave."

Mom noticed how excited we became as the Realtor showed us the bedroom that, besides the master bedroom, was the biggest. Mirroring the design of most of the other bedrooms, it was rectangular. With walnut-colored wood paneling on all but one, wallpapered, wall, the room had a built-in bureau and closet that matched the paneling.

"Nice," Sean said, nodding his ever-tan head as he surveyed the space. "I call this room."

"Nah," Brian replied, the freckles speckling his fair-skinned face blurring under his brunette buzz cut as he shook his head and smiled. "I call dibs."

"I think *I* should get it," I piped up.

"It *is* big enough for your equipment." Mom hugged me as she held me from behind.

I grinned and looked from Sean and Brian. *You hear that, guys?*

The Realtor laughed along with my family as she asked us to follow her out of the room.

Mom watched how we excitedly ran across the backyard. With the bounty of Angela's green thumb—lilacs, daffodils, and hydrangeas, among others—and her white knee-high statues of Jesus, Mary, and Saint Francis of Assisi, it was like a park. It even had a circular fountain featuring a stone child standing with a fish woven around his legs and torso. No water cascading, it housed orange daylilies, their emerald stems holding the blossoms high above the basin.

"So?" Angela asked after the tour's conclusion. "What do you think?"

"We love it," Mom exclaimed. "It's nice and level for Meg. The kids love it—this is the first house we've looked at that they haven't asked to go home. I'd love to raise them here."

She told Angela that she wanted to make an offer and just had to check out the school system first. Phoning Middlebury Elementary, the school in Regional School District 15 that Angela's neighborhood was assigned to, she learned of its freeze on enrollment. So many families had moved into the region that the school was at capacity. New students were sent to Long Meadow Elementary, another Region 15 school serving half of Middlebury and a portion of neighboring Southbury.

"Why don't you just go look at Long Meadow?" the secretary suggested, hearing Mom's disappointment that we wouldn't go to school with neighbors. "I think you'll like it."

Mom couldn't understand why the secretary laughed while saying that. She later understood—it was the nicest of the elementary schools. She had heard of the school when it was built in 1997, the year of my birth (she later joked that it was built for me). She saw the article in the paper and, as she and Da were looking into moving to Middlebury, she saved it, thinking it might be a school to look at.

At the time, the boys were at Saint Mary's School in Waterbury, and I was at our beloved friend Lois Carrington's house, but I imagine my mother walking into LMES's lobby, the glass window wall looking into the office to her right, each pane outlined in forest-green borders. I can picture her exchanging smiles with the staff upon entering the office.

"Can I wait until he is free then?" she asked the secretary who had informed her that the principal, Richard Gusenburg, was tied up in a meeting. "I need to make a decision on a house, and it all depends on whether I like the school system."

I imagine Mr. Gusenburg striding into the office in his suit, a broad smile spread across his fair-skinned face framed by short gray hair. He showed her around the school—the classrooms and the tan playscape and sprawling field outside, among other areas.

He brought Mom to meet the preschool teacher, Ms. Gillian Tripp. I imagine Ms. Tripp, tall and lean, her sandy-colored hair sitting on her shoulders as she grinned at Mom.

"I have a background in working with kids with cerebral palsy," she told Mom as she took her through the stations of the room—the dress-up station with a heap of costumes in front of a rectangular mirror, the play kitchen with its wooden appliances, the cluster of small tables in the back pushed together to form one big table. Ms. Tripp shared her experience working with children who had cerebral palsy at a school in Fairfield County.

My mother liked what she saw so much that she drove directly to my old school afterward, retrieving my special education files and returning to LMES to enroll me immediately.

Now it was just a matter of securing the house. Mom meticulously analyzed our finances, trying to find a way to close the gap between the asking price and the amount we could afford. She was determined to buy the house without getting a mortgage and adding yet another burden to her mind.

"This is all I can do," she explained as she presented Angela with a dollar amount well below the asking price, afraid it would not be enough.

"Let me ask you this," Angela began after a moment of thought. "Are you Catholic?"

Having built the house with her husband in the 1950s, Angela wanted to handpick the family that moved in. Raised by nuns after her parents died, her faith was at the forefront of life—she even had a small alcove-like room in the house with a Catholic sanctuary and kneeler.

"Yes," Mom said, stunned. "We go to the Immaculate Conception Church in Waterbury."

"No kidding," she replied. "So do I."

Angela accepted the offer. Later in my life, I joked with my mother, speculating what might have happened had we not been Catholic. Perhaps there would have been no deal.

❧

With a closing date in August and school starting shortly after, packing became the main event of each day. Friends from church and school gladly lent a hand. Everybody in the house was put to work. Everybody had a role to play.

I recall the dull *thud* of the box Mom set down next to my chair in the playroom one day.

"You didn't think you were getting out of helping with packing, did you?" she said with a smile.

"No," I laughed.

Since I was a toddler, my mother had assigned me chores just like the boys. My chores consisted of helping her fold T-shirts and dish towels. Now, rolling me next to the wooden rack holding small red, blue, and yellow bins of toys, she asked me to toss the toys into the box.

"Don't worry if you drop some," she said as she went to return to her packing in another area. "We'll all be walking through here. We'll pick them up."

I remember picking up my Basketball Barbie doll, with her blonde hair pulled back into a long ponytail sitting over the back of the turquoise jersey that matched her shorts and shoes. Looking at her for a moment, I noted how my packing was just like shooting hoops—aiming and tossing the dolls, blocks, and other toys and waiting to see if they made it in.

Throughout my life, after hearing about or seeing my chores, people were horrified.

"Your mother makes you do work like that, even with all your challenges?" they gaped.

The first time this happened, I was shocked. I had been raised to view myself as a normal kid who just needed a little extra help to complete life's daily actions. I could take on small tasks, and it only seemed fair that I do my part to help in any way possible.

<hr>

It occurred to me in my adulthood how exhausting this move must have been for my mom. Constantly making arrangements with Realtors, buyers of our house, Angela, and the school while packing and driving between Middlebury and Waterbury must have enervated her in mind and body. Her fatigue hardly showed, except briefly at the end of the day, when she suggested we call it a night and do something fun like take a walk in the park. I imagine those were just as much for her as they were for the boys and me. She, too, needed to decompress.

"I was just glad to find a place where we could get homecooked, healthy food," she often said when recalling the move later, remembering our new favorite, Maples Restaurant, in Middlebury.

Mom loved to cook and distrusted fast food and its lack of nutrition, but once the appliances and kitchen items were packed, she had to find another option.

On our last night in that little yellow house, Ed Garrity came over for one last Waterbury sleepover, and we lined up our sleeping bags on the floor in our otherwise empty family room. I remember we asked Mom if we could take a trip up to the attic, the only space in the house we had never seen. There was a regular wooden staircase leading up there—no ladders or crazy steps—so she allowed it.

"It's kind of creepy up here." Brian grinned like that was his favorite aspect of the space.

We lingered there for a while, looking up at the slanted ceiling, at the wood planks lining it. There was a strong sense of peace and comfort in the house that night—my family and I all noticed it. It was like we were enveloped in memories. This was the home our parents had shared, the place that welcomed the boys and me home as newborns, the last dwelling in which Da lived and breathed. It was a strange feeling—we looked forward to our new home, yet we were leaving the site of so much love, of so many milestones and tribulations.

Photo Credit: Anne Mulville Moore

I imagine my brothers had mixed emotions about moving. They had already established close-knit friendships in and outside of school. Middlebury was just a town over, but not seeing their friends every day was still a big change. It wouldn't really hit them until school started.

I don't remember thinking about missing my friends—Mom said we would come back to see them and have them over to our new home. I never thought of missing school—I was really happy about not going back. I imagine I was curious about the new school—my first education experience had been positive. The second had been negative, teaching me that schooling could go either way. I had never been to this new school. Mom raved about how nice the staff and building were, but I imagine that I wondered how I would be received, what would happen in this new classroom, which trend was to continue on the other side of summer's night.

Chapter 6

Hall of Miracles

"I didn't know you could just do that anywhere," I said to my mother as we placed knickknacks—family photos, plaques displaying Irish blessings, decorative pillows embroidered with sayings like "Home is where the heart is"—around the rectangle of our living room, transforming the new house into our home.

She had already replaced the aged mural on the wall, pulling down the faded scene of an Italian fountain to make room for one of a beach, ocean, and palm trees as seen from a porch.

"Here, see if this looks good on the couch there." She handed me a small pillow and inched my wheelchair closer to the pastel-yellow, daisy-printed couch as I reached to put it near a bolster armrest. "But yeah, you can have Mass in a house. They do all sorts of ceremonies if you request them. Monsignor Coleman used to deliver Communion to Grampy when he was too sick to go to church."

"Oh, yeah."

"I don't know what he has in mind, but maybe we can have you and the boys bring the gifts up to him during Communion. He may station himself with everything in one spot, but I'll ask him if you guys can do something during Mass."

"Cool!"

Time has blurred the image, but my mind can still conjure the visual of the Mass that was said in our living room. I don't remember who else came, just that a group of friends joined us by Mom's invitation. I don't even remember if the boys and I got to help in the Mass—I just recall Monsignor Coleman standing by the new mural, leading us in prayer, his arms raised beneath his vestment and a broad smile across his face.

Monsignor Coleman was our family priest—Mom considered him so, even through my adulthood. He had married my parents in 1989, performed our christenings, and said Mass at all the family funerals. He was close to my grandparents and my parents, often spending Super Bowl Sunday with them, sitting in a recliner next to Da, watching the game as Mom prepared her famous chili in the kitchen. I can almost see him lounging in the chair, his short, dark gray hair falling over the top of his head while another strip tapered along the back, his shoulders touching both sides of the chair. Hoping to bring the family traditions, friendship, and beliefs to our new life in Middlebury, Mom had invited him to bless the house.

While I don't remember his full homily, I do recall the main blessing invoked as he consecrated the Communion hosts and sprinkled holy water across the room with a gold-handled aspergillum.

"And we pray for our friends the Moores, Lord, bless them and keep them safe as they adjust to their beautiful new home. May they grow and prosper in You as they move about these rooms."

At four years old, it didn't occur to me how hard it must have been for a single mother to move a family and set up a new home while also transitioning three children into a new school system. Years later, Mom recounted stories of how she managed to finish painting and wallpapering by spending the nights working on areas far away from the bedroom wings, letting the chilly autumn air seep through the screens of the open windows so we wouldn't inhale paint and glue fumes, while also expediting the furnishing of our home. She caught a few hours of sleep in the wee hours of the morning, enough of a recharge to be able to jump up in the morning and get us up, fed, dressed, and on the bus. After we were off to school, she worked on the bedrooms, timing it so that everything would be dry and aired out by the time we got home. She napped briefly in the afternoon, and by the time our buses came, she was ready to play, take the boys to baseball and soccer practice, help with homework, and do play dates, baths, dinner, and the bedtime routine. I don't know how she found the energy. She knew she was doing the right things, though. She knew this move was going to be worth it.

A vague image of my first day at Long Meadow Elementary School's preschool remains in my mind even as an adult. I don't remember who rolled my wheelchair down to the classroom; I imagine it was one of the numerous aides who assisted with the class. I remember Ms. Tripp appearing in the pine-green doorway, smiling as she took in my appearance. She crouched down so that she was at my eye level, a pearly smile spreading across her face.

"Hi, Meg," she said, making eye contact. "I'm Ms. Tripp. I'm your teacher this year. It's so nice to finally meet you; I've heard so much about you! I'm excited to have you in my class. We're going to have a lot of fun this year."

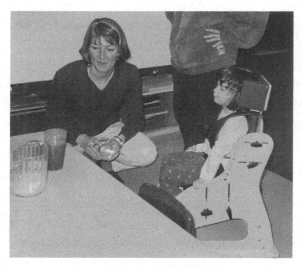

Photo Credit: Anne Mulville Moore

I remember grinning at her for a moment before she welcomed me into the classroom. I don't recall consciously making the comparison between Ms. Tripp and Miss Treet, but it struck me, even at four years old, how friendly and genuinely happy Ms. Tripp was about having me there—and, as time proved, how she maintained this aura. Compared to the preceding school year, it was like night and day, an experience that even a four-year-old notices. No longer was school a place where my teacher yelled at me, belittled me, excluded me. No longer did I pass the hours puzzling through confusion, wondering if I had done something wrong without realizing it that made me deserve punishment. School became an environment I loved again, the way I had in Mrs. Sierra's class.

I don't remember my transition into this new class and school being difficult. From my memory, it was practically seamless. I loved sitting cross-legged on the multicolored area rug beside my classmates, an aide spotting me from behind as Ms. Tripp guided us through the alphabet and numbers and led us through reciting the days of the week, often to the tune of *The Addams Family* theme song. I loved being dismissed from the rug, set free to choose among the classroom stations for playtime. I remember being gently placed back in the chair provided by the school—a wooden chair padded with navy-blue cushions matching the curved headrest. The classroom aides rolled me around the classroom on the chair's four small black wheels—the kind on office chairs.

"What would you like to do first today, Meg?" they would ask.

My hand would shoot outward. I didn't have the fine motor skills to gesture with much precision, but the aides knew I was pointing to one of my two favorite stations—the play kitchen or the dress-up station.

I remember playing at the pretend kitchen alongside the other children, picking up plastic cups and bowls, putting them in the wooden pretend oven and on the wooden stove, waiting for the plastic hamburgers, french fries, and other food to cook as we carefully consulted the timer that only ticked in our imaginations. (We wouldn't want the nonexistent heat of the appliances to burn the fake food, would we?)

Mostly, though, I spent my time laughing as the aides rolled me in front of a full-length mirror and helped me into extravagant clothes—red and white–pinstriped button-downs that, adult-sized, looked more like a dress on my small body; boas made of fluffy, hot-pink feathers; hats; and sunglasses. They laughed just as much as I did.

For the first few weeks, the classroom aides took turns helping me. From what I can remember, they rotated themselves on an activity-to-activity basis. I didn't mind. Whether it was Mrs. Kowtko helping me, her golden hair falling around her face as she flashed me a pearly smile framed with fuchsia-colored lips; Mrs. Tyburski, with her bob of thick black curls and cream-colored skin; or any of the others, I was happy.

It made sense, though, that they hired a new one-on-one paraprofessional—someone who could be devoted to constantly helping me. She appeared one afternoon at a Town Meeting—a monthly school assembly (later renamed Leopard's Pride in honor of the school mascot) that showcased student talents and accomplishments, highlighting at least one class in each grade and a selection of students who had reached outstanding achievement in academics, community service, or the arts. I don't know when she came, but after our principal, Mr. Gusenburg, dismissed the school to go back to class following his closing remarks, she appeared. Somehow my mind has preserved an image of the first time I saw her. Her blonde hair fell onto her shoulders and tapered across her warm-ivory face. She wore a black and white–striped shirt with a white sweater tied around her neck, the sleeves neatly tucked beneath the small gold heart necklace that I would never see absent from her appearance. She gently pushed my chair forward with one hand, sliding her body behind it and gripping either side of the handle-less back before turning me and rolling me out of the cafeteria ahead of the six-hundred-member student body plus the faculty and staff lining up to flow through the doorway.

"Hi, Meg," she said once we were outside in the much quieter lobby. "I'm Mrs. Caleca—Mrs. C."

I turned my head to look at her behind me, acknowledging her comment with a smile that she returned.

This was the only real introduction I remember with Mrs. C. Though it is possible that my mind did not record memories of the training she received from other staff, I don't recall her going through a period of acclimation to my needs; she was practically a natural, knowing what to do and unhesitatingly jumping in to help me. Even as young as I was, I could tell who was uncertain about their competency in helping me; those who were uncomfortable always held me at arms-length. Their arms trembled beneath mine as they held me up so that I could stand and walk with their support. It was a different kind of trembling than that of someone who did not possess the physical strength to complete the action—I knew how that felt too. When new people quivered as they helped me, I could somehow tell that it was because of their nerves. They were afraid they were not doing it properly, that they were hurting me, that they were providing inadequate support. I don't remember any of this happening with Mrs. Caleca. In fact, I remember thinking, even at four years old, how amazing it was that she caught on to my school routine so quickly—it was as if she had always known me.

Most of my preschool memories take place on the Circle Time rug, with Mrs. Caleca sitting on the floor behind me, spotting my back as I balanced myself while sitting cross-legged among my classmates. (It was physically beneficial for me to sit without my wheelchair for a while each day; it helped me develop my balance and core strength. Plus, it allowed me to be at the same level as my peers.) I remember Ms. Tripp would get the day's lesson under way, explaining and posing questions about numbers, shapes, the calendar, and so on. Suddenly I would hear a whisper in my ear, a quiet joke being delivered solely to me. The distance between preschool and adulthood has eroded my memory of what the specific jokes were, but I remember Mrs. Caleca would take part of the lesson and twist it in some way to make it comical—singing or speaking about the topic in a cartoonishly deep or squeaky voice, inserting key words into nonsensical songs, the kind of comedy that hits a four-year-old like a tidal wave, sweeping me off even ground and pulling me hopelessly into hysterics.

"What's so funny?" other students always asked, turning and taking in our appearance—the two of us hunched forward or sometimes even backward if the joke had sent a fierce enough case of laughter through me, making me lose my balance and topple into a chuckling Mrs. Caleca's arms. "What's so funny? Come on, what's the joke?"

"*Mrs. Caleca?*" Ms. Tripp or one of the classroom aides would call, her voice coated in amusement. "Are you behaving? Are you getting Meg into trouble again?"

"Oh, no," she would say, hysterics still rattling her voice as she gently lifted my torso off her and guided me into sitting position, my hands returning to the floor to act as stabilizers. "We're fine. Maybe we will share the joke at snack or playtime. Why don't we all go back to giving Ms. Tripp our eyes and ears?"

I could hardly wait to return to school each day, both because of the kindness I was shown by adults and students alike and because of the humor spontaneously emerging from Mrs. Caleca.

Photo Credit: Anne Mulville Moore

One of the greatest highlights of school, though, was simply seeing my siblings during the day. The three of us, each in different grades—Brian in third and Sean in fourth—always thought it was so exciting to run into one another. It was the first thing we told our mother after school.

"I saw Sean today," I recall exclaiming as soon as the preschool bus dropped me off. "I saw Brian!"

Even as an adult, I can still visualize being rolled through the hallway and seeing a line of students tapering along the walls, quietly chatting among themselves while trailing behind a teacher. I remember scanning the lines with my eyes, wondering if my brother was in them. I would suddenly see a familiar figure with a brunette buzz cut leave the formation, jogging over and squatting in front of my chair.

"Hey! What's up?" my brother would ask. "You having a good day?"

"Yeah! Are you?"

"Yeah! Where you heading?"

"The therapy room," I might say, thinking of the stretching and exercising session with my physical and occupational therapists I was heading toward.

"Cool! We just got out of Gym. I should get back. What do you wanna do after school? Mom'll probably be ready to take us on a walk around the block, right? Maybe we can play a game or something too."

"Yeah!"

"Alright; think about what you wanna play, and we can do that. See you later!"

Whether it was Sean or Brian, the conversation would typically conclude with a high five, and the boys would return to the class line, smiling at their teacher, who had paused and was grinning too. I could always see my brothers stepping back into the line and turning to their friends, gesturing to me and telling them I was their sister. They all smiled and waved as we passed each other.

I recall, too, spotting them among the students lining either side of the hallway on Halloween. Sitting on the green-carpeted floor in front of the arctic-blue lockers that ran along the walls, the older students, faculty, and staff awaited Long Meadow's traditional pre-school Halloween parade and cheered when my class marched by in costume. I was dressed as my favorite animal, a monkey, wearing a fuzzy one-piece brown suit complete with a tail and a hood from which little ears protruded.

"Look! There she is—there's Meg," Sean said to his friends as he waved to me. I could hear him describing details of the costume covered by my chair—the tail and the rubber bottom we had laughed at when Mom and her friend Lisa showed us the costume for the first time—and how we had plans to trick-or-treat with our neighbors.

Photo Credit: Anne Mulville Moore

Yet there was something missing in my new life in Middlebury—something I subconsciously knew was absent but that, at four years old, I'm not sure I had the words to name. It always became abundantly clear during playtime, snack time, and Circle Time. I was making friends in class, but my connection to them was limited, one-way even. I was the only student with a physical disability. I don't know if there were children with other types of disabilities, but the class was considered mainstreamed, following the normal preschool curriculum and gearing students toward kindergarten and all the future grade levels. My classmates had reacted well to my disability. From what I remember, they always treated me as part of the class, running to sit by me at Circle Time, at the classroom tables for crafts and snack time, and on the bus.

"Hey! Come on, we talked about this yesterday," I recall one of my classmates, Jacob, saying to another classmate, Dan, while walking to the back of our pineapple-yellow minibus, his face shocked under his fuzzy brown buzz cut. "It's my turn—you sat with her yesterday."

"Oh, alright," Dan sighed, picking up his backpack from the floor in front of the seatback near our feet and moving to the seat in front of mine. He slid in sideways, sitting so that his face, framed by kinky brown curls, pointed toward me as the other boy settled down next to my car seat. "But I get to sit there tomorrow."

"Fine," Jacob replied. "So you guys wanna hear a joke?"

As the other kids offered jokes on the bus and at school, my mind ran rapidly, filling with responses I would have liked to share—funny remarks that would have furthered the humor. I never allowed myself to speak to the other kids, though. Whether on the bus or in the classroom, all I would permit myself to do is laugh at their jokes and nod or shake my head in response to their questions.

At an incredibly young age, I understood that a very small number of people—mainly my family—could decipher my words. When I was not around them, I transformed into a mute in order to avoid the blank, "I have no idea what you just said but maybe if I just nod and smile you won't notice" expression I so often received when attempting to converse with others. I spent the beginning of my schooling in silence, really only verbalizing in speech therapy, when my speech therapist, Mrs. McCleary, prompted me to practice saying simple words, such as my name or a greeting. ("Can you practice telling me your name? Remember, close your lips as best as you can for the 'M' sound like we've been working on.") I had grown accustomed to silencing myself when I arrived at school each morning and to unmuting when I was reunited with my family afterward.

"You'll never guess what Devon said today—it was *so* funny," I'd say, talking a mile a minute, enjoying returning to the company of people who understood my words.

I don't recall being particularly bothered by the communication barrier between myself and my classmates. Though there were jokes and sentiments I longed to share, this was the way it had always been for me. Even when the Waterbury school system put the ancient speech box in front of me, my communication was still limited to the three options it offered: "hi," "yes," and "no." I couldn't share any thoughts beyond those words. I assumed it was the only way it could be.

Fortunately, those around me knew of a solution. A major reason Mom had moved us to Middlebury was to get me into a school system that was up on modern assistive technology trends. My mother heard me speak every day and recognized how intelligent I was. She knew that I needed to be able to show others who I was beyond my disability, to thrive by the intellect already apparent in my young life.

My mother knew I needed some type of technology, but she didn't know what it would be. Fortunately, Ms. Tripp and Mrs. McCleary accepted the baton from my mother and carried it the rest of the way to the finish. My mother does not remember hearing too many details ahead of the solution's delivery; she just remembers the remarks here and there as Ms. Tripp observed my performance in her classroom.

"She'll need a communication device," she repeatedly told Mom. "She really needs a communication device."

I don't remember hearing any discussion on the matter. All my mind recorded is the life-changing trip to the hallway.

I remember sitting outside of my preschool classroom with my mother and my teacher, listening to the post-dismissal silence. We were waiting for Mrs. McCleary to come out of her office, though I did not yet know why.

Mrs. McCleary finally came strolling out, a broad smile spread across her face. She was carrying something with the greatest of care, as if handling a newborn baby. It looked like a portable computer monitor—the kind that prevailed before laptops or flat-screen monitors—with no keyboard or mouse attached.

"Hey, Meg! This is called a DynaVox," Mrs. McCleary explained. "It's something that will help you talk to people. We still want you to use your words like we have been working on, but this will help too. Watch this."

She sat down cross-legged on the floor and tapped the screen a few times. Suddenly a girl's voice came from the machine.

"Hi, Meg."

Whoa, now *that* was cool! Mrs. McCleary smiled at my amazed reaction.

"Would you like to try now?"

I nodded, still staring in wonder at the device. She straightened up so that she was kneeling beside me and then she moved to the front of my chair. She held the device up to me, and I studied it for a moment.

It was a white box with navy-blue accents. On the top were big, round, white speakers. In the center was a huge screen, currently showing the first twelve letters of the alphabet. Covering the screen was a thick piece of hard plastic. It had holes that matched up with the letters and a rectangular hole that ran all the way across the top of the screen. This plastic grid was a keyguard—an accessory that prevented my fingers from accidentally selecting more than one button at once.

Hesitantly, I extended my arm and ran my fingers over the holes, pressing various letters to compose my very first message. As I was typing, the adults started talking.

"Has Meg had a device before?"

"No," Mom replied. "Well, nothing like this. The old school found an ancient box in the closet, so they literally dusted it off and let her use that—but, I mean, it only had three buttons: 'Hi,' 'Yes,' and 'No.' But this . . ."

I could hear the smile start to form as she trailed off. Sighing at the thought of an antiquated three-button box, Ms. Tripp and Mrs. McCleary began to discuss having me go to training for the DynaVox. Quietly listening, I finished typing.

Now how do I make it talk like she did? I wondered. *Maybe the top rectangle.*

I touched the white space where my words had appeared.

"My name is Meg."

Hey, it worked! What else can I make it say?

I pushed the "Close" button and found a "Social" page. The pages looked somewhat similar to what the home screen of an iPad looks like today. Brightly colored squares filled the screen, each with a little icon and text label. To get into the "Social" page, for example, I had to click a key among the twelve options for buttons on the home screen. In thin, black font, the top of the square read "SOCIAL," while the rest of it was occupied by a picture of a group of cartoon people who all had their arms around one another as they smiled. Pushing this button revealed a page with common greetings, salutations, and facts about myself (already programmed in by my speech therapist), such as my age, favorite color, where I lived, and who my family members were. Each key had an icon corresponding to a particular saying or fact. The combination of the preprogrammed keys and access to the alphabet keyboard promoted my efficiency in using the device, while also giving me the freedom to say anything that came to mind.

Pushing the "Hi" button and then my message again, the computer projected "Hi! My name is Meg." Off to the alphabet page, I experimented with more messages. The adults grew quiet as they observed me curiously.

"Actually, she might not need training after all."

I never ended up having the training. Instead, I learned by exploring the device in speech therapy, in class, and at home. Whenever thick raindrops and snowflakes beat relentlessly against my windows, I found myself inside at my kitchen table, teaching myself the ins and outs of my device to cure my bad-weather boredom. Studying the location of the words and letters enabled me to increase my typing rate and ultimately share my thoughts and ideas more quickly.

What I thought was mindless entertainment educated me on both the computer and the English language. Having access to a complete picture dictionary and pages of many words of the English language at my fingertips at four years old broadened my vocabulary—a benefit my mother later believed laid the foundation for my writing talents.

I was finally able to show Ms. Tripp and the staff how much I was absorbing in class. Ms. Tripp, Mrs. Caleca, or one of the other aides set up the DynaVox in front of me in each setting, gently swinging the two thin, hard-plastic legs out from the back and placing the device on the table as I sat in my chair behind it, or on the floor as I sat on the rug during Circle Time.

"Can anyone tell me what day it will be on the day that comes *after* tomorrow?" Ms. Tripp would ask, surveying the class as she sat on the rug with the blackboard behind her and the huge laminated calendar beside her. "Meg? Can you give us the answer, please? Take your time; we'll wait for you."

Even when I had grown accustomed to using the device, and even with the preprogrammed options—days of the week, classmates' and staff members' names, descriptors for the weather, and other common words—it took me a few moments to type what I wanted to say. I don't remember this bothering me in preschool or in most grade levels that followed. The teacher always waited patiently and, in turn, taught the other students to be just as patient in waiting for my response.

"Wednesday," my device projected at my touch of the buttons.

"Very good." Ms. Tripp always beamed after I answered.

It was as if the faculty and staff members were just getting to know me—not physically or emotionally, but intellectually. They could finally see what was going through my mind and why my mother insisted I be enrolled in a regular preschool as opposed to special education. They could finally see that, on the inside, I was as bright and on-the-ball as typical kids my age.

What was even better than that, though, was my new access to the world of socialization. Before I received my device, my classmates tended to want to help me rather than treating me as their equal. During craft time, they noticed when I stretched my arm to try to retrieve a crayon or marker on the other side of the table. They quickly put down their own projects to hand me the supplies. They made sure to show me the toy or book they were looking at, pointing out and describing each part as if I was a significantly younger child. I loved the time I spent with my classmates, but I noticed the way they treated me was much different than how they regarded one another.

I think Ms. Tripp described this best when she told Mom that they used to treat me like a doll—always wanting to help take care of me. With my newfound ability to communicate, they began to realize that I was just a typical kid. Suddenly, crafts, snack, and playtime were enhanced by conversation, and they could hear my feelings, ideas, and thoughts during class.

"That's funny," I now had the ability to say in addition to laughing at their jokes. "I have a joke too—knock, knock!"

I began to reveal who I was. I began to build real, meaningful relationships with my peers, teacher, and all who crossed my path.

Photo Credit: Anne Mulville Moore

My new device left the staff and administrators in a quandary, though. Since it had been purchased by the school, the device was technically owned by the region. At the time, the devices cost about $8,400 (with technological advances, the price climbed to $10,000 and then even $15,000). The school, understandably, wanted to ensure that nothing happened to the device. They worried that it might get knocked to the ground if my friends and I got too frisky during our playdates. They also worried that my brothers wouldn't treat it delicately. They proposed that it should stay at school for nights and weekends.

My mother understood their concerns, but she also knew the limitations that restricting my use of the device to school would impose. Although my speech therapist and, later in my life, close friends could interpret my natural speech, my mother knew I needed a way to speak to those beyond my immediate circle. She wanted me to be like a typical kid, able to make and talk to friends outside of school. She didn't want me to have to rely on her and my brothers to translate what I was trying to say to others. She wanted me to have the ability to speak for myself and knew how imperative it would be for my quality of life.

"That's ridiculous," she said over the phone to the district's director of Special Education. My mother wanted to be respectful, but she couldn't mask her feelings. "What is she supposed to do outside of school? She needs a voice. She needs to be able to talk to friends and relatives beyond her brothers and me."

She assured the director that we had never had an issue with my brothers being around my equipment; at a very young age, they had gleaned its delicacy and importance. They understood that none of my equipment was a toy and knew how instrumental it was to my functionality.

"What if I put it on my homeowners' insurance policy?" she asked. "That way I'm responsible for it at home. We will be very careful with it; I'll guard it with my life."

With the director's approval, the device was packed in its navy-blue padded computer bag and sent home with me each afternoon.

I don't remember the boys having to adjust to this new assistive technology. By then, they were used to new equipment coming home with the directives to be extremely careful and to wait for our mother to show them how to handle it gently if I needed them to help move it.

I remember their reactions—their sheer excitement that I had this device.

"It's called a DynaVox, but Meg calls it a Dyna for short—we all do now," I remember my brothers explaining to friends as they walked down the hallway of our house and found me at the kitchen table with the device. "It talks for her—whatever she wants to say, she types it in, hits a button, and it says what she typed. She can talk to you now without needing us to tell you what she's saying. Meg, show them."

"Hi! My name is Meg," the device announced at my touch of a button.

"That's so cool," their friends always exclaimed.

"Yeah, and it's all touch screen," Sean once replied, his eyes alight with his amazement (touch screens were new technology at the time). "Hey, Meg, push the one that explains what the Dyna is. I wanna see if I'm any better at imitating it."

The Dyna had come with a preprogrammed button that gave a simple explanation so I could tell people of all ages what the device was for. "How do you like my DynaVox?" it asked. "It helps me talk to you." Most of the words and phrases the device spoke sounded relatively human, with only a faint machinelike quality. These two sentences, though, came out with a heavy robotic cadence, as if it was designed to speak to the rhythm of a metronome. I imagine that some device users might have found this dehumanizing, as it emphasized the computerized quality of the voice. At four years old, I was too young and too amazed by the device to be self-conscious about this. Plus, my brothers had unconsciously provided comic relief when I first brought the device home, making a game of imitating the device reading the two sentences, trying to master the cadence, and making me, Mom, and our friends break into hysterics.

What I remember most, though, amid the bouts of laughter provoked by my brothers, my friends, and me after my device had read my latest joke or my funny response to theirs, are the moments that I could share my own thoughts for the first time at gatherings where I previously couldn't.

121

I remember the first Thanksgiving that I had my Dyna. I can still picture being in the circle of guests surrounding a crowded, oval wooden dining room table at the house of our friends Betty Jayne and Hugh St. Ledger, who had known our Grammy from guilds at church and who were now fellow parishioners with us at the Immaculate Conception Church. Betty Jayne and Hugh had begun the traditional sharing of what they were thankful for, inviting the person next to them to do the same afterward. As one guest spoke and invited the person neighboring them to do so, I caught Mom's whisper in my ear.

"Hey, you can actually do this yourself now," she said, the thought just dawning on her.

In prior years, I had spent the first few moments of this tradition quietly whispering to my family what I would like them to say for me when it was my turn. The three of them took turns speaking for me, designating someone to say my piece each year.

"I'm thankful for my family and my friends," my mom or brothers would say. "And Meg is also thankful for her family and friends and for our gathering today."

My mother's words reminded me of the new independence I had in speaking for myself. Taking her suggestion, I leaned down to reach the device on the semitransparent wheelchair tray in front of me and began typing while the first few people were still talking. This was something I quickly learned to do during that first year with the Dyna—thinking ahead when I knew I would be asked the same question as the rest of the group and typing my response as others were voicing theirs. Most people would patiently wait for my response if I was put on the spot and didn't have time to prepare in advance. I rapidly discovered, though, that it made it easier if I took advantage of any time I had to prepare in advance; it gave me time to form my responses how I wanted without feeling rushed, and perhaps choosing the least words possible rather than the full response running through

122

my mind. It also relieved the pressure—most likely just a figment of my imagination—that sometimes came from having a roomful of people staring at me, waiting for my response, as I finished typing.

"I'm thankful for my three wonderful children, Sean, Brian, and Meg; for our family and friends; and for being able to spend this holiday with you all," Mom said as she beamed at those around the table for a moment before turning to me. "How about you, Meg? What are you thankful for?"

The room seemed to fall even more silent. I could feel dozens of faces turning to try to catch a glimpse of me. As I reached for the top of the Dyna's screen, I saw their faces out of the corner of my eye—they seemed curious, as if wondering what was about to happen.

"I am thankful for my mom and my brothers and my friends and teachers and all of you," the Dyna projected.

I peered around the table in astonishment, grinning when the room's silence transformed into applause and cheers.

When everybody had shared the blessings for which they were thankful, they filled their plates and dispersed throughout the house, as the crowd of fifty or so was bigger than the dining room could seat. A small group joined my family and me at one of the folding tables in the living room. Many drew close to me, squeezing into places next to my mother, who was sitting beside me, and into the spots between the boys and me. Some even chose to sit with their plates on their laps and their chairs a few feet from the table, so as to not overcrowd it while still holding a spot among us. Our tablemates asked me to show them how the Dyna worked and watched my fingers gently drum across the screen as I did. They began to slip into normal conversation with me, asking how I liked my new school.

"I love it! I have a nice teacher and a lot of new friends."

"Wow, that's great," some replied, laughing at the novelty of conversing with me. "That's so cool!"

We had spent Thanksgiving and Easter with the St. Ledgers for years. They always drew the same core crowd, adding a few new faces here and there. With my family translating my words, I had spoken to them. Yet this was the first time I was able to show them the thoughts that came to me as they spoke and, for that, I would always be thankful.

Photo Credit: Anne Mulville Moore

When school ended that June, it was only the beginning of my communication feats. While most of my summer was a break from school and a time for trips to the lake, playdates, and the boys' baseball games, I still found myself spending a month in the school environment. Like most school systems, Region 15 runs a special education program in the summer called Extended School Year, or summer school, as my family and I called it. Running about a half day for four or five four-day weeks, ESY is designed to maintain academic, social, emotional, behavioral, and communication skills obtained during the normal school year and to provide a continued regimen of therapies. For my elementary school years, I attended full-time. As I had no learning disabilities, I became a walk-in student for middle school and high school, only going for thirty minutes to an hour of therapy a few times a week.

Thinking about summer school later in life, my mind instantly conjured scenes of field trips to Ballantine Park in Southbury every Thursday. I remembered swimming laps in the in-ground outdoor pool as my teachers and therapists surrounded me, their arms around my torso as I splashed and kicked through the cool water with my arms and legs.

Photo Credit: Anne Mulville Moore

I recalled, too, the moments of laughter and excitement as, supported by my aide Meghan—a college student working for the school for the summer—I ran up the squishy steps of the giant inflatable waterslide in the center of a grassy field. I suppose we had it down to a science. She would help me run to the top of the slide and would sit me down on the landing. Still supporting my back and shoulders with both hands, she sat herself down behind me, stretching her legs out on either side of me, and wrapping her arms snugly around my waist.

"Ready?" she asked, stretching her neck to look at my face as I nodded, grinning wildly.

"Here we go," she shouted, almost singing.

She scooched us forward to the slope, where the water trickled down onto the slide's surface from a hose on the slide. The water sent us flying down, the wind blowing Meghan's long chestnut locks and my shaggy chocolate brown bob back as laughter filled our bodies. We would sail to the landing mat at the bottom—or sometimes past it, right into the mud beyond, as we sank into hysterics.

"Wanna go again?" Meghan always asked as I nodded through my giggles.

I recall, too, my time in the classroom. For many summers I had Mrs. Erica Harrington as a teacher. I was often the only girl in her class, and this became a point of humor between the two of us.

Photo Credit: Anne Mulville Moore

"I have two brothers," I told her on one of the first days through my Dyna. "And I'm around only boys here; there are crazy boys everywhere I go!"

She tossed her head back as she clapped her hands and laughed. Each time the boys did something silly—drawing a crazy picture, making an outrageous joke, busting a dance move while walking across the classroom—she always called to me, saying, "Meg, he's at it again." I instantly turned to my Dyna to type.

"You cuckoo boys always act like the craziest people I have ever seen," it would project, launching into my daily spiel and making everybody smile and laugh.

In my child mind, these moments seemed like the highlights of the experience. They infused it with fun and humor, and, especially in summer, that seemed the most important part.

Later in my life, I heard my mother reflect on that first summer in the ESY program, describing it as a transformative season for me. It was the memories in my mind's periphery—the happenings beyond the waterslides and the jokes—that she held at the center, considering them to have set me up for lifelong success. That was the summer I was introduced to Tracy Kirk, a speech therapist who worked at the middle school and high school but covered summer school that year. Unbeknownst to me, Tracy was called in to help set up the Dyna before it was presented to me. She had a sister with cerebral palsy who needed a communication device—presumably serving as the inspiration behind Tracy's speech pathology career. Tracy came very well-versed in assistive and augmentative communication devices, knowing the types of vocabulary and page sets I would most benefit from. It was Tracy who had loaded the picture dictionary before I received the device.

"She's very bright," my mother remembers Tracy saying as she observed me using my device that summer. "We need to load the device up, more than it already is. She'll definitely make use of more vocabulary."

I imagine Tracy sitting in front of my device, gently tapping the screen, adding more pages, programming more keys with basic words and selecting a vibrant icon to pair with each word. I vaguely remember the Dyna being returned to me with a new "Feelings" page, vibrant with pastel-yellow smiley faces that depicted every emotion thinkable as the small black labels defined what they were showing. A smiling face appeared with the word "happy"; another button showed a face cocked slightly sideways and bore the descriptor "confused." There was a button for frustration, showing the face's eyes looking off to the side under arched eyebrows. These were more than just the simple terms to describe how I was happy, sad, or mad—these were words that were more substantial, more descriptive, more human.

I remember, too, the new "Family" page. It was one I could never forget. Tracy had programmed several keys so that I could explain to others what had happened to my father. One key, bearing an icon of an angel, spoke the sentence "My Da is up in Heaven." The next said, "When he died, I was a little baby and cried a lot." A few others explained how he had stomach cancer, how we all missed him, and how we considered him to be our guardian angel. Sometimes, when people outside of a communication device user's family program the device with the user's personal or family details, they might inaccurately assume that certain emotions and thoughts have been experienced and will need to be expressed with the device. I never told Tracy how I felt about my father. This page, though, even when I was in preschool, seemed to adequately depict our story and my emotions. I recall opening it from time to time, both when I wanted to tell others about my family and when I was just exploring the device's contents on my own. It always brought a sense of awe, inspiring me to relish my access to such beautiful words to tell my family's story.

I don't think I realized the gift my mother gave me when she moved our family to Middlebury. At the time, it seemed like a natural event—lots of families move. Lots of families find a new home and school that perfectly suit them. It occurs to me as an adult, though, the incredible wonders that my mom afforded me in our move. I was part of a miracle that day in the hallway, and I was blessed to be on its receiving end. She had found the means to transform the whole trajectory of my life, leading me to have a voice that all the world could understand. Though she undoubtedly realized my new school's impact on my life, I often wonder as an adult if she ever anticipated back then the density and depths of the atmosphere I was to enter next.

Chapter 7

To Mirror the Rising Sun

What if she had forgotten me?

What if she had left me out?

Gathered on the classroom's vibrant area rug, our attention was captivated by our kindergarten teacher, Mrs. McGovern, standing before us.

Photo Credit: Anne Mulville Moore

One by one, smiles began to spread across my friends' faces as Mrs. McGovern announced who was assigned the roles of the planets and astronauts in our solar system class play. As the last few names were called, my curiosity and excitement transformed into concern. I never believed I always had to be chosen first for activities, but I couldn't help but worry that I was being left out. My teacher had been very nice and welcoming when I entered her class that fall, but still I couldn't shake the memories of waiting for my name to be called for certain activities at my old school, only to find that it never would be.

"And Meg," Mrs. McGovern finally said, smiling at me, her blue eyes glowing with excitement. "You will be our sun."

A hum of "oohs" rose as my classmates turned to look at me. I beamed in disbelief—of the fifteen to twenty students in the class, I was the one chosen for the coveted role of the sun. The child the Waterbury teacher had tried to exclude from class pictures and activities was now going to be at the center for all to see. No longer was I made to feel like a burden or an outsider in the classroom. I was regarded with the same respect as my peers and was even considered important enough by my teacher to serve as a main fixture in the play.

Photo Credit: Anne Mulville Moore

On the day of the show, it all seemed to run so smoothly, just as we had practiced during the preceding weeks. Our families smiled with cameras in hand as they turned their attention to the circle we formed on the rug. Waddling forward in their planet costumes, each of my classmates spoke a few sentences about their function in the solar system. When the last of the planets had introduced themselves, those in the front parted, and I was rolled forward toward the smiling crowd. As a mirroring grin spread across my face, I heaved myself forward in my yellow costume and reached down to my DynaVox, situated on a chair off to the side. Poking the square key my speech therapist had labeled "Sun"—complemented by a golden cartoon sun icon—I straightened up and smiled at the audience as my part began to play.

"I am the sun. I light up the universe. . . ."

Afterwards, I was rolled into the center of the circle, and the orbit commenced. The class slowly pivoted to the left and began to make their way around me, twirling themselves after each step. I looked out into the audience, grinning back at my mother and brothers as they watched.

The sun and the sky were the limit that year as I began to see new heights of what was possible for me despite my disability.

I attended school for the full day, enrolled in Mrs. McGovern's class in the morning and Mrs. Sussman's class in the afternoon. Mrs. McGovern's class was regular education kindergarten; Mrs. Sussman's class was special education. I was the only girl in Mrs. Sussman's class.

Photo Credit: Anne Mulville Moore

"Wait," I asked my mom later in life. "Why'd I need the special ed. class if I didn't have cognitive impairments?"

"It was more for your therapies," she explained. "They couldn't fit them all in in the morning."

Both teachers brimmed with positivity when interacting with me.

I still remember the day Mrs. Sussman introduced the cutout project. I watched her gesture to the giant rolls of white paper on the table behind her, explaining that we would each lie down while she, the classroom assistants, and our classmates traced the outlines of our bodies in pencil.

"How about we get you out of this chair?" she asked after finishing giving the project instructions, squatting in front of me so that her face was at my eye level. "We'll lay you on a piece of paper, trace you, and then get you back in so you can paint it yourself."

"Okay," I exclaimed through my Dyna.

Supporting me under the arms as she stood me up on my wheel-chair's footrest, she helped my aide lift me, gently placing me on the paper stretched across the navy carpet. It reminded me of being on an exam table at the doctor's office (except, of course, this was so much more fun). Even the slightest movement rustled the page loudly, and the constant muscle movements caused by my cerebral palsy made it quite audible.

"Try to hold still, honey," an aide said. "I know it's hard. Do you mind if I help you? I could put my hand on yours to keep it steady while we trace your fingers."

I nodded in agreement. She gently rested her hand on the back of mine, helping my fingers stay fanned as Mrs. Sussman and the aides sketched around them with pencil. The pencil practically vibrated the page, tickling the edge of my skin as it wove around my contours.

"Meg, do you want pants or a skirt in the picture?" Mrs. Sussman asked from beyond my feet. "I know you don't have your Dyna. Try to use your words; we'll understand you."

"Skirt," I said, stumbling over the *s* sound, almost skipping it completely.

She nodded and smiled, leaning down to make one big swoop with the pencil around both feet. Finishing the drawing, they lifted me back into my chair, handed me a paintbrush, and rolled me in front of an easel. I stretched to reach the top of the shoulders, coming slightly below them as I spread violet paint across the torso in wavering strokes. When I had decorated the skirt royal blue and the hair mocha brown, the staff helped me, hand over hand, mark

135

the face with three brown dots for the eyes and nose and a swoop of cherry red for the lips.

"The boys are going to fill this out by hand," Mrs. Sussman explained, showing me a large, fill-in-the-blanks worksheet that would be affixed to the cutout.

In large bold, black font, the paper read, **"When I grow up, I want to be a _____. I will need to _____ and _____. I will use a _____ and a _____."**

"I brought in some ink and alphabet stamps for you. I thought you might like to fill it in yourself."

I remember smiling, knowing what she was getting at. Even at that age, I appreciated how far in advance my teacher had thought. Handwriting was out of the question—with my weak fine motor skills, my writing looked like chicken scratch, a mess of squiggly lines that bore only a faint resemblance to the shapes of letters. I relied on family and school staff to write down thoughts I dictated to them with my Dyna or, mostly at home, with my own voice. I never minded—those around me usually were glad to help and did so without modifying my words. When Mrs. Sussman presented the idea of the stamps, I was excited about having a project I could complete a little more independently.

"I even got you purple ink," she exclaimed as she lifted the thin, white plastic lid of the ink pad to reveal my favorite color. "Well, purply blue anyway. So, Meg, can you tell me what you want to be when you grow up?"

"A teacher," I said through my Dyna.

"Just like me! That's fantastic! You'll be a great teacher," she said with a grin. "What do you think you will need to do when you teach your class? What are two things we do at school?"

"We read and sing."

"Good! And what will you need to read and sing to your class?"

"A book and a song."

"Yep! Here, I'll lay out the letters for you, and you can start pressing them into the ink. Maybe I'll line them up on the page for you, and you can press them down on the paper."

I took the small wooden stamps one by one and pushed their rubber bottoms into the spongy pad of ink, staining my fingers blue-violet in the process. Mrs. Sussman gently took them from my hand and placed them on the worksheet's lines. I plopped my palm onto their glossy wooden heads, pressing down on each. When she lifted them, my message stood boldly against the white paper.

❧

"When I grow up, I want to be a TEACHER. I will need to READ and SING. I will use a BOOK and a SONG."

❧

When the cutout came home with me a few days later, my mother held it up, smiling as she examined it and listened to my narrative of how each part had been completed.

"This is great! This is really cool," she exclaimed. "Hey, maybe we can hang this up."

"Really?"

"Yeah! I'll get it framed when you're at school, and we can hang it in your room or in the hall or somewhere that everybody can see it."

Mounted against a royal blue background and set in a silver chrome frame, my self-portrait hung in our center hallway for years.

Photo Credit: Anne Mulville Moore

I was allowed to dream in kindergarten. When I told my family and teachers that I dreamt of growing up to become a teacher and that I wanted to do the same activities—crafts, sports, extracurricular activities—as my peers, they were supportive and helped me to keep up with those my age. I was treated as a normal kindergartener who simply needed a little extra help.

Photo Credit: Anne Mulville Moore

My classmates followed our teachers' leads and treated me like everybody else. Years later, I laughed and talked, only half-jokingly, with my best friend, Nikki—whom I had met in Mrs. McGovern's class—about how some of the best people we ever met were those we met in kindergarten. I don't remember them ever being standoffish about interacting with me. They talked and played with me like everyone else. I don't recall them getting much of an introduction to my disability or equipment until later years, when the classroom became less about playing and more about studying. I just remember how they waited patiently for me to finish typing my thoughts into my Dyna and how playing with them was so natural—they understood that I

139

might need help picking up a toy or craft, but that I could play just like them. They understood why I needed an aide, and they accepted the aides as part of the class.

Photo Credit: Anne Mulville Moore

"Could you imagine if Mrs. Caleca had followed you up to high school?" Nikki asked me one day as we hung out during a holiday recess in college. Her face was already breaking into a grin as her wildly curly blonde hair fell around it. "Dude, that would have been *so* much fun. I mean, most of the people you had were nice, but she definitely was the most fun, and she was joking right along with us. Couldn't you just picture her sitting down at lunch with us in high school like, 'Okay girls, what is the 4-1-1? Give me all the latest scoops.'"

"Yeah, that would have been awesome! We still keep in touch," I replied. "She hasn't changed a bit—she's still absolutely hilarious."

Photo Credit: Anne Mulville Moore

I remember, too, how quickly my peers caught on to my sense of humor and how well I could take a joke and dish it right back to them. It became abundantly evident when Mrs. McGovern announced that, together with the third-grade class we partnered with for activities that year, we would be performing the play *Jack and the Beanstalk*.

"And our cow will be," our teacher began, pausing to allow suspense to creep into the quiet classroom, "Meg!"

There was pin-drop silence for a moment. My friends looked around at one another as if making some sort of silent agreement. They turned to me almost in unison, inhaled, and bellowed one drawn-out "*MOOOOOOOOO!*" I bypassed the Dyna for this one, feeling the urgent need to respond immediately and unaided. I gathered my breath and exhaled a moo of my own before falling into hysterics with everyone else.

A few days later, Mrs. McGovern once again stood before us, this time holding a cow stuffed animal.

"Meg, this is my son's favorite stuffed animal," she explained. "It moos when you squeeze it. See?"

She gave its stomach a good, hard squeeze, and an oddly realistic cow noise sounded.

"I'm going to cut it open and take the device that makes the noise out so you can use it in the play."

I, along with the rest of the girls, gasped loudly in a "not the cow!" sort of way while the boys cheered and shouted, "Cool!"

Mrs. McGovern assured us that she would put the mooer back in and sew the cow back together after the show.

No stuffed animal was permanently harmed in the production of this play.

The next day, she Velcroed the little white moo box to a strap that fastened to my pant leg. From then on, I spent rehearsals anxiously awaiting my cue, slightly paranoid that I would push the button too soon (because, obviously, a single *moo* out of place would throw the whole play off).

Each day, after a successful session of mooing and practicing, my friends moseyed over to me on stage, props—giant plastic leaves, a golden egg, or a shepherd's staff—still in hand. Before they could say anything, I pressed the button, letting my cow call echo and sending them into hysterical laughter.

"So, Mego," my friend Colleen once began, tucking a long strand of chestnut-colored hair behind her ear. "How—"

I clicked the button, cutting her off with a potent cow noise. She giggled and began a second attempt.

"How's it go—"

I pushed the button again, no longer able to hold in my chuckle.

"Why did they let you have this thing again?" she asked, still laughing, as she reached to press the button herself.

"What?" I looked at her as innocently as possible as my Dyna projected my thoughts. "I'm just practicing my lines like they told us to."

"Yeah, *sure* you are."

◦◦◦

On the day of the play, my family, sitting among the sea of students' loved ones in padded folding chairs on the cafeteria floor, watched the stage as I was exchanged for three magic beans. Dressed in green lederhosen, my classmate pushed my wheelchair—the sides decorated in laminated cow patterns by my classmates' parents—across the stage. I clicked my mooer and turned my head slightly to peer past the hat of my black-and-white cow costume at my family and the rest of the audience laughing. I couldn't contain my own laughter as the farmers rolled me next to the risers housing the rest of the class on the other side of the stage.

Photo Credit: Anne Mulville Moore

"I'm just saying she's worth more than three beans," I heard Sean say to Brian and Mom as I was rolled to my family after the play.

They turned and praised me for a moo well conveyed before Mom filled me in on my brother's outrage at the price paid for my cow-self.

"Yeah, I guess I am worth more than that," I laughed, shrugging.

144

My brother was right, though. I was worth more than three magic beans. My family and I had visions of me flourishing in environments besides just the stage, and we began advancing toward them that school year.

As my mother believed I should enjoy all the same adventures as other kids my age, she sought opportunities for me to join fun activities both in and outside of school. She remembers seeing an advertisement somewhere for Girl Scouts. I vaguely recall her explaining what Girl Scouts was—a gathering of a troop of girls in the same age group interested in doing community service and crafts together. A smile had grown on my face as she talked about how I would meet more new friends and do fun activities with them each week.

Mostly, though, I remember entering Middlebury's Shepardson Community Center with my mother one afternoon and seeing the event hall bustling with girls ranging from kindergarteners to high schoolers in clusters with their moms and other girls their age. It was an open house, and new girls and their parents were welcome to meander through the room to see what troop they might like to join.

"Look, there's Donna," Mom said, waving at our neighbor who was greeting families across the room. "How about we go say hi and see if you can join her troop?"

"Okay!"

A smile crossed Donna's face when we approached. With a daughter my age, she was starting a troop for Daisies—the first level of Girl Scouting, the classification for kindergarteners.

"We'd love to have Meg," she exclaimed when Mom told her I was interested in becoming a Daisy. "We're going to meet here every Tuesday after school."

Each Tuesday, my mother and I entered Shepardson, joining the other girls and moms at the tables. The core principles of Daisies were to engage in crafts, activities, and service projects that taught us good values endorsed by the Girl Scouts, including courage, honesty, fairness, and respect of authority for others and for oneself. Each principle was represented by a flower-petal patch earned by completing projects throughout the year. By the end-of-the-year awards ceremony, girls would be able to display a full flower—a blue circular center patch and petals in shades of blue, green, purple, yellow, pink, red, and orange—on the front of their royal blue Daisy apron.

Years later, it dawned on me how easy my mom made my participation seem. With my poor fine motor skills, small objects often slipped through my fingers. I often found myself staring for a moment at the colorful beads, googly eyes, and other fine materials on the table, watching as my mother gathered them into a pile on the table before me. Part of my instinct was to dive right in and try to manipulate them, but something inside me told me not to, that it would only lead to a symphony of percussion as the materials dropped and bounced on the floor. I sat with my hands in my lap, looking on as Mom's fingers worked nimbly.

"Uh, excuse me," she once said, smiling. "You don't think I'm going to put this together myself, do you? I already did my time as a girl in Girl Scouts. It's your turn now. Come on; I'll help you pick everything up. Here, let's start by getting some glue on the paper."

She flipped a bottle of glue over and held it above the page, waiting for me to reach out and squeeze the white paste out. She then took the materials we were using—beads, thread, Popsicle sticks—and placed them in my hand before gently enveloping my hand with her own, securing the materials as she guided my hand to the page.

"There! Nice job! What do you want on there next?"

With her support, I hand-made all my crafts and earned my petals.

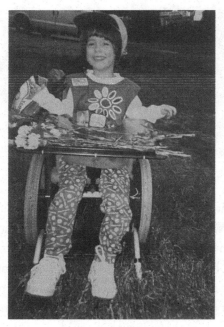

Photo Credit: Anne Mulville Moore

Meetings and ceremonies began and/or concluded with the reciting of the Girl Scout Promise and Law. Girls were asked to hold up the first three fingers of their right hand during both recitations.

Even in adulthood, I can still picture my first time doing this. The leaders had gathered everybody into a circle and demonstrated the Girl Scout sign, asking us to mirror their hands. It seemed so easy for them. Their hands slipped into position at the slightest jerk of the muscle. Mine did everything it could to keep my fingers apart—my pinky and thumb going the opposite directions than they were supposed to the harder I tried to bring them together, the pinky staying straight up as my thumb folded into my palm, and the entire hand clenching into a fist when I attempted to bend my pinky. I sighed, looking from my hand to the leader. She was looking around at the girls with their hands in position, smiling, appearing as if she was getting ready to proceed with the next step.

Come on, I thought. *It can't be that hard to figure this out.*

I don't remember dwelling on my inability to do this for more than a moment. I was more concerned with keeping up—I didn't want to miss the activity just because I was still trying to make it through the first step.

"I can't get it," I whispered to my mom, showing her how, despite my best efforts, my pinky and my thumb would not bend toward each other. "Can you just help me quick before they start?"

"Yeah, come here," she said, taking my hand and easing my fingers into position.

She held them like that each time as we professed the Promise and Law.

"On my honor, I will try: to serve God and my country, to help people at all times, and to live by the Girl Scout Law."

"Good," Donna would say, beaming. "And the Girl Scout Law?"

"I will do my best to be honest and fair, friendly and helpful, considerate and caring, courageous and strong, and responsible for what I say and do, and to respect myself and others, respect authority, use resources wisely, make the world a better place, and be a sister to every Girl Scout."

149

My mother managed to think through every adventure, making every activity that first year of Girl Scouts—and the years that followed it—accessible and possible for me. Even at five and six years old, I started to realize the extent that she had done so—and that handicap accessibility was only part of it. As the year inched toward its end, my friends at school and in my troop began bustling with excitement. It was tradition for a Someone Special and Me Dance to be held, and we were approaching our first. Free moments at school were spent gabbing about the fancy dresses we were planning to wear and the boutonnieres we would get those who were accompanying us.

"Wait, Meg," Colleen said one day as we sat on Mrs. McGovern's Circle Time rug before the lesson began. "Will you even go? I mean, without your dad?"

"Oh yeah, I'm going," I replied through my DynaVox. "My mom got my uncle to go."

"That's cool! What are you wearing?"

"Purple!"

"Wow, what a surprise," she laughed, gesturing to my almost-all-purple outfit.

"Yeah, and my uncle said he would wear purple too," I said, thinking of the promise my mother's brother Billy had made. "We're getting him a purple flower and everything."

"Cool!"

It was a strange feeling, being at what was primarily a father-daughter dance without my father—it always would be strange and a little sad. Beneath my excitement and enthrallment with the event, I would always feel a faint lump in my throat as I watched my friends dance with their dads. I was grateful for Uncle Billy's presence, but nobody

150

could quite fit into Da's shoes. I couldn't help but picture what the dance would be like if he were there. I imagine he would have been one of those goofy dads that popped onto the dance floor, moving wildly just to make my friends and me laugh. Perhaps he would have scooped me up at the start of each slow dance, holding me close as we moved until the very last note of the song.

On the evening of the dance, Uncle Billy met us at Middlebury's Trucking Museum, and we lined up to go down the red carpet rolled out in the venue's lobby. Looking dapper in a gray suit with a lavender shirt and purple-striped tie, a smile spread across his white-bearded face as he revealed a clear plastic box housing a lavender rose resting among tiny white blossoms of baby's breath.

"I was trying to get one that matched your dress perfectly," he said, opening the box and sliding the lace wristband onto my arm as he mirrored my smile. "I think I was pretty close, huh?"

"Yeah," I exclaimed, staring at the corsage now accessorizing my wrist.

"And," Mom began, shifting her camera to one hand as she reached into her purse to pull out the box containing the boutonniere almost perfectly matching my corsage. "You want to give this to Uncle Billy?"

I took the box from her with both hands and turned to place it in his hands. He smiled, remarking how we both had great taste in flowers.

"Here, I'll get it," Mom said, gently swinging her purse and my DynaVox case further up her shoulder and pinning the flower to his jacket before getting the camera back out. "Okay, now smile, guys!"

The flashes of the camera were the first of many she and the official dance photographer would initiate that evening.

151

Following our red-carpet photo shoot, we entered the event hall and found my friends and their dads on the already-packed dance floor. My friends and I began dancing almost immediately to the heartbeat-like bass thumping from the DJ's speakers. We laughed as my friends began hopping, skipping, and twirling all around on the balls of their ballet flats while I twisted and turned my upper body in my chair and threw my hands up in the air. The guys hung just beyond our circle, chatting in a group and smiling as they watched us, occasionally bursting in to bust a move when a popular song came on.

"Alright, we're going to slow things down a bit," the DJ announced as a gentle tempo replaced the previous fast-paced one. "Gentlemen, please join those lovely young ladies on the dance floor."

Uncle Billy appeared before me, taking my hands as my friends took their fathers'. He swayed us back and forth as we exchanged grins.

"Hey," Mom said, appearing beside us. "Do you want to get out of your chair for a bit? Dance with Uncle Billy standing up?"

"Yeah!"

She unbuckled me from my wheelchair and lifted me out, standing me up and getting behind me while my uncle put one hand around my back and took my hand in his other one. When I was secure in his arms, Mom stepped back, smiling and capturing the moment on camera. It felt wonderfully aberrant to dance outside of my wheelchair—to have nothing to restrict my movements and be able to sway freely. With rigid little movements, I took steps back and forth, and my uncle had me place my feet on his so he could lead me in the dance steps.

Photo Credit: Anne Mulville Moore

"Ready for the twirl?" Mom asked, approaching and putting her hands beneath my arms as Uncle Billy released one hand and as Mom spun me in her arms, filling me with giggles.

I was glad Mom had encouraged me to attend with my uncle. Years later, I remembered how much fun these dances were and what a blast my friends and I always had being the last ones off the dance floor. It was hard to watch my friends have these beautiful father-daughter moments and to know that Da and I had missed out on so many of them. But it dawned on me early on that it would have been worse

153

to stay home on the nights of the dances, knowing how much fun my friends were having while I stayed in and sulked about the loss of my father. I was glad my mother had encouraged me to go. It resulted in some of my best childhood memories.

We had to take periodic breaks when my leg muscles and my uncle's arms burned with fatigue. Mostly, though, we left the wheelchair off to the side and showed how I could work the dance floor without letting cerebral palsy limit my moves.

___

Later in life, it occurred to me how fortunate I was that my mother was not one to accept that, because I was in a wheelchair, I was confined to the sidelines. She believed in getting me out of the chair as much as possible—in finding a way to involve me in exercise, sports, and games even if they were not wheelchair accessible. This was the best thing for me.

With cerebral palsy, it is critical to stay active to maintain circulation, muscle flexibility, and overall health. Otherwise, muscles are at risk of atrophy—the saying "move it or lose it" comes into play quite literally. On days when the common cold or a virus has rattled my body and left me without energy to do much more than lie in bed, I can feel my muscles grow tighter than usual and the normal bodily functions slow to a stop, making me feel worse than the cold would ordinarily make a person feel. Fortunately, my mother grasped the importance of exercise in my life years before I was mature enough to understand it myself.

Mom and my therapists not only wanted to promote the level of exercise I engaged in, but they also wanted to give me access to all the childhood experiences my able-bodied peers had. From the time I entered Long Meadow's pre-K through kindergarten or first grade, I used the school's red adaptive bicycle a few times a week to navigate from one side of the school to another or across the playground at recess. My therapists incorporated this into my routine because of the health benefits of bike riding—the strengthening of my legs from pedaling, the muscle coordination needed to grasp the handlebars, and maintaining good posture and trunk control among other advantages. I was enthralled with riding, with the way the breeze blew back the strands of my short hair under my helmet, and with my ability to propel the bike as fast as my legs could go (of course there were strict speed limits imposed at school). I don't think I had experienced bike riding before this, and I often filled my family's ears with chatter about how much fun I had pedaling through the school.

My occupational therapist Ms. Gerry Campbell and I taking the bike for a ride on the school field.
Photo Credit: Anne Mulville Moore

"She absolutely loves that bike," Mom vaguely recalls telling Lisa Williams, the mother of Sean's friend Mitch, one day as the boys hung out at the Williams' house. "She's always talking about it."

Mom mentioned how she would love to have the means to get me a bike at home. Our neighborhood sat on level ground that would be easy to ride on. She knew, though, that this would not be covered by insurance. The insurance companies only covered, at least in part, equipment they deemed a "necessity," such as a wheelchair; and sometimes, even getting the necessities approved was challenging. Back then, adaptive bikes ran for just over $3,000—money my mother knew we couldn't spare for equipment that was more of a luxury.

As Mrs. Williams was a teacher at Long Meadow, I imagine she remembered the delight on my face as I biked by her in the hallway. Shortly after this conversation with my mother—when I was seven years old—her oldest daughter, Taylor, seventeen at the time, launched a fundraiser to buy me a bike. In the periphery of my memory are recollections of hearing my mother and Taylor describe the steps and status of negotiating a reduction to the price; arranging for special pedals that had a heel cup and Velcro straps to be put on the bike, which would stabilize my feet in ways standard pedals could not; and even talking the vendor into selling them the demo model because it came in my favorite color, purple, while the retail version did not.

What remains in my mind clearly is the crisp New England day I received the bike. I sat on the black seat—which resembled the typical bike seat in shape and size but perhaps was made from a foamier material. Behind me, a U-shaped cushion supported my back, and the exterior side housed a handle and brake to be operated by a companion. The violet frame protruded from beneath me, supporting two huge black tires on either side and one up front. A horseshoe-shaped handlebar sat before me, its chrome surface peeking out at the ends while the rest was enveloped in squishy black foam. All over the frame were various levers and knobs, where the height of each section could be adjusted. This bike was meant to grow with me and was a gift I cherished all through life.

"Ready?" Taylor asked, leaning around from behind me so I could see her face, framed by long blonde hair, once my helmet and the straps for my chest, waist, and feet were fastened.

Smiling, I nodded as I reached to the far edge of the handlebars to ring the small purple bell. As the bold, sweet tone sounded, I gripped the handlebars and began to pedal, pushing one foot forward and down as I brought the other up and over an invisible curve, repeating these movements and building momentum. We were on the Williams' quiet road, gradually making our way across the straightaway and beginning to climb a hill. My legs began to push the pedals harder and faster, propelling the bike at a speed I had never approached on the school bike. My laughter mingled with Taylor's as we passed our families watching from the curb for the first of many laps we would take that afternoon.

Photo Credit: Anne Mulville Moore

157

In the years that followed, I spent innumerable spring and summer afternoons racing friends through local parks as they rode their bikes parallel with mine.

Photo Credit: Anne Mulville Moore

These laughter-filled moments remain among my favorite childhood memories. None, though, are greater than the feeling of the wind rushing over me, the burn of my muscles as my legs pedaled on, and the laughter rumbling through my body on that inaugural ride of that shiny purple bike I was so excited to have as my own.

◦◦◦

My mother didn't just want me to experience the ordinary experiences of childhood. She sought to give me admission to the extraordinary activities that were both physically beneficial to my body and astonishing to the mind. When she learned of an adaptive horseback riding program from another mother at school, she didn't hesitate to sign me up in kindergarten. I remember there being talk of how beneficial this was for kids with CP. I recall therapists at school and the farm commending my mother for finding a way to get me on a horse. The activity increases the chance of somebody with CP developing the ability to walk, as it allows them to experience movements similar to the human gait.

My mother was intrigued by the therapeutic prospects—they were prominent reasons for her signing me up—but I don't remember her being overly insistent that it would make me walk independently, that it would *have* to work. I'm glad this was not her focus. Too often in the years that followed, I would see parents put their children through rigorous exercise and surgeries in an effort to make them walk on their own. When the results did not amount to what they had hoped, the parents grew too disappointed to celebrate the progress and joy the child experienced. Some kids seemed to sense their parents' disappointment, which dampened their spirits, perhaps assuming they had failed. My mother wanted me to develop strength to sit, stand, walk, and complete the basic activities of daily life more

159

independently, but she didn't dwell on what wasn't yet achievable. Instead, she celebrated even the smallest gains I made and the joy that filled me during the activities.

The possibility that horseback riding could help me to walk on my own was more like background noise—something I heard and was aware of, but not the focal point on which my mind centered. My attention was instead fixed on spending time with horses. I loved animals and relished any chance I was given to be up close with them.

I remember the excitement buzzing through me each week as my mother supported me while we stood on a wooden platform. I could hardly stand still, wiggling in Mom's arms as I watched the high school– or college-age girl mount the chestnut-colored horse, sliding to the back edge of the saddle to make room for me. Three women always surrounded the horse. The two on either side were therapists who walked beside us during the rides, reminding me to sit with my torso straight and tall and asking me to stretch my arms to various parts of the saddle and the horse's neck to get some therapy into the session. Leading the horse was Joyce Smilie, who owned the farm and ran the program. Once the rider who would sit behind me was settled, the therapists gathered beside us and helped Mom hoist me onto the horse named Flurt. The back rider's arms came around me like a harness, holding my body up.

"You good, Meg?" Mom always asked, waiting to see me nod under the baseball cap–like brim of my black riding helmet before turning to the back rider, chuckling at my grin. "She's already smiling. She needs support at her trunk—she tends to tip back and to either side. I know I say it every week and probably sound like a broken record, but just to make sure."

The back rider assured her that I was in good hands. I'm sure the staff was used to parents reminding them about the specifics of their children's impairments. I'm certain my mother couldn't help it; she took motherhood very seriously, listening intently to her heart when it told her, many times over, to review the details that would ensure my brothers' and my safety and happiness. Mom smiled, wishing us a good ride before taking her place against the railing of the fence, camera in hand as always.

Joyce led us around the field, circling its perimeter to start then weaving through various bales of hay in the middle.

"Hey, Meg," one of the therapists always began shortly into the ride. "Can you try stretching your arms toward Flurt's left ear? Keep holding on, but *stretch*! Good! How about the other side?"

The therapy seemed like it was in the background during those rides. I hardly noticed it. My mind was too preoccupied with other phenomena. Holding tightly to the reins while also keeping my hands close to Flurt's thick brown fur so I could feel the fuzziness of its texture and the silkiness of the long black mane that tapered down her neck, I remember spending my rides laughing at the bouncing sensation created by Flurt's gait.

"Alright ladies, I hate to be the bearer of bad news, but the hour is just about up. Meg, time always flies when you're here," Joyce smiled at me from in front. "Would you like to trot Flurt back to your mom?"

I never refused a trot, giving Joyce a big nod each time she asked.

"Okay, Flurt, trot!"

My entire being filled with laughter as the horse sped up, galloping across the field. My stomach did a somersault, tickling me as my body bounced up and down on the saddle. The breeze seemed to increase around me, rushing over my face and blowing my hair backward as we raced toward my mother. Commanded by Joyce, the horse slowed her hooves and halted sideways by my mother, leaving me already looking forward to my next trip to the field.

Photo Credit: Anne Mulville Moore

That was just one of many fields I found myself traipsing on beginning that year. I had grown up watching my brothers' athletics and loved my place among the spectators. My family had me play sports with them in our yard and at parks, helping me hit a Wiffle ball, shoot a basketball hand over hand, and running alongside my walker or holding my body up as I ran in fields or around baseball diamonds. I don't remember feeling like I was missing out. Because my family played with me this way, it seemed like I actually was playing sports.

162

Of course I recognized how different my experience with athletics was from that of my brothers and friends. They all had their teams and could jump into action in official practices and games, whereas my time on the field was limited to times after their sporting events, when the fields were clear of the real competition. I don't think I knew it could be any different.

Photo Credit: Anne Mulville Moore

One flyer began to change all that. It was dropped off in the main office of Long Meadow Elementary School and was sent down to the OT/PT room. My physical therapist later shared the information with my mother, figuring it might be something I'd like to try.

The Outreach Program for Soccer (TOPSoccer) was starting a league in Middlebury. TOPSoccer was for children with physical and mental impairments and other special needs. A volunteer-based program geared toward fostering physical, social, and emotional growth, therapists came to the twice-weekly practices to work with participants as they ran through drills and played mini-scrimmages against other teammates.

I was thrilled when Mom told me about it and how she was planning to take me to check out the first practice. I can't recall whether I had ever played soccer before then, though part of my mind very vaguely recalls kicking around a ball in the yard with my family and friends.

As Mom drove into the Shepardson Community Center parking lot, I stretched up in my car seat to get a better look at what was happening on the field. Shepardson didn't have an official soccer field, but between the ornate brick buildings of Town Hall and Shepardson was a grassy, rolling hill and a vast field of grass at the bottom. Two yellow portable goals were already set up, and soccer balls were scattered toward the edge, just before the grass met the parking lot. Families were migrating there—some with assistive equipment and others without, parents lifting their children out of cars and helping them into walkers and crutches before walking with them onto the field.

"Huh," Brian said, also looking out the window. "So *that's* what we look like when we're helping Meg."

"Yeah, it's cool, but it's weird," Sean remarked. "I feel like I'm watching myself right now."

"It does look similar," Mom agreed. "Alright, when I park, can you guys start unbuckling Meg while I get the walker out of the trunk?"

"Yeah."

❧

I soon found myself running down the field in my walker, gripping the rubber handles tightly as my legs pounded against the grass, propelling me forward, dribbling and chasing after the ball I had just kicked. Pulling my legs to the back edge of the walker frame, I swung

164

one leg forward and launched the ball another several feet before beginning to run again. I don't remember ever feeling fatigued during practices until I was seated afterward. When I was on the field, I was too busy playing to notice. I couldn't get enough of the sport; using my legs to kick the ball, run after it, and move from side to side in the goal to block shots as I played goalie enthralled me. I couldn't wait for Tuesday and Thursday afternoons to come and bring the next opportunity to get out on the field.

Photo Credit: Anne Mulville Moore

165

TOPSoccer didn't follow the structure of a regular soccer league. The focus was not on competition, and there were no games against other teams. Occasionally, the volunteers divided the team in two and let us play a quick scrimmage against each other.

Mostly, though, we did drills. The physical therapists, who volunteered their time to the program, typically led the drills, instructing us to dribble the ball from the side of the goal, out and around a cone several feet in front of the goal, and to send the ball sailing into the net. They often paired us up, usually with the teammates they had seen us developing friendships with, and asked us to practice passing the ball.

I had made some friends with other girls who had cerebral palsy, drawn to them not because of the disability we shared, but because of our common interests—our similar senses of humor, spirits of positivity and determination, tastes in clothes and color schemes—the qualities that typically draw people together. I remember beaming when I was paired up with my friend Emily, who was my age. Emily had very similar impairments, with the exception of speech. She stood across from me in her walker, passing the ball back and forth as she made jokes and inspired laughter for both of us.

"Get away from me, ball! Go to Meg," she'd say as she whacked the ball with her foot, her black hair swinging around her short body from the power and effort of her kick. "I thought I told you to go to Meg! You're coming back? Get out of here!"

We'd laugh until the whistle blew to signify that it was time for a water break or new drill.

Photo Credit: Anne Mulville Moore

Mom, Sean, and Brian quickly became avid volunteers at TOP-Soccer, eventually stepping up to coordinate major logistics of the program.

The boys helped with drills, stationing themselves at the cones and directing the players to go around it.

"I'm expecting a goal here," Sean once called to me as I rounded the cone. "Or else."

"Or else what?" I asked as I pushed through the thick grass with my walker. I could see the smug look on his face, signifying that a joke was brewing.

"You'll have to walk home!"

"It's Mom's car, so she gets to pick who gets a ride," I giggled.

"Well then, if you miss, I'll have to send you to the back of the line."

"You have to send me to the back of the line anyway so I can do the next round," I said, laughing even harder.

"Still expecting a goal. That's all I'm saying."

I rounded the last curve around the cone, letting the ball roll a short distance ahead of me so I could run up to it and kick it with extra momentum, making it speed into the net. A grin crossed my face as I glanced back at Sean, who was giving me an exaggerated round of applause and a genuine nod and smile of approval. I turned and ran to the back of the line, slapping hands with Brian on the way as he pulled the ball out of the goal and kicked it over to the therapist for the next kid.

❧

Our mother took on some of the administrative work of organizing the league, making the arrangements for each end-of-season banquet at a local restaurant in the fall and at Quassy Amusement Park in the spring.

Noticing when watching our team get called up at the Connecticut Junior Soccer Association annual banquet that we were the only league not being presented with trophies, Mom contacted the higher-ups and arranged for awards to be given to us in front of everybody, just like the other teams. Volunteering her time, she dedicated so much effort and energy to making every minor and monumental detail of the program as spectacular as it could be.

Excitement flooded my mind and body as the CJSA banquet's emcee announced our team and called each player up by name. I couldn't stop smiling as I zigzagged through the tables of the banquet hall in my walker and walked across the hardwood floor, listening to the thunderous applause and stopping in the center with my teammates. I beamed as I accepted my trophy, feeling its cool, gold soccer player figurine beneath my fingers as we had our picture taken. I looked out to my family, seated at a front table, grinning at me as they held every digital, disposable, and video camera we owned. In the moment and even more so years later, it dawned on me how fortunate and grateful I was that they were there to celebrate how agile I could be on my feet.

⁓⦿⦿⁓

A few weeks after the spring soccer season ended, I found myself not at all nifty on my feet. Actually, I found myself not able to be on my feet whatsoever. I remember the morning my body sent up the red flag. My mother had come into my bedroom to help me get out of bed, gently shaking my shoulder to wake me.

"Hey, Mego, come on. It's time to get up. Time for school."

I swung my legs over the side of the bed and offered her my hands. She helped me sit up on the edge of the mattress, pausing for a moment before standing me up and helping me walk to the bathroom.

"What are you doing?" she asked, noticing my limp as we took the first few steps together. "Does something hurt?"

"I don't know. I'm not doing that on purpose. It doesn't hurt."

"Not at all? You just can't put pressure on it?"

"I guess."

169

She picked me up and carried me the rest of the way to the bathroom and then back to my wheelchair in my room. Squatting down to my footrest, she took my foot in her hand and gently turned it to look at all of its sides and angles.

"Does anything hurt as I'm moving it?"

"No."

In the days and weeks that followed, doctors and therapists removed my shoes, braces, and socks to look closely at my feet, searching for any physical clue that might solve the puzzle of my sudden inability to bear weight. Nobody could find any answers, though.

Though my mother did not know the injury that was causing my limp, she knew the cause. Not long before it surfaced, I had received a new pair of braces, having outgrown my previous pair. The local orthotist had fitted me for them as he was supposed to, wrapping my feet in plaster and letting them dry into casts as if I had broken legs. When the plaster was dry, he cut both casts off, slicing through them with a motorized razor that looked like a pizza cutter as I, six years old then, cringed at how there was nothing between my skin and the cast and how one false move could leave a gash by mistake. Removing the casts without difficulty or injury, he scheduled an appointment for us to return to pick up the finished braces.

When my mother and I sat in the white-walled exam room weeks later and watched the orthotist walk in with my new braces, multiple reactions flashed across my mind. At first, I was thrilled with their appearance. The clinic had recently gained the capacity to print images on the plastic. The pair I had just grown out of featured one soccer ball on the center of the otherwise plain white plastic that covered my calf. This new pair showed purple butterflies on every inch of the surface. Matched with violet Velcro straps for the top of the calf and the ankle, their appearance was quite pleasing to my eyes.

When the orthotist fastened them onto my legs for the first time, though, puzzlement replaced my excitement.

These can't be right, I thought.

Every time I got new braces, the end of each brace had come to the tips of my toes, fitting my foot to a T. My toes only reached about half of these braces' length.

"Why are they so *big*?" Mom asked, voicing the question that was also running through my mind.

"We make them for growth," he explained. "Insurance companies only cover these once a year, so we make them big so they last."

"But won't that hurt her feet?" Mom asked, looking horrified. "They're huge!"

"They'll work for her. She won't have a problem. Just have her use them as she did her old ones."

And yet there I was, confined to my chair, only walking for the purpose of showing medical professionals my limp. Finally, at wit's end and not finding the source of the problem, my doctors ordered an X-ray, telling my mother to get the imaging done at a local general hospital.

"Can't they do that at the doctor's office?" I remember asking when she told me the plan.

Although cerebral palsy mandated that I visit medical facilities every few months for orthopedic and neurological checkups, I was afraid of hospitals and preferred to stay out of them unless I knew that a typical-looking doctor's office was my destination inside. I could never pinpoint the reason for this phobia; I was comfortable with doctors and nurses. Perhaps it was the thought of the needles, the sharp instruments, or how many times people get cut open or lose their lives there—I could never say for certain.

"I asked them that, but they have better technology down at the hospital," she explained. "Sean, Brian, and I will be with you the whole time. It'll be quick, and then we can go do something fun."

I remember her pulling the van up to the sliding glass doors of the hospital. She spotted a vacant hospital wheelchair deserted on the sidewalk and asked if I would be okay with using that one, already set up and ready to go, as opposed to my own that was packed in the trunk. I agreed, although as soon as I sat down, I started to shiver—not from the cold, but simply from the association it had to the hospital. Its large brown seat could have held two of me.

"Want me to sit with you?" Brian asked.

I nodded, sliding myself to the side to make room. Putting his arm around me as he climbed in, he began to dispense every joke he had recently heard or thought of, making me laugh all the way to the X-ray wing.

❧

When my X-ray revealed nothing more than fully intact bones, my doctors expressed their befuddlement to my mother. They had conducted every test and exam they could think of and simply couldn't find an answer.

If they don't know what's wrong, who will? I wondered. *Aren't doctors supposed to know what's wrong?*

Mom assured me that she was already looking into more doctors and would find somebody who could figure everything out. It soon occurred to her that someone had already given her the answer months before my limp began.

It all started at the boys' baseball game. A woman approached Mom and me as we watched the game from the bleachers. She introduced herself as Kathy D'Andrea, the mother of one of Sean and Brian's friends and teammates, Louis.

"Have you ever considered taking Meg to Shriners Hospital for Children? My dad is a Shriner."

Mrs. D'Andrea began to describe the work her father did as a Mason that raised funds and awareness for the hospital and how Shriners Hospitals had a reputation for providing excellent health care to children with special needs. Mom recounted the story of how she and Da had registered me as a patient at the Springfield, Massachusetts hospital when I was a year old, just in case I needed their services when I got older. She always remembered how positive the staff had been, telling my parents how much potential I had for improvement. They had even projected a possibility that I might walk on my own someday.

Mom thanked Mrs. D'Andrea for the information, telling her that she would keep it in mind.

When the memory of this conversation crossed her mind, she called Shriners. Able to schedule an appointment immediately, we soon found ourselves in the van, driving for what seemed to me like a life-time. Mom had explained to me a thousand times that we were going to another hospital, but never once during the commute did it hit me. My mind was occupied with other things—joking around with the boys and Brian's best friend, Ed, who had come along as Mom had promised the boys a visit to the Basketball Hall of Fame after the appointment since it was in Springfield, and excitedly searching for a familiar house outside the window to satisfy a burning inquiry in my six-year-old brain: Homer Simpson and his family lived in Springfield. Would we get to meet them?

Before I could vocalize this question, it occurred to me that the Simpsons lived in Springfield, Illinois, not Springfield, Massachusetts.

~~∞~~

It was only when we were passing through the sliding glass doors that my mother's words hit me. Without even glancing at my surroundings, I lowered my head to my clear plastic wheelchair tray and framed my face with my folded arms. This was another hospital. This visit didn't come with a guarantee of a quick, in-and-out trip to the X-ray wing like the trip to the local hospital had.

"I want to go home," I sobbed. "Please! Let me go home. Please, let me go home . . ."

A friendly nurse joined my family and Ed in trying to cheer me up. They begged me to look up, to see where I was, assuring me that it was perfectly fine. After some serious coaxing, I obliged, lifting my head and wiping away the tears, feeling confusion settle in as soon as I took in the bright colors, cozy couches, innumerable bins of toys, and life-sized Lego statues of firefighter clowns and Mickey Mouse. There had to be some sort of mistake—this was not a hospital; this was a kid's wonderland!

It seemed as though the boys and I had hardly scratched the surface of the gold mine of toys and games in the waiting room when we heard "MARGARET?" shouted from the far corner. We returned the toys to their bins and followed a smiling nurse to an exam room. My eyes widened at the multicolored carpet, the stuffed Big Bird and Sully life-sized figures, the fluorescent light covers that depicted multicolored hot air balloons floating across a baby-blue sky, and, most of all, the genuine, gigantic smiles of the entire staff. It was astonishing that such a kid-friendly environment could be classified as a hospital.

I soon found myself in my walker, hobbling down the hallway toward Big Bird and back to my new doctor, who was squatting in the center, telling me how great I was doing as he observed. I did this a few more times, first barefoot then with shoes and braces.

175

After consulting with a team of physical therapists and occupational therapists, the doctor sent me to the Orthotics and Prosthetics department on the opposite side of the waiting room, where I was cast for new braces.

Even at six years old, I noticed how different the care was here—how it was centered on protecting and promoting the health and happiness of the child. It was the little things that struck me, like the way the orthotist had put a tube in between my legs and the casts to protect me from the scissors when she cut them off.

She released my feet from the stiflingly hot casts and handed me a ring with several samples of uniquely-patterned plastic dangling from it—rainbows, pictures of cats, navy-blue camouflage, pink camouflage, and flowers among other designs. While she filled out paperwork, I flipped through each sample and decided on a psychedelic pattern.

A few weeks later, my new orthotist revealed a pair of braces that displayed stripes of every color of the rainbow, topped off with royal purple Velcro straps. They fit like a glove, molded to the precise shape and size of my feet. We went out into the vacant waiting room, where the real test was administered. Mom helped me transfer from my chair to my forest-green walker for the first time in months. Then, as if I was an astronaut taking my first step on the moon, I lifted my foot and let it fall ever so slowly. I took another step, then a few more, noticing that my limp had suddenly disappeared.

One small step for Meg, one giant step for Meg-kind.

I smiled and started to initiate the action I had dreamed of taking for months. I took off running, sprinting around the play area bordered by dozens of chairs. Only slowing briefly to take each corner, I ran as fast and for as long as I could before having to take a break. My body heaved with breath while also emitting laughter as I ran.

Little did I know, now that I was back on my feet, I was about to find that there was some unique terrain waiting for me outside the hospital. While some of it was anticipated by my family, there also was territory we never expected I'd step into.

Chapter 8

Flying on Many a Frozen Pond

It was as if I was flying.

The only sensation telling me I was still grounded was the vibration of the skates sliding across the ice beneath me.

The frigid New York air of Rocking Horse Ranch Resort rushed over my face as we circled the frozen pond. A Girl Scout weekend trip, many of my friends had come with their families too.

We had already gone tubing before hitting the ice. I think we left my chair at the bottom of the slope and my family helped me to walk up partway before Brian gave me a piggyback ride to the top. Somebody tossed a wide, multicolored inner tube near us, and it landed on the glittering snow with a bounce. My friends' fathers caught the rebound, steadying it as Brian climbed into the black center seat. Once he had settled into a cross-legged position, Mom and Sean helped me into Brian's lap. After quadruple-checking to make sure I was snugly wedged inside the tube and secured by his bear-hug grip, Mom hurried down the hill as Sean climbed into his tube.

The fathers received the wave from Mom when she arrived at the lowest point, and they gave our tubes a hefty shove. We hit a pocket of wind shortly after launching and began to spin. The world surrounding us became a blur as if we had been swallowed up by a tornado funnel cloud. My stomach did somersaults, tickling me, conjuring hysterical laughter as the wind rushed roughly over our faces. The spinning ceased abruptly as Mom caught both tubes as they slowed with the transition to level ground. Before she could ask about the ride, the three of us spoke almost simultaneously.

"Can we go again? Can we? Please?"

❧

Though it was easy enough to make tubing accessible—I had been sledding down small hills with my brothers for many winters—ice skating posed a challenge.

No one was certain how or if I would navigate the ice, but my family decided to try anyway. Having heard before the trip that the other girls were scheduled for an ice-skating session, Mom devised a plan for me to skate right along with them. Borrowing a pair of double-bladed skates from my friend's family, she reasoned that double blades, together with my braces and walker, would give me as much stability as I could possibly get.

My excursion didn't come with lessons—there was no manual for using assistive technology to skate. It was a matter of trial and error, learning that the slippery ice left me leaning backward into my walker's thick strip of cushioning, which wrapped around my torso, keeping me upright. To compensate, I needed to pull my upper body forward by engaging my abs and gripping my walker handles so that my head was over my feet, helping me stay in a straighter and taller position. I learned to swish my feet from side to side, moving myself forward as my blades carved chalklike marks on the smooth surface of the ice.

When I had the basics down, I increased my speed, laughing as Mom and the boys, all chuckling, scrambled to reach a speed identical to mine. Catching up to my friends and their families, my eyes met those of my friends and our laughter amplified, filling the air with a sweet melody as our breath hung in the air like wisps of clouds. Side by side, my friends and I tested our gracefulness and swiftness on the ice.

Photo Credit: Anne Mulville Moore

I didn't realize at the time how much of a frozen pond my life was back then, at six years old. No one knew how I would navigate the terrain I approached that year, but those who cared for me were certain that it was the key for me to prosper in life.

The teachers and administrators at Long Meadow Elementary School completely agreed with my mother when she expressed her desire for me to be mainstreamed—to be in a regular education classroom completing the same assignments and being held to the same academic standards as my able-bodied peers. This, I would learn later in life, was not always a given—students with physical disabilities like mine are often stereotyped, labeled as incapable, and put in a room where they play with toys long outgrown by their age group and where they work to develop basic life skills, such as cooking, baking, and doing laundry. Fortunately, the staff had recognized my intelligence as soon as they had given me my DynaVox.

"There's a lot going on in there—she's very bright. There's no question about if she is understanding what I'm teaching in class," Ms. Tripp had said after observing me in preschool.

My mother later told me how wonderful the school was with making my classroom accommodations. Seeing how well I was able to convey my thoughts with my DynaVox, the school administrators reasoned that I could complete my work on a desktop computer (communication devices were still about four years away from having the capacity to run word processors and all other programs other than the speech software). Each year, always on a wheeled computer table, my computer was rolled to my new classroom before I arrived on the first day. Aligned with rows of normal school desks to enable me to sit beside my peers, the table housed a flat-screen computer monitor and an adaptive keyboard on one side and had enough room on the other for my DynaVox and the small wooden tabletop easel used to prop up my books and paperwork.

In front of the computer monitor sat a large, turquoise Intel-liKeys keyboard. Supported by its thick built-in black stand, about three-quarters of the surface was occupied by an interchangeable papery overlay showing the QWERTY keyboard, each letter shown in bold, black font within a pastel-yellow square and each number in a pastel-yellow circle in a row above the letters. It also had buttons that allowed me to control the mouse, since I did not have the fine motor skills to control a regular mouse (every time I placed a hand on a regular mouse and tried to bring the cursor to an icon, it flew wildly over the screen like a bee flying in looping circles). Like my DynaVox, the surface was covered by a keyguard—a hard plastic grid adorned with holes that lined up with the keys of the keyboard to help me push my desired key without accidentally hitting those next to it.

Except for word prediction and math programs that allowed me to write out longhand equations independently, the computer had the same software as all other computers in the school—Microsoft Office, Internet Explorer, and Storybook Weaver among other applications.

Photo Credit: Anne Mulville Moore

As I progressed to higher grade levels, the computer and, later, my communication device became my sole means of completing my schoolwork. In the earlier grades, though, like first grade, I used my DynaVox to dictate my answers to my aides, who handwrote them, word for word, on worksheets that, in the early 2000s, could not be transmitted into my computer. When the class worked silently and independently on assignments, my aide pulled her chair close to mine, reading my screen without my having to push the "Speak" button. My process for homework was almost identical—family members sat by me each night and wrote down my answers without changing the words I had given them. At home, though, I used my own voice to give my answers, since my family understood my verbalizations.

My teachers were told to treat me as a regular student who simply needed help physically manipulating materials, and that is how I felt. I didn't see myself as too much different than my classmates. I was doing the work and was making friends like everybody else. The only unique elements were my use of assistive technology and the support I received from my teachers, aides, and therapists to promote my physical progression as well as my intellectual growth.

My therapists always collaborated with my teacher to make sure I was prompted to maintain good posture, to use my left hand—which, as one of the tightest and weakest parts of my body, benefited from routinely attempting fine motor activities to promote its flexibility and strength—to hold pages or craft materials steady as my right hand worked on creating a masterpiece, and to use my own speech as often as possible. I recall how well my teachers balanced my academic and physical needs. It started in first grade, when classroom playtime faded into the background and regular schoolwork emerged.

One particular moment, as brief and minor as it appeared at the time, remains in my mind. My teacher, Mrs. Burke, stood at the overhead projector, her bob of brown hair and her face illuminated by the overhead's light bulb—the only source of brightness in the room at the time. She was calling on students to read their answers to our morning math work as she wrote them on the overhead transparency in vibrant Expo marker—red, blue, green, or simply black.

"Meg," she called, looking over the ruby brim of her reading glasses to meet my eyes. "What did you get for the next one, girlfriend? Can you tell us?"

Smiling and nodding, I looked down at my worksheet. My hand automatically flew to my Dyna even before my eyes left the page. My fingers, though, hadn't yet reached the "0" key when Mrs. Burke spoke again.

"Ah," she said, stopping me in my tracks. "How about you do this one with your voice?"

When a child receives a communication device, especially at a young age, it is easy for them to fall into the trap of perpetually relying on the device. This impedes the improvement of speech and could leave the child without any means to communicate when the device malfunctions. It is for this reason that I always used my own voice with my immediate family and that my teacher sometimes asked me to verbalize my answers without the Dyna.

"None," I said, smiling at the simplicity of the word as my tongue touched the roof of my mouth and dropped back down for each "n" sound.

"And what is the number form of none?" Mrs. Burke asked.

It was the "z" sound that would trip me up—I just knew it, even before I set out to say it. It always had, and it would until I learned an effective way to arrange my mouth to say it somewhat clearly as an adult. As a child, I tended to skip over the sound completely. I wonder if the cringe that occurred inside showed on my face, because Mrs. Burke encouraged me to take my time with voicing the syllables. "Eero" is the word I produced, my teeth and tongue simply unwilling to coordinate to make the appropriate sound.

I don't remember being self-conscious about this exchange happening in front of my friends—many of them had been with me since kindergarten and, even as six-year-olds, had always commended any progress and effort they saw me making. Some had even begun to understand what I said without my device at recess and playdates, and as we grew up, they practically became experts.

"Let's try that word again. See if you can really focus on getting that first sound out," Mrs. Burke said. "Take your time—I'm not going anywhere. Neither are these goofs."

Mrs. Burke was known among the students as one of the funniest teachers in the school, sliding jokes into her lessons, reminding us of her obsession with chocolate and her willingness to accept it in any form and at any time, and often making use of her famous catchphrases, "Heads are gonna roll" and "RUN SCREAMING FROM THE ROOM," when her plan had gone awry, and "run like the wind" when she knew we would be playing sports in gym class or after school. She typically had the class in hysterics within minutes of the day's start.

On this day, though, her eyes didn't show that a joke was imminent. They were calm with patience and alight with eagerness, as if she wanted to see me discover that I could make the sounds clearer than I thought.

I took a deep breath, adding sound to it as I exhaled. An "s" sound emerged, turning into a "d" then a "j," before I could get my tongue in the right spot to form the "z."

"Jah-zah-eero—zero." I smiled, relieved that the proper sound had finally emerged.

I laughed silently as my friends Nikki and Colleen nodded in a goofy sort of way and gave me the "okay" sign with their fingers from across the room, each of them grinning.

"Nice job," Mrs. Burke exclaimed. "And that is correct."

Photo Credit: Anne Mulville Moore

This was only part of the physical regimen I followed. Throughout elementary school, I was pulled out of class for therapy. Each session of physical, occupational, and speech therapy lasted about half an hour and usually occurred semiweekly.

Though my school therapy guaranteed hard work, I was intrigued by it, loving the prospects of getting active during the school day and of exercising in general. Admittedly, too, though I loved school, the therapy sessions were a nice break from class.

I remember the coolness of the mat beneath me as I lay on it. It was squishy in texture and vibrant in color, each section of the folding mat a different one—red, blue, yellow, and green. I spent my physical therapy sessions with my back pressed against it for at least part of the time. My PT, Tina Meyers, always sat below me, cradling one of my legs in her arms, one hand pushing the sole of my foot upward as she used her other hand to push my knee down, igniting a fire-like stretch from the back of my thigh to my ankle—the hamstring stretch. Being the tightest part of my body, that stretch made me squirm for its duration. It didn't hurt—it was just a very potent stretch that inched me out of my comfort zone.

"Relax, relax, relax, relax," Tina always urged, her voice almost a whisper as a smile spread across her lean face framed by wisps of sandy brown hair that had escaped from her ponytail. "Almost there. Thirty more seconds—you got this! Watch any good TV shows lately? What was that one you said you liked?"

"*Lizzie McGuire*," I replied, my voice a little strained from the stretch.

"And that's on Disney Channel?" she asked, sometimes having me repeat my words for better clarity.

"Yeah."

"Cool! And what about music? What have you been listening to?"

Our chitchat made the stretch fade slightly into the background.

I typically went from lying down to trying to balance on my hands and knees. As Tina counted backwards from the number of seconds she wanted me to hold the position for, each time starting with a slightly higher number, I could feel the weight of my body at my elbows and at the bend of my wrists as my fingers curled into fists despite my best attempts to keep them fanned.

"Nine, eight, seven—come on, come on," she'd exclaimed as she noticed my elbows trembling with fatigue. "Hold it, hold it, hold it—you've got this! A few more seconds—six, five, four, three, two, one! Good job! Take a rest."

She'd help me lower myself, guiding my body as I bent my elbows and rolled over.

Eventually, I sat on the big blue therapy ball, trying to stay upright as Tina rolled it slightly from side to side and back and forth.

"Don't let me knock you over! Don't let me knock you over," she'd say as she gently gave my shoulders a gentle shove backwards. "Use those tummy muscles—pull them tight!"

A dull burn ignited in my abs as I pulled my torso forward and held it there with my head parallel to my knees. I'd hold it until fatigue set in, throwing me backwards onto the squishy surface of the ball.

∾⁗

Tina also attended gym class with me from time to time. Observing me as I ran across the hardwood floor in my walker alongside my friends, she'd slide into line with us to nudge the walker over so that I walked in a straighter pattern.

After hearing that I was interested in participating in the six-week gymnastics unit just like my friends, she came, helping me tuck my chin and hug my arms around my legs so I could do somersaults across the mats covering the gym floor. With my aide spotting me on one side and Tina on the other, each taking and supporting one of my arms, I walked a short way across the padded wooden balance beam, putting one foot in front of the other.

I didn't mind being the only one who needed extra help in P. E.. What mattered to me was having an opportunity to try what was being offered to my peers—it looked like too much fun to choose an alternative activity that was guaranteed to be accessible, such as running or dribbling a soccer ball in the empty edges of the gym. Fortunately, my mother, teachers, and therapist agreed.

Photo Credit: Anne Mulville Moore

My occupational therapist, Ms. Gerry Campbell, also saw me inside and outside of the therapy room. Ms. Gerry, my friends and peers

189

always said, looked just like my mother, with pale ivory skin and red waves cascading down to her shoulders. Throughout my elementary school years, kids would mistake Mom for Ms. Gerry, running up and hugging and high-fiving her as she made her way into the school or around town. She got used to it and was amused; she had always wanted a twin.

"Alright, darlin'," Ms. Gerry always said as she rolled my chair into the therapy room, passing the mats on the floor to get to the table in the back. "How about we start with stretching out those hands and arms, and then we can do something fun—putty or something? Sound good?"

"Yeah," I'd say with my natural voice.

Sitting in a chair beside me, she took one of my arms in her hands. Gently guiding my elbow into extension, she pressed her palm into mine, pushing my wrist into a vertical angle, holding it there for a few seconds as a soft burn of a stretch settled in. Lifting my arm over my head, she helped me keep it up for a moment, the burn crawling from my armpit to my fingertips. She repeated the process with the other arm and later guided both arms up simultaneously, igniting a burn on both sides of my body. After bringing them down and giving me a moment's rest, she took my hand. Dragging her thumbs from the center of my palm outward, she stretched my muscles, slightly tugging my skin in opposite directions as the tiniest of burning sensations prickled it.

"Okay," she said, reaching across the table for a small tub of neon pink putty. "Let's see if I can stump you this time."

Pulling out the putty and taking a handful of small, golf tee–like pegs from another container, she kneaded them into the putty.

"There are ten in there for you to find," she said, plopping the putty on the table in front of me. "Don't forget to use both hands."

Considering the task to be a game, I pulled the ball apart, first taking it in both hands in front of me, then yanking it in either direction at once, creating long, taffy-like strands that decreased in thickness the more I pulled. Separating the two halves, I placed one piece on the table and began tearing the other in two. As my left hand was tighter than my right, I mainly used it to hold the putty as my right worked to make finer pinches, separating the parts that, from the hard lumps protruding, clearly contained tees.

"Don't forget to work that left hand just like the right," Ms. Gerry coached from beside me.

Using my nail to peel away the last of the putty, I transferred the peg from my left hand to the right and reached to put it in a small container on the table, sometimes feeling it slip through my fingers on the way, the peg clattering to the azure-tiled floor. Ms. Gerry retrieved and held the peg in her palm at a height that made me stretch to reach.

"I think I'll have to find a better way to hide these if you keep doing it this fast. Nice job," she exclaimed as I dropped the last one into the container, a small *plink* sounding as the peg landed on the others. "Oh, your paintbrushes came in—and just in time too. Mrs. Porter-Hahn says you're painting on Thursday. I'm coming to your class this week, but let me show you—"

She'd produce the latest adaptive gizmos: paintbrushes with widened tops in the shape of turkey basters; pencils with chunky grips; scissors that stood up, the blades becoming like the mouth of an alligator, moving down to cut paper with the simple touch of a lever-like handle; eating utensils with thick handles—tools that enabled me to partake in normal school activities as independently as possible. She let me hold them and practice the motion needed to use them, giving me a preview of what she would help me work on when she visited my art class or friend-filled lunch table a few times a month.

Photo Credit: Anne Mulville Moore

Ms. Gerry also collaborated with my speech therapist, Mrs. Sarah Moreira. Every few weeks, she met us in Mrs. Moreira's office for a joint therapy session in which they fused their respective areas of expertise to devise the best practices and positioning for feeding.

"Meg, when I popped into lunch the other day, I noticed you started out with a nice, straight head," Ms. Gerry sometimes said.

192

"But when you were talking to your friends and then went back to take a bite, you were tilting your head. I just don't want food to go down the wrong way—can we practice turning and keeping our heads straight?"

They had me turn toward them, to my left and right, and practice turning back while maintaining a straight head, keeping my positioning steady during and after my movement.

"Hey, girlfriend. I grabbed your lunch box as I was rolling you out of class," Mrs. Moreira sometimes said, flashing me a broad smile as her wild, cinnamon-shaded curls fell around her face. "It's almost snack time for your class anyway—do you mind having yours here with us today? That way I can see how you're doing with working that mouth and tongue when eating."

"Sure," I'd say using my own voice.

In her office, I didn't feel self-conscious about using my natural voice, or about talking to somebody outside my family without my communication device. I didn't worry whether she understood or was just agreeing, nodding and yessing whatever I said as others tended to do when they didn't know what I was saying but tried unsuccessfully not to make it evident. She could decipher my words and hold a normal conversation with me, only occasionally having me repeat myself to clarify what she couldn't quite understand or what she wanted me to work on enunciating better.

"Let's try that again—really focus on making that *sh* sound. Watch me—*s*ure. Sh-ure."

"Ja—sha—err," I'd stumble over that first sound before getting it out with some clarity. "Sure."

"Great job! That is getting better, you know. We'll keep working on it."

She would unpack the cereal bar, two colorful dishcloths, and the bottle of the nutritional supplement PediaSure my mother had sent.

"Apple cinnamon? Are you sure you want this?" she always asked, keeping a straight face only for a moment before breaking into a laugh as she held up the cereal bar with its metallic green wrapper. "I haven't tried this kind yet. I'd be happy to take it off your hands."

The three of us always laughed, and then Mrs. Moreira would don plastic gloves, open the snack, and feed it to me. She held the cereal bar up to my mouth for each bite and carefully observed how my mouth and throat moved as I chewed, swallowed, and drank my PediaSure from my semitransparent turquoise nosy cup—a cup that had part of the top lip missing, making it easy for therapists and caregivers to see how much liquid was getting to the person being fed. Ms. Gerry watched my body and positioning as I ate. At different times, they each made suggestions for how I could be better positioned for safer, more efficient eating.

"I wonder if she would have more stability by being a little more forward while drinking," Ms. Gerry once pondered aloud. "Meg, can you try that for us? Don't lean all the way forward so that you're taking a nap on the table, but put your arms on the table and lean a little on your forearms."

"Yeah, I like that better for her head positioning," Mrs. Moreira replied after giving me a drink of my banana-flavored PediaSure (which I actually enjoyed, as its taste resembled flavored milk). "But, Meg, remember to keep your head straight when you swallow; you started to put it back a little. Look straight ahead after we take the cup away if that helps you to remember."

I didn't mind getting these reminders—having been in speech therapy since I was only a few weeks old, they seemed a natural part of my life. I just incorporated them into my routine, sometimes remembering with the help of my mother and school staff.

On days when I solely had speech therapy, Mrs. Moreira rolled me down to her office with my DynaVox over her shoulder, hanging by its long black carrying strap. She typically had a funny story about her cat to tell as she parked my chair at the table and set up my communication device.

"Do you know my cat slept on my head again last night? I woke up this morning and she was literally lying on top of my head with her paws tangled in my hair. I don't know what I'm going to do with her, Meg."

"Crazy cat," I'd laugh, not quite getting the "z" sound, almost skipping it completely.

"What was that? What kind of cat? Try that "z" again; put your tongue behind your teeth and blow, like this—cray-*zee*. Cray-*zee*."

"Cray-eee."

"Almost. Try one more time. Cray-*zee*."

I inhaled, fueling my sounds with the air. "Cray-zee."

"Great job! Remember that breathing is the key," she said. "Okay, so today I wanted to do your oral motor exercises, go through that list of words you wanted to work on, and then get some of that speech for your presentation programmed into the Dyna—I'll probably snag the device when you're in your walker in Gym and do the bulk of it then, but I thought I could do some with you here."

Until I took over the task myself in fourth grade, my speech therapists and my mother took care of saving preprogrammed messages to the Dyna, taking lines I would be reciting in school, Girl Scouts, and CCD class at church, as well as common words, phrases, and names I used frequently, and keying them, letter by letter back then, into a button on the device. It wasn't that hard to do once you were familiar with the process, but it did take some time to navigate the settings.

Speech devices also stumble over unique and even basic words, mispronouncing and leaving programmers to puzzle through the best way to spell them phonetically.

Mrs. Moreira once struggled for days on end with the word "Australia," which came out as "Austra-lee-uh." Fortunately, she was able to correct the pronunciation in time for my class presentation.

But rumor has it that the poor woman still has nightmares about the word.

Photo Credit: Anne Mulville Moore

Mostly, though, my time in speech therapy was dedicated to improving my natural verbalizations and working through oral motor exercises to strengthen my jaw, lips, and tongue. My personal exercises involved moving my tongue from side to side, puckering and pursing my lips, lifting my tongue to the roof of my mouth and pulling it down quickly to produce a clicking sound, and more. Clicking my tongue seemed to become second nature for me shortly after Mrs.

Moreira introduced it, and it even seemed amusing—I often found myself doing it in bored moments waiting to proceed down the school hallway or elsewhere.

Some exercises, though, had much more appeal. Jaw strengthening came with a method I looked forward to even before my speech therapist arrived at my classroom to retrieve me each week: chewing bubblegum. Because my muscles didn't operate normally or have typical reflexes, I wasn't really allowed to chew gum as a kid (I could have lollipops and—thank God—chocolate), as my family and therapists feared I would accidentally swallow it. Mrs. Moreira got creative when she decided that gum would be beneficial for me, putting it in a piece of cheesecloth—a gauzelike material ordinarily used for baking—and holding onto the end as I chewed. She was pleased with the physical outcomes of the exercise, and I was just happy about how potently the sweet flavor soaked through the cloth.

Not all exercises and movements came as easily as chewing, though. Bringing my tongue from side to side was very hard—no matter how much I tried, my tongue only stuck straight out and back in. Attempting to entice the muscle to bank left and right, Mrs. Moreira held a Dum-Dum Pop to either side of my mouth, encouraging me to work to situate my tongue so that it touched the flavor of my choice—almost always Blu Raspberry. When I had inched my tongue to the side and tasted the zing of sourness amid the thick sweetness, she moved the pop to be just above my upper lip and, later, below my lower lip, asking me to stretch my tongue to reach it. Afterward, she put it in my mouth, holding the stick for me, and asked me to work on closing my lips around it. She sent me back to class with a blue tongue.

When I had been quietly rolled back to my desk, my friends always turned around, smiling and giving a small wave. I had my fun in these moments, sticking out my blue tongue, making them do double takes. *Where'd you get candy?* they'd mouth, looking a bit jealous.

I always smiled and turned my attention to the lesson the teacher was giving, leaving my friends wondering until we had the freedom to chat at lunch and recess.

As my mother has always said, sometimes it pays to be disabled.

My friends understood a remarkable amount about my disability at a young age. They understood that I needed help standing, sitting, and walking and why I needed each piece of my assistive technology. They knew I did the same work they did, only using a computer or a scribe to help me write my thoughts down rather than writing by hand. They knew I could play and attend playdates, sleepovers, birthday parties, and other events just like them and that my mom had to come along to help me with my personal care needs and with transferring in and out of equipment and furniture. They knew why and how I rode the elevator at school—two classmates, a different pair each time, got to accompany me and my aide whenever the class traveled to a different level of the school. They knew why I left our classroom a few times a week, why therapists showed up in our art and gym classes, and that my therapists helped me strengthen and stretch my muscles and have access to the same activities they were doing.

There was a part of my experience that, up until about the first grade, was a mystery to them, though. I was open to letting them know what it was like to be me, but I didn't quite know what words to use when, at recess or at gatherings beyond school, they asked questions like "Is it hard to use all that equipment you have at school?" and "What's it feel like when you move?" I did my best to answer them, explaining that because I had been doing it for so long, it seemed easy and natural to use my equipment and to have help moving. Still, my mind pondered these questions, trying to find words to paint my classmates a more detailed picture.

What's it like to do all this? I mused. *And why is it so hard to figure out how to explain it? I've used all this stuff my whole life.*

Years later, it dawned on me that it was so difficult to describe because I didn't know life without the support and equipment. I think able-bodied people would probably have the same struggle if I asked them what it felt like to stand and walk unassisted; there is simply a gap between the experiences of abled and disabled people that makes it impossible for one party to fully understand what the other must contend with.

I don't know if they ever overheard my friends expressing their curiosity, but in any case, the school staff wanted the other students to understand what it was like for me to navigate the world with a disability. Each year, my therapists teamed up with my teachers to organize an in-class event deemed "Meg Day." My therapists brought equipment from their rooms that they hoped would simulate what it was like for me to move and function. Each therapist set up a station that demonstrated movement and functioning of the actions they worked on with me.

"Are you still up for helping me at the Dyna station?" Mrs. Moreira asked annually before the event.

"Yeah!"

"Good, because you're the expert—you'll probably run the show again," she said as she beamed.

For the hour or so that Meg Day took place, the two of us always sat at a small table in the back of the classroom with the Dyna halfway between us. When it was time to rotate groups, we welcomed the newcomers, inviting them to gather around the table as Mrs. Moreira gave a brief introduction.

"Of course you guys know that Meg's DynaVox helps her talk," she began.

"Quite the chatterbox if you ask me," my friend Colleen once said, a smug smile on her freckled face. "And I'm not talking about the Dyna."

"Hey," I laughed as the word slipped out of my mouth.

"Does anybody else think it's ironic that Colleen is the one calling someone else a chatterbox?" my friend Gabby asked, a broad smile spreading over her face.

"*Yes*, Gabby," I laughed.

"Very funny," Colleen replied as she stuck out her tongue.

"Anyway," Mrs. Moreira laughed, turning the device so they could see the alphabet on the screen—each bold, black letter sitting at the heart of a white square framed by the clear plastic keyguard holes. "I don't know how closely you have watched Meg work the device, but she pushes each letter, and it appears in the white rectangle on the top. When she wants to make it talk, she hits the message window where the words show up."

She always had me demonstrate as the group gathered behind me, watching in a way that they had not before—following my fingers with their eyes, observing which button I used to make the device speak, leaning in close to see how I cleared the message window of old messages, tapping the small red key labeled "Clear" that showed an icon of an upside-down pencil with its pink eraser touching a page.

"And notice how gentle Meg is being with her fingers? She really doesn't have to tap it hard at all. So please remember to be *very very* gentle," Mrs. Moreira said. "Okay, why don't you guys form a line near me? Who wants to go first?"

Each classmate was allowed to type and have a sentence read by the device. I watched the concentration appear on their faces as their fingers drummed delicately on the screen. I tried to read their expressions for hints, but it was hard to tell whether their amused grins meant that something comical was about to sound or if my classmates were simply entertained by the novelty of trying the device.

All I could see of the device was its thick white frame. It was strange to be on the other side, to be the one waiting to hear what message would emerge from the speakers.

Most used their time to type in an introduction for themselves ("*Hi! My name is . . .*"), while others seized the opportunity to type in a cool or funny phrase ("*Hey dude, what's up?*"). We all laughed after each utterance before quickly hushing ourselves to see what the next person would come up with.

I vaguely recall my friends sharing their reactions with me after the event.

"I knew you made that look easy," one friend said. "But, *man*, I was really sweating it trying to figure out where all the letters were, and then trying to make the thing talk, and even just touching it hard enough to click but not too hard—that's, like, tough to do."

"Yeah, but you get used to it," I replied through my DynaVox. "Like if you did that every day, you'd catch onto it quick. I almost don't even have to think about all that anymore."

☙❧

From the Dyna station, I could catch glimpses of the stations across the room. By the chalkboard, Ms. Gerry had laid out my adaptive art supplies and was letting my peers hold them or perhaps even try to make some lines on paper.

Tina's station was the one that captured my eyes and mind while waiting for a new person or group to settle in at the Dyna. Tina had put out a line of therapy tools, among them a balance board.

As I watched people step onto the square wooden board and try to maintain stability as it seesawed on the two half-moon–shaped pieces of wood beneath, I could hear Tina begin her explanation.

"This is how it feels for Meg to stand and walk. Her body doesn't have too much balance, so it kind of feels like a seesaw motion."

I turned these sentences over in my mind repeatedly, deliberating on their levels of accuracy. Did I really feel like I was seesawing when I walked?

Well, kind of, I guess, I thought, reflecting on the way my whole body tended to sway from side to side when people took steps with me while holding me up.

⁓∾⧸⁓

My classmates had varied reactions to Meg Day. Most, especially close friends, loved every minute, relishing the hands-on challenge of using the equipment. For others the event was an eye-opener, and I imagine it left them hungering for more experience of what a day in the life of a physically challenged child was like.

My mother was shocked when the phone rang in the hours after Meg Day one year.

It was the mother of my classmate, who I'll call Carrie. She was flabbergasted by the reaction Carrie had brought home.

"She's been asking me to help her walk around the house. She asked me to help her get to the bathroom too," she explained. "She said it has something to do with what they did in school today? Something to do with Meg?"

My mother didn't quite know what to say, other than to explain the purpose of Meg Day.

"They just want to help the kids understand what Meg has to go through to navigate the world."

My mother said Carrie's mom seemed shocked throughout the conversation. Perhaps Meg Day was an education for both students and their families, a humbling experience showing them not only the rugged terrain I had to face each day but also how my family had to support me in the simplest of tasks.

As I grew older, I noticed a difference between the friends who had been with me through elementary school and those who had come into my life later. My Long Meadow friends were more in tune to my needs, anticipating them before I could even ask. They ran over to pick up items I dropped. They didn't hesitate to speak up and show others that I needed to be included just like everyone else.

"Of course Meg can do this," some said when others questioned whether to invite me to a go-carting birthday party or other unique activities. "Meg can do anything we do. She might need to make modifications to help her use that kind of stuff. But she will do it—you'll see."

When my therapists first told me they were going to start having Meg Day, I thought it was cool to have something dedicated to me; but at six or seven years old, I didn't understand why they felt it was so important. In fact, I was surprised that it was such a priority for them each year—I saw myself as a typical student who needed a little extra help. When I looked back later, I saw how much it had impacted me and those surrounding me, creating a more tolerant and inclusive community by giving them a close look at my family's often-challenging reality.

There was a part of our family life, though, that came as unfamiliar territory to our friends and even to us sometimes. We never knew when our plans for the day would be disrupted by a malfunctioning piece of equipment or a family matter. Being a single-parent household, every member of our immediate family was affected by these obstacles, having to adjust the day's expectations and go with the flow as our mother worked to cope with the issue while also continuing to care for us herself. An unexpected family affair in 2003 provided a prominent reminder of this aspect of our lives, emerging as a ring of my mother's cell phone.

Having been driving Brian and me to school (Sean was already in middle school and had started his school day an hour before), she pulled off to the side of the road.

"Hold on, guys," she said, explaining that it was her brother calling and that she had to take it—he never phoned this early.

We were on a quiet side road in Middlebury, parked on a tree-lined edge of the pavement. I remember feeling like we were there for an eternity. The van was silent other than Mom's voice. Brian, Mom, and I had been chatting excitedly about the day ahead. It was the last day before Christmas vacation, and Long Meadow always sent students out with a day of holiday celebrations. We had looked forward to this day for weeks. My brother and I didn't continue this conversation as our mom was on the phone—we were too distracted by the sound of her voice growing increasingly upset as she uttered words like "What? When? What happened? Oh, oh my gosh—I can't believe it. Okay, I'm going to drop Brian and Meg at school and then I'll be right there."

She closed her flip phone, holding it over the steering wheel as she let out a heavy sigh. She stared out at the trees for a moment before speaking.

"Grammy died."

I remember Brian's body erupting into sobs immediately, a pool of tears welling up in his hazel eyes. The news hadn't registered with me yet, caught somewhere between my ears and my mind.

Grammy's gone? I thought. *No—we just saw her the other day. How could she be gone?*

"I know you guys are really sad right now—I am too," Mom said with a slow sigh. "But could you be strong for me and Grammy and still go to school? All I'm going to be doing is going to the funeral home to make the plans—you'll have a much better time doing the holiday festivities; then, I promise, we can go home and lay low."

Resuming the drive, she pulled around to the student drop-off circle a few moments later. Wiping his eyes, Brian exited the van. My aide, Mrs. Calzone, greeted my mother as she lifted my backpack out and handed it to her. Mrs. Calzone took in Mom's glum expression and asked if anything was the matter.

"M-my mother just died," Mom replied, the words coming out as if they didn't seem real or familiar yet.

"Oh, *Anne!* I'm so sorry!"

"Thanks," Mom sighed. "I have to go make the arrangements as soon as I leave here. These guys said they could be strong and still come in. I figured being around all the holiday celebrations would be better than coming with me."

She lifted me out of my car seat and into my chair before hugging me and Brian tightly.

❧

Mom called Mrs. Burke and Brian's fifth-grade teacher, Mr. Vesneski, to let them know and ask them not to be surprised if we got upset.

I remember Mrs. Burke casually making her way over throughout that day, looking down at the craft I was working on.

"How are you doing?" she asked after complimenting my creation. "Need anything from me?"

205

I vaguely recall, even at six years old, connecting the dots, realizing that she was really asking about how I was taking the news.

"I'm good," my Dyna projected.

I didn't really know what other answer to give. The loss of my grandmother was still a shock. Part of me still felt like I would go home for break and go with my family to visit her at my uncle's house like Mom had planned.

"That's good to hear," she replied, reminding me that she was there if I needed anything.

Sean wore a teary-eyed expression when he greeted Brian and me at home that afternoon. Mom had broken the news to him when his school day ended. The three of us sat huddled together on the sunroom's couch in sad silence as we waited for Mom to join us. She strode through the doorway and sat down in front of us with a long face.

"Listen, guys, Christmas isn't gonna be that big this year. We'll still celebrate of course, but Grammy had asked me to be in charge of her arrangements, so I need to handle those," she explained. "I know I had promised we'd get a real tree when you got out for break. I'm just not going to have time to do that now. *But* we do have Da's old tabletop tree. What if we use that?"

We all nodded, smiles touching our lips at the reminder of our father.

It was the tree our father had set up in his hospital room when he was admitted during the holiday season. With its green branches, it was no more than a foot or two tall and was adorned with small lights. It seemed comforting as I decorated and admired it. In a way, it—and Christmas trees in general—reminded me of a favorite memory of Grammy too.

For our first Christmas in Middlebury in 2001, my father's friend Frank Hartnett took the boys to cut down a real tree at a farm and returned with an eight-foot-tall, six-foot-wide tree.

"Get one that's tall and narrow," Mom had instructed. "The doorways aren't overly wide here."

A few hours later, Mom and I took a break from laying out stockings, festive stuffed animals, and more to answer the door. Sean was the first one in, grinning from ear to ear.

"I got the biggest, fattest tree I could find," he said.

Our mouths hung open as they attempted to squeeze it through the front door.

"What happened to tall and narrow?" Mom was still in shock.

"I couldn't refuse?" Frank looked around at Mom meekly.

"Really?" Mom looked at Frank with an amused yet disbelieving look. "How are you going to get it in here?"

By then, it was evident that, even after trimming the branches, the tree was not coming in through the front door. Their next approach was bringing it through the garage. After more trimming, it just fit. We put it in the foyer—partly because of the high ceiling—and began to hang ornaments so that it looked evenly decorated. Mom had to go out and buy more lights just to cover the entire surface.

Photo Credit: Anne Mulville Moore

What I remember most, though, is Grammy's reaction to the tree. She had been diagnosed with dementia by then, and it seemed like she was losing her memory by the minute. Mom had her over for Christmas dinner, and she sat for hours, mesmerized by the tree.

"That is such a beautiful tree," she kept saying. "It's so beautiful."

Her face was alight with her amazement and joy as she maintained her gaze for practically the whole day. Watching how much she delighted in the simple beauty was a gift I took with me to ponder and cherish throughout life.

Photo Credit: Anne Mulville Moore

When our grandmother's health began to decline, my mother's already-full hands were handed another load to juggle: Grammy's final care and the details to be handled before and after she passed. Wanting to fulfill her mother's wishes, Mom found a way to balance between tending to them and continuing with her single-mother routine. She stripped the routine of any extravagant events with the promise of returning to them when things settled down.

"Do you mind if we postpone your birthday party?" she asked me ahead of my seventh birthday. "We'll still do something at home on your day—and I know you were really excited about celebrating with your friends—but if we could do something with them a little later in the year, that would help me so much."

My mother had asked Brian the same question in September, and two months after posing it to me, she would be asking Sean too. It was of course a little disappointing not to celebrate with friends outside of school right away, but I don't remember any of us objecting or raising any complaints. I recall watching how hard she was working and how she came to pick us up from school with stories of her day of running to appointments for the final loose ends of Grammy's care and hurrying back for school dismissal. As an adult, I realize how exhausted she must have been—fatigue she concealed very well. As a kid, it simply made sense that the time that would have been spent on our birthday parties would help Mom get everything done quicker. This is something children in single-parent households learn quickly—the parent is trying to do the job of two adults. It's a juggling act that sometimes, when extenuating circumstances arise, requires compromises from the parent and the child. When she asked me, I agreed, knowing she always kept her word.

That was her first order of business when the school year ended. Rather than planning three separate parties on three separate days with three separate groups of kids, she scheduled all three parties on the same day with the same start time.

It had been a tradition ever since we were little to have our parties at Quassy Amusement Park in Middlebury, owned and operated by our family friends, the Frantzises. They had stepped up when Da got sick, making it their mission to bring us a little joy by putting on our birthday parties, even calling each year if Mom had not already scheduled them.

Photo Credit: Anne Mulville Moore

Remaining loyal as we grew older, the Frantzises were happy to grant her request of booking the birthday party room for an entire day in the summer of 2004. On that sunny day, about sixty of us assembled in the center of the park. The parents of Sean's, Brian's, and my friends gathered before us, talking to Mom about the plan. When they had finished, Sean's group followed his friends' parents, and Brian's and mine followed suit. We disappeared into the depths of the park as Mom took off in the other direction to set up the birthday party room.

I spent the day being lifted in and out of my chair by friends' parents before being the meat in the parent-friend sandwich as we sat on each ride.

We screamed loudly as the train chugged steadily through the pitch-black tunnel, listening as the shrill sounds echoed.

Photo Credit: Anne Mulville Moore

We giggled at the flipping sensation of our stomachs as the kiddie roller coaster crept up the steep incline a centimeter per minute. The train of yellow and royal blue cars paused dramatically at the peak of the incline, and everybody drew a sharp, collective breath as we peered down the steep incline. The coaster sped down and took a jackknife turn before slowing and calmly looping back to the entrance, leaving me and my friends laughing and windblown.

Seated on the benches of the great green glazed body of The Dragon, we were lifted up, around, and down in several circular swoops. Elevating us to the treetops, the ride slowed to give us a chance to take in the semi–sky view of the park—over the rainbow of rides, the beaming families and friends, the concession stands and carnival-like game shacks, the white-painted office building, and the turquoise waters of Lake Quassapaug shimmering in the sun. The view was the reason this ride was my favorite.

The day ended in the birthday party pavilion—Mom's third shift of serving cake, pizza, and presents. Looking fatigued yet energized by adrenaline and excitement, she listened as my friends and I detailed the day's adventures. The boys had already bid their friends goodbye and were now helping to video and celebrate with me. Once the pizza had been devoured, Mom gently set a flaming, purple-frosted cake in front of me, singing the first note of "Happy Birthday" as everybody else joined in. When they finished, I extinguished the candles with an effortful blow—an action that was always challenging for me to coordinate my muscles to do and that had taken years to learn.

I don't remember what I wished for that year as I worked hard to gather air, sucking it through my nostrils and holding it in my diaphragm before sending it over the twinkling flames. I don't recall if it came true. What I do know is that the next year of my life brought me new blessings beyond anything I could have hoped for in that one little birthday wish. Sitting around that table with my family and friends, I didn't know how much the trajectory of my life was about to change.

Chapter 9

Cardinal Visions

"Something wrong, Meg?" Mrs. Ahern, my second-grade teacher, asked, smirking.

The shock rushed over my body, leaving my mouth hanging wide open. Her long, manicured pink nails rhythmically tapped the side of her bronze Diet Coke can. Her blue eyes followed the expressions of my classmates as they filed into the classroom and laid their eyes on what awaited me at my desk that morning.

The entire table was covered with them.

She had even balanced some of the figurines on the edge of my computer monitor.

I knew she had been too quiet the day before. Her reaction to my little stunt had been a surprise to my friends and me. She had remained subdued, only making a few jokes, asking if it had been pitch-black in my bedroom when I was dressing that morning because she found my outfit to be an eyesore, just as I had anticipated.

She had brought it up on the first day of school. She had gone through the typical introduction, telling us about herself, her family, how she had a daughter, Michaela, who was our age and in a classroom just down the hall. Michaela and I would become inseparable friends about two years later.

Photo Credit: Anne Mulville Moore

She told us she loved cardinals, gesturing to the stuffed animals and figurines of the red bird scattered about the room. She told us, too, that the Cardinals were her favorite baseball team, pointing out the St. Louis logos on the walls.

"And you should know," she had said, "that I absolutely *hate* the Yankees."

I calculated the amount of time I should wait until I showed up to school in my Yankees jersey, concluding that I should hold off for a few weeks, giving my teacher an opportunity to see how I was a well-behaved, hardworking kid before revealing the full caliber of my sense of humor.

I remember the look on my best friend Nikki's face the morning I traipsed through the second- and third-grade wing in my white and navy-blue pinstriped jersey, wearing navy-blue shorts and a hair scrunchy to match. She slammed her locker, adding to the melody of cymbal-like crashes resounding throughout the hallway and, gathering her binders, hurried to where my aide had parked my chair against the wall next to the still-locked classroom door.

215

"You actually wore it?"

Nikki's hazel eyes were wild with disbelief.

"Yeah," I replied, knowing she could decipher my words without my DynaVox. "I told you yesterday I was gonna."

"I know, but dude! You're *all* Yankees! She'll freak."

"I wear this every time I go to Shriners, and that's like *in* Red Sox territory. I make it out of there alive. If I can do that, this will be no big deal."

✦

The next day, my friends and I understood why our teacher had been so ominously quiet about my attire. Payback had dawned with the sun. Mrs. Ahern had turned my table into a St. Louis Cardinal collage, with numerous magnets and one-dimensional decals depicting the team logo filling every space around the computer and adaptive keyboard. Stuffed cardinal birds were balanced on the top edge of the flat-screen computer monitor.

As Mrs. Ahern made her way to the front of the class, I turned to see my friends. They, too, gaped at the clutter before me; their faces, like mine, were stunned, frozen with their mouths slightly ajar for a moment before quiet laughter broke out.

"*No one,*" Mrs. Ahern began, gesturing to my desk, "is to take any of this down before the end of the day."

My teacher seemed to call on me as frequently as she could that day, pausing between saying my name and asking me to answer a question. An amused smile on her lips, she gazed for a moment at the sight of me among the cardinals.

As a seven-year-old, I didn't know that the word "cardinal" could also function as an adjective, but later it would be easy to see how thoroughly it described second grade. Something that is cardinal means it is of great importance—a central idea or value.

School was not in session for long when my teacher and my family began to reveal the cardinal visions they had for my life.

I remember the Andrew Sisters. I remember how excited Mrs. Ahern was to make me a part of the iconic World War II–era singing group. The second grade had just finished the social studies unit on the war, and we were to put on a musical show about the war and its heroes.

I remember my mother picking me up from school and asking if Mrs. Ahern had shared what role I would play. My teacher had told her beforehand, and Mom had waited for me to hear it at school before talking to me about it.

"She's so excited—she has it all figured out," Mom exclaimed. "She says it's the perfect part for you."

At seven or eight years old, I wasn't thinking about the steps my teachers took to ensure that I could participate. My mind was instead thinking typical girlie-girl thoughts—what would I get to wear? The rumblings from the teachers of lacy dresses enthralled my friends and me. We couldn't wait to see the costumes and the accessories that were in store.

I took the stage with a group of other girls during the class's rendition of the Andrew Sisters' hit "Don't Sit Under the Apple Tree." The teachers had asked my classmate Kevin, who was playing the soldier in the number, to loop around the stage after he had marched across the hardwood to the beat of the music and bring my wheelchair from my spot in front of the silver risers where the rest of the class stood. With impeccable timing, he rolled me out to center stage just as the other "Andrew Sisters" were stepping off the risers. Each of us holding an umbrella over one shoulder, we formed a line and pivoted to the right, the other girls bebopping to the music as they walked in a circle while Kevin and I followed.

"Don't sit under the apple tree with anyone else but me, anyone else but me, anyone else but me, 'til I come marching home."

As the class held out the last note of "home," we turned to face the audience and went in for the big umbrella-spinning finale.

The first run-through of the spin remains in my memory. I was doing well until this point, holding the cold, silver rod between my thumb and fingers in one hand, resting it on my shoulder as the other hand gripped the curved plastic handle at the end.

Photo Credit: Anne Mulville Moore

I tipped the umbrella forward so that the multicolored canopy was in front of me. When I removed one hand from the umbrella to use for the spin, the rod slipped from the fingers of the other hand and the umbrella clattered to the floor.

I don't remember feeling embarrassed when the soundtrack was shut off or when a teacher and classmates ran to give the umbrella back to me. I recall looking down at the fallen prop for a moment, doing the calculations in my head. The muscles in my hand wanted to grip the umbrella as tightly as they could, but I needed to loosen them just enough for the umbrella to have the freedom to spin. With my cerebral palsy, my hands typically offered an all-or-nothing-type deal, letting me either grasp an object very tightly or not at all. It was not impossible for me to learn to do the move—even at that age, I knew I could work on it with my occupational therapist. But I wondered if I could learn in time for the show and what kind of guarantee would come with that—just because I practiced didn't mean I wouldn't drop it during the show.

"Hey, Meg," one of the other teachers called, walking across the cafeteria floor and eventually resting her forearms on the edge of the stage. "What if Kevin helped you with the spin? Would that be okay?"

I nodded, smiling, relieved.

"Kevin, can you try that?" she asked. "Act like you just got Meg's chair in line and practice taking the umbrella."

Kevin's hand moved from the back of my chair, stretching toward my shoulder as I lifted the rod back until I felt him take it. Leaning the umbrella forward in front of me, he began to twirl it.

"You can't even tell who is doing it," the teacher said, walking backward slowly to view it at a distance. "It still looks like you, Meg."

I'd like to thank my stunt double for making all parts of the dance run smoothly.

Photo Credit: Anne Mulville Moore

The Long Meadow staff never hesitated to have me front and center in activities—something, I would later learn, that was not always the case for disabled students.

The holiday season saw another curtain opening as the second-grade teachers prepared us to put on another music-filled show, this time featuring selections of songs about an array of holiday traditions. Some songs were comical, calling for my classmate to be the goofy Santa Claus dancing on stage, shuffling his black boots almost as if he was running in place, a Hawaiian button-down shirt on top, red velvet Santa pants on the bottom to go with the fake beard and red hat as we sang about Santa getting a sunburn on his post-Christmas vacation. Others played on a more serious theme, depicting events and influential figures that embodied the spirit of the season.

Envisioning me as a source of light, Mrs. Ahern gave me the role of Santa Lucia. Santa Lucia was an early Christian martyr who faced brutal persecution for her religious beliefs. It is said that her perpetrators first tried to end her life by setting a fire around her; miraculously, the flames never touched her. She is seen as a symbol of brightness and hope.

I remember my mother and my teacher brimming with excitement over my role, telling me how glorious it was. I didn't think too deeply about it as a kid. Like a typical girl, my mind was focused on fashion, looking forward to the elegant gown I'd get to wear. I grinned from ear to ear as I sat in the silky white dress that cascaded down to my ankles on stage. The last notes of the preceding up-tempo carol faded into a slow and graceful melody as my classmates sang the syllables "San-ta Lu-chia" to the quiet rhythms of the new song.

"San-ta Lu-chia," they continued to repeat as a classmate pushed my chair across the stage, looping around in a great circle in front of the risers and bringing me parallel to the edge to give the audience a closer look.

I tried to hold my upper body as straight as it would go to give the audience the full effect of my costume, pulling my abs tight to keep myself at full height without leaning back into the cushions. I kept my head up tall and level, hoping to show the best view possible of my crown—an artificial green wreath from which thick white candlesticks, lit by small light bulbs, protruded. I beamed at my family and the rest of the audience as their eyes and smiles sparkled back at me.

Photo Credit: Anne Mulville Moore

I'm not sure if I knew then the extent of the vision of faith, hope, and light my family and my teacher had for my life.

Early in childhood, just like my brothers and peers, I began Confraternity of Christian Doctrine (CCD) classes. Each Sunday morning, my mother drove my brothers and me to the Immaculate Conception Church (later to become a basilica) in Waterbury, timing our arrival carefully in the hopes of beating the mad rush to the church's few handicapped parking spaces.

Despite the church's grandiose, cathedral-like design, there was no elevator leading to the basement, where classes were held. As I grew older, the lack of accessibility would become more of an obstacle, but back then, with my mother supporting me under my arms, I would stand on the concrete top step leading from outside into the church basement as a few of the dads carried my small pink wheelchair down the stairs. My brothers waited at the bottom, helping set the chair down gently and moving the buckles off the seat. My mother would help me twirl around to face her; then, lifting me up onto her hip, with my arms looping around her neck, she slowly carried me downstairs as other parents spotted her in the front and back. Together, my family set me up in the chair when we reached the bottom, my mother guiding me gently into the bubblegum-pink seat and my brothers sliding the semitransparent tray over the black leather armrests. The boys then dispersed, joining their peers at the tables between the dividers that segmented the vast event hall into several makeshift classrooms.

Turning on my DynaVox and placing it on my tray, Mom wheeled me over to my class, taking a seat in the folding chair next to me. While the other parents dropped their children off and went for coffee or to run errands in their free hour before returning for Mass, my mother attended class with me, perhaps going through Sunday school education for the second time in her life. She spent the full hour helping me turn pages of the reading my teacher went over, coloring with me hand over hand as I worked to decorate biblical-themed coloring pages, and acting as my scribe when I had to complete a worksheet. Although it was plain to see that I was the only one accompanied by a parent, it really didn't faze me that I was doing anything out of the ordinary. I knew that, as with every other activity in my life, having somebody with me enabled my participation.

My teachers always treated me as they did every other student, asking me to recite answers in class. The only difference was the extra few minutes they gave to allow me type my responses into my Dyna. I journeyed through the program on the same course as everybody else and prepared to make my First Holy Communion in second grade.

"What's it taste like?" I remember asking my family in the days leading up to it.

"Kind of like a Nilla Wafer," Sean replied, his brown eyes looking far in the distance as he searched for fitting words. "Just not as sweet. The practice ones they give you at the rehearsal don't taste that good, but the regular ones are better. Literally all you do is go up to Father Bevins, open your mouth, and he'll place it on your tongue for you—which will actually work out for you. Mom won't have to ask him to feed it to you. Everybody takes it on their tongue anyway."

My Communion preparations were identical to those of my friends'. Mom and I coordinated with my close friend Kate from school and her mom to go dress shopping. Using my walker to run with Kate down the aisles of a bridal store owned by their family's friend, I felt a smile spread across my face, much like the one Kate wore on hers. Letting go of one of the two walker handles, I ran a hand along the dresses like Kate did as we passed racks upon racks of gauzy white lace. I chose a simple, lacy gown that touched the tops of my shoes. Small pearls stippled the bodice, and the sleeves were poofs of lace. I was fitted with a simple veil that had a sparkly silver tiara comb—an accessory that, given my love of princesses, enthused me.

"I just can't wait to wear my dress," Kate gushed as we waited for our moms to finish at the register. "It's so pretty that I'm counting down the days to my Communion!"

"Me too," I exclaimed, smiling even more as the words emerged from my mouth.

Photo Credit: Anne Mulville Moore

Some moments I encountered as Communion approached, though, were unique and divergent from those my able-bodied friends would ever endure. Most were enjoyable, coming as welcome surprises.

When Brian's friend's mom, an artist, asked if I would like her to decorate my walker for the special occasion, Mom and I jumped at the offer, knowing how much room there was for the walker to be revamped—the paint was chipping in several spots, and one of the handle grippers, having fallen off somewhere unknown, had been temporarily replaced with tomato-red duct tape.

When she brought it back a few days later, it was transformed into elegance. Aside from the handles being replaced with new, custom-made red rubber grippers, thick strands of white lace had been wrapped all around the frame, with some thin strips of lavender lace hanging here and there. Lace had even been stretched over the thick strip of cushioning that encircled my torso. Clusters of artificial baby's breath flowers were carefully placed throughout its frame.

Never having thought about decorating my walker, I was enthralled with its new beauty and eager to walk down the aisle in it.

Other moments, though, were unwelcome and didn't belong in church.

Our pastor, Father Bevins, and my CCD teachers were always supportive of my religious endeavors. One staff member did not share the same mentality, though.

As the rest of the class filed out of the cathedral-like nave one day, the coordinator held Mom and me back to talk about the procession, explaining that it would be ordered by height, with the tallest kids in the front and the shortest bringing up the rear.

"We figured it would be best to have Meg come in at the end," she explained, standing before us, peering through glasses that sat atop her face.

"Why?" Mom asked. "She isn't the shortest."

"There will be more room for her walker there. It will be easier for her."

I watched my mother's ivory skin pinken to red. My mom was a very even-keeled person. Having dealt with many adversities—caring for her parents and my father in the final stages of their lives, becoming a young single mother, and dealing with my disability—she knew which issues were worth combatting. The one thing she could not tolerate was discrimination. To her, I, and everybody else, should be treated equally and fairly.

At eight years old, I'm not sure that I really understood what was going on. My mother explained it to me later that day. "Think about it," she said. "If everybody else is lined up by height and you're not the shortest, is it fair to have you as the last person?"

"No," I said.

"Exactly. She was trying to classify you by your disability instead of your height," she replied. "She was trying to treat you differently than everybody else just because you have a disability."

Though my mother tried to explain it to me in kid-friendly terms, I would not fully understand discrimination and its detriments until I was older. In a way, it was better that way. It was like a cushion—something to ease the blow of what I would later learn could be a devastating experience. I didn't feel the heartbreak I would when dealing with this type of experience as I grew older. I had the vague sense of why it was wrong, and the tension between my mom and this woman made me feel ill at ease, but I don't remember feeling that upset. I was too young to understand the magnitude of the situation.

I was not too young to grasp the power and cleverness of my mother's response to the woman, though.

"What if you put Meg in the front?" she asked, keeping her face straight and her voice calm but direct. "There's plenty of extra space there, just as much as in the back."

"N-no, I-I don't think that's—" The woman stammered for a moment before clearing her throat and producing a coherent response. "We can make room for her in the middle where she would be based on her height."

"No, no," Mom opposed. "I think the front will be good."

As I watched the coordinator's jaw drop, my mind worked to understand what was happening. Even at age eight, I had a vague idea of her theory. Since the coordinator wanted to stick me in the back because of my disability, my mother wanted her and everybody else to see that I was just as important as everybody else and that my disability did not define my place at this event or in society. Perhaps the Bible verse of Matthew 20:16—a saying my mother would reference throughout my life—says it all: "The last shall be first and the first shall be last." Those acting as superior in society will be regarded with little importance, and those treated as inferior will have high importance.

The gold chandeliers lining the high ceilings of Immaculate Conception Church seemed to glow with an increased brilliance as I led my peers down the marble-floored aisle on the morning of our First Holy Communion. Turning my head slightly, I looked down the rows of glossy mahogany pews to see my family, our family friends, and some of my friends from school and their parents sitting there, smiling back at me. In a matter of minutes, they would see me rise from the pew my mother had sat me down in next to my classmates, reenter my walker, and walk up to Father Bevins to give him an "Amen" with my own vocals, accepting the host on my tongue. They would grin at me, whispering words of congratulations as I walked in a loop around the pews to my seat; later, we would gather at Da's friend Danny's catering venue to celebrate. In the moment, though, they smiled while watching me stride toward something greater in life.

A scene from the morning of my Communion, before the pomp and circumstance even began, has remained clear in my memory. In the flurry of activity in the church basement, I remember my mother coming to get me from where I sat with my class, waiting to line up.

"Mrs. Ahern's here," she exclaimed, pushing my chair across the room. "She came to see you before she heads to Michaela's Communion."

We had invited my teacher to celebrate with us, but, like many of my friends from school, her daughter was making her own Communion the same day.

I remember sitting with her for a few minutes, grinning as she complimented my dress and gave me a gift box with a small golden locket inside.

"I thought you might like to put a picture of your father in there," she said.

"Wow, that's gorgeous, Rose! You didn't have to do that," my mother said. "Thank you so much! What do you say, Meg?"

"Thank you," I exclaimed with my own speech as my eyes flew between the shiny gold necklace on my wheelchair tray and my teacher's face.

"You are very welcome," she replied.

I remember Mrs. Ahern taking a moment to look around at our surroundings, checking out the interior of the church for perhaps the first time. Years later, the irony dawned on me—she was standing in the setting I had depicted on a page for her months earlier.

For our first major assignment of second grade, Mrs. Ahern asked each student to craft a fictional story about a main character with a first name, a last name, and a nickname partaking in any activity our minds brewed. This would be my first real story—there would be no crayon doodlings to accompany it, no single-sentence storyline. The teacher expected real plotlines and pages filled with paragraphs.

When released to grapple with the infinite possibilities, I found myself staring at the stark white page of a Word document, the cursor blinking impatiently. Leaning back on the soft surface of my seat, I began to sort through the tangled web of ideas weaving its way through my brain.

I could make up a story that takes place in school, but so many other people do that. I could write about an adventure I had gone on—at the beach or on Da's sailboat or at the park—and twist parts of the plot to make it fiction. No, I need something new. What have I done lately? Where have I been that I have never written about at school?

I flipped through a mental photo album of memories from the past few days, thinking about everywhere I had been and everything I had seen—home, school, soccer, scouts, church—church! I had never written anything about church before. It was perfect.

Now I just needed a character and a storyline. My mind flashed back to the most recent Sunday. It was the usual routine: We had gone to CCD followed by Mass. CCD, as always, had introduced new concepts and new questions—oh, and that chatterbox girl had gotten yelled at again right before Father Bevins called all the classes to attention for the closing prayer.

Huh, I thought. *I wonder what would happen if somebody else did the talking one Sunday and she was blamed anyway. What if she had to prove it hadn't been her?*

I set to work to the soundtrack of the faint beep each keystroke of my adaptive keyboard produced. For the next several days, I wrote for the allotted writing time in its entirety, documenting the scenes materializing in my mind like a movie until I absolutely had to stop. When I was not writing and was instead daydreaming during free moments in and outside of school, I found myself thinking about my story, pondering the details I would put down next. I just couldn't wait to get back to my pages.

After days of weaving my ideas into one unified piece, I concluded with everybody's surprised realization that, for once, it was not my character, Isabel Jabber Jaws, who had spoken and disrupted the focus of the class.

I remember watching as my aide, Mrs. Calzone, returned to the room and carried my pages, hot off the library's printer, to Mrs. Ahern. Mrs. Calzone's head was tilted down as she set her eyes on the first page. I tried to read her expression. I couldn't help it—curiosity was burning inside me. Did she like them? Did she want to keep reading?

The feeling only intensified when the paper landed in Mrs. Ahern's grasp. Perhaps it was my imagination, but I thought I saw her eyes linger on the first page for a prolonged moment before she laid the stapled packet on the pile with the other students' stories. I pondered what her reaction to the piece would be—I had loved writing it and was very proud of my work, but it was only my first real story. How good could it be?

That story changed my life.

A few days after I submitted my story, Mom picked me up after school. Since she had been volunteering in the school that day anyway, she met me outside of Mrs. Ahern's classroom. My friends and I greeted her excitedly as we poured out of the room and into the hallway, stopping to tell her about our day. Mrs. Ahern appeared in the doorway, smiling.

"Hi, Anne! Have a minute?"

"Sure," my mother exclaimed and followed her a short distance down the hallway.

My friends and I had noticed them strolling along the row of lockers but had become too engrossed with telling jokes as everybody retrieved their belongings to follow any of the conversation. After a few moments, they returned, both smiling. Mrs. Ahern called for the rest of the class to line up and bid me goodbye as she led the class upstairs, pausing briefly to take in my appearance, her sapphire eyes glittering brightly.

In the van, Mom told me about how Mrs. Ahern had wanted to talk about my story, how much she had loved it, and how it indicated that I had great talent in writing.

"She said, 'I tossed and turned one night worrying about what Meg could do for a living.'"

My mother told me about my teacher's theory about my future and how I could write a book—and many more after that—about my life. Since I had experienced so many unique events and had overcome so many obstacles right from my beginning, she thought that my life's story had the potential of inspiring other individuals with disabilities.

Of course! Why had I not thought of being a writer before? Around preschool, I dreamed of becoming a doctor, giving compassionate care that would enable kids to thrive as so many doctors had done for me. When my doctor administered the first immunization I remembered, I realized that, as a doctor, I would have to stick kids with needles and decided that this line of work was not for me. Shortly after, I hoped to be a teacher, perhaps because I had been surrounded by so many great teachers at Long Meadow. While this dream never died, a focus on writing seemed so exciting; I loved the idea of sharing my stories with the world.

I began to dream about scrawling my signature onto the pages of millions of copies of my books, chatting with readers about the impact my work had made, appearing on prominent talk shows to unveil the story behind my stories, and spending my days crafting literary masterpieces. I began to look at the world differently, catching myself daydreaming about how I might write a scene depicting the moment I was experiencing at that time. The unique happenings that made up my days suddenly became my muses, most of them eventually landing as ink on a page. Occasions like my mom's cousin Helen and her husband, Don, visiting from Oklahoma, filling our house with laughter and stories of Helen and Mom's early days, called me to craft an essay titled "Meet the Cousins."

❧

When the school invited children's authors to the library to give keynote speeches to the student body a few times a year, I sat in the audience and began to envision myself in the author's place. I pictured the librarian, Mrs. Groman, standing before the dozens of students sitting on the floor, a grin spread across her face as she raised her arm, gesturing toward me as she spoke the words "Children, please help me welcome our author guest, Margaret Moore!"

❧

Two years later, perhaps a very ambitious ten-year-old, I set out to record the greatest moments of my life in a memoir. Over a long weekend, after nearly two years of listening to family, friends, and teachers talk about the great book I was going to write, I decided I would start writing it. At our kitchen table, I sat with my DynaVox, gently drumming my fingers along the screen consistently for hours.

"What are you up to?" Mom asked as she entered, noting the charcoal blankness of our TV and the soft, rhythmic beat of my fingertips on my DynaVox screen.

"Starting my book."

"Really?" she gasped.

We both agreed that we should give Mrs. Ahern a call to share the good news.

"Wait, Mom," I said as she turned to retrieve the cordless house phone. "When I was born, after the cord dropped, was I blue?"

That was the first of many times I would interview my mother about the details of my earliest days. She paused to contemplate her answer—the background information, the emotions, and the reactions that emerged from the events of my birth and their repercussions. I took her responses and, like pieces of a puzzle, figured out how and where they fit. Once I had passed through the events of no-memory lane, I wrote about my own memories and how I felt throughout my childhood. I wrote about the good times, the bad times, the minor details, and the monumental ones. My family, friends, and teachers encouraged me to keep going, to keep writing down everything that seemed important about my life.

Years later, I would sit and laugh about what my fourth-grade-self had written, reading various excerpts to my family as we laughed about the oh-so-sophisticated language and spelling ("Lois made me delishus chocolate pudding and it was yummy!"), realizing that the draft I had thought would only need minor editing before being published would actually need substantial revision. I would snicker at my idea of a paragraph (about three very short sentences) and of a chapter—about four paragraphs packed with details about not only the big events of my life but what I did on a daily basis during the most recent years of my childhood.

While time revealed that this draft was nowhere near ready for the *New York Times* "Best Seller" list, it came in handy. Rereading these pages as an adult helped me remember exactly how it felt to face life with cerebral palsy as a child so that I could re-create an adequate and vivid picture for readers.

It was not easy to be known as the kid who was writing a book. I admit that I started and stopped writing my book frequently during my childhood and adolescent years. I'd get stuck and put it away until the next wave of inspiration hit—sometimes months or even years later. During the times of writer's block, I always inevitably had those few people, adults and peers my family and I encountered at school and in our community, who tossed me those questions that made my head swim: Didn't I want to finish what I started? All I had to do was write down what had already happened to me—what was the holdup? Didn't I know how cool it would be if I could get it done in my youth and be a child author? Given the number of times I had taken breaks, was I really going to see the project through?

I could never put my finger on the reasoning for this start-and-stop nature of my work—I did want to produce new chapters, but I felt stuck, and being approached with so many questions about why I wasn't working to finish quickly, an ache of guilt settled in my core.

Years later, as I pursued my college and graduate degrees at Fairfield University, I learned the concept of selection and arrangement in creative nonfiction writing, and my struggles as a child writer suddenly made sense to me. As a kid, I didn't know how to write a book, and as none of my supporters had ever written a book either, the best advice loved ones and school staff could offer—which was undoubtedly sound—was to write down the events of my life and the emotions that accompanied them. I remember calculating as a very young child how broad life was, and my mind flooded with questions of how I would ever get it all in. As an adult, I learned to pick and choose the scenes that should fill my book and that the book should have a certain purpose that these scenes work to demonstrate. As my life turned from childhood to adulthood, a few things about my dream of writing books remained consistent: I couldn't wait to sculpt my life story in artful words, and I couldn't wait to see the world change for the better in response to learning about my experiences.

In a way, though, I didn't have to wait to see how my life impacted others. It wasn't long into second grade that I befriended Rebecca Fischer. We were like Velcro, always gravitating to each other as soon as the teacher called the class to pair up for a team project or to go somewhere else in the school. She was among the cluster of friends who, without being asked, waited beside my walker in the gym, holding off on beginning the assigned exercise until my aide had transferred me from my chair so that we could run across the gym together.

Our house phone played its tune one warm spring afternoon. Mom picked up to hear Mrs. Fischer's voice inquiring about a playdate at their house.

Like every other child, playdates were prominent parts of my social life. Unlike most kids, though, I needed my mother to accompany me, at least until my friends' families had gotten to know me and my needs well. Mom would chat with my friends' parents as we played. She helped me move from room to room (most houses were not accessible), fed me if a snack was offered—essentially, she bridged the gap between my limitations and what a "normal" playdate entailed.

As this was my first playdate with Rebecca, Mom assumed she would attend with me. Running a finger over a coffee table–size calendar, she sighed and asked for alternate dates.

Mrs. Fischer's response was a solid no.

"How about if I pick the girls up from school? I can borrow an extra car seat from my friend, and you can just meet us at the house after your appointment."

My mother still looked shocked when she hung up and told me about the invitation and conversation.

∽⚭∽

A few days later, my aide followed Rebecca, her younger sister, Jessie, their mother, and me to the van and helped Mrs. Fischer transfer me from my walker to my seat and fold up my walker. Once harnesses had been fastened and belongings had been stowed, everybody settled into their seats and pivoted to greet their baby brother Jackson.

Rebecca looked from her blond-haired, blue-eyed brother to me and back again.

"Aw, *Mom!* Why'd you have to get a car seat that looks just like Jack's? She's not a baby."

Mrs. Fischer explained that it was the only one she could borrow. Raised to find humor and positivity in every unique situation, I smiled, grateful for her efforts. Then I turned to Rebecca, who had been around me long enough to begin to understand my natural speech. Laughter was already welling up inside of me.

"Hey, Rebecca, look! I'm a baby."

With my best infant imitation, I sent the carload into roaring hysterics. My friend followed my lead, mustering a realistic baby wail as I answered her in "goo-goo ga-gas." The vehicle was filled with lingering laughter all the way to their home.

After many rounds of board games, Rebecca sighed and plunged backward into the plush couch cushions next to me. We sat there for a moment, pondering our next action. We had run through a verbal list of the possibilities and, reaching the end, had fallen into a thoughtful silence. Rebecca abruptly sprang upward, smiling.

"Hey, wanna go in your walker so we can run around?"

The word "yes" had barely projected from my DynaVox when she ran for the kitchen. As the chatter of fresh conversation emerged, I slid myself upward on the couch, glancing at the front door. I had been carried from the car to the couch by Mrs. Fischer. With a sigh, it dawned on me that Mom was not due for a little while longer and that, as she was the only one of the bunch who knew how to help me into my walker, our plan would have to wait.

Down the hall, I heard the unmistakable clicking of walker wheels growing near, and soon Rebecca and her mother appeared, half rolling and half carrying my folded walker. Setting it down in front of the couch, Mrs. Fischer looked at it for a minute, a puzzled expression on her face. Rebecca was miles ahead of her.

"Okay, Mom, start by lifting up these latches."

She turned to me.

"Right?" she asked, looking at me while holding up her index finger in front of her mother, signaling her to wait for me to type a response on the Dyna.

"Yeah, but you have to do both sides at the same time or else it won't work," I explained.

Each taking a side, they slid the thin, black latches upward and pulled the frame back until it clicked into place. Getting into the walker herself to demonstrate the next steps, Rebecca showed how the harness went and explained how her mother needed to support me. Afterward, she slid past the harness and moved next to her mom to spot her as she stood me up. With one smooth motion, Mrs. Fischer placed me in the center of the walker and began to secure the buckles. Rebecca and I thanked her as we began our marathon through the house.

On our second lap, we were joined by Rebecca's younger siblings, Jackson and Jessica. Contributing to our chorus of laughter, they trailed behind us as we sprinted. The doorbell echoed loudly as we passed the front door, and Mrs. Fischer opened it to find my mother on the other side. We breezed through, shouting greetings behind us.

"Hi, Mom!"

"Hi, Mrs. Moore!"

"Hi!" she exclaimed. "You're in your walker! Wow, you guys are good!"

"Rebecca showed me how to put her in," Mrs. Fischer replied.

"That's amazing."

We rounded out our last few laps before joining them in the kitchen. Upon transferring to the seat next to Mom, a fit of giggles hit me as Rebecca took my place in the walker, strutting around the room. Jessica gave it a whirl after, replenishing everybody's amusement. Little Jackson took the cake, though, being too short to reach the handles and discovering that he could move it by grasping the bottom of the harness and pulling.

❧

All the Fischers, we found out, were comfortable with my disability and acted like tending to my needs was no big deal.

Each year, Long Meadow Elementary held an event called PJ Story Hour—an evening where the kids went back to the school dressed in pajamas and carried their favorite stuffed animals as they traveled from room to room to listen to staff and parent volunteers read from picture books.

In second grade, the event conflicted with my brothers' basketball practice. My mother had it all figured out, dropping the boys off a few minutes early. She had told me that we would have to leave PJ Story Hour shortly before it ended to pick them up.

"Mego," she whispered in an almost singsong voice from behind me. "You ready? Time to go get the boys."

"Hm? Yeah, okay, I'm good," I replied, seated on the floor next to Rebecca, my eyes and ears still captivated by the reader sitting in a chair at the head of the cafeteria.

"You don't look ready," she chuckled quietly.

I raised my arms slightly, preparing for her to lift me from behind.

"Where are you headed?" Mr. Fischer asked from beside her.

"Just down to the middle school to the boys' basketball practice—it's one of those nights when everybody's in different directions at once," she laughed.

"Well, I don't know if you want to come back this way," he said. "But I'd be happy to stay with her while you go pick them up."

"Really? That would be wonderful. What do you think, Meg?"

I nodded, still engrossed in the reader's words.

"Is that even a question? Of course she wants to stay," my mother laughed. "This is really so nice of you—most parents wouldn't offer like this until knowing Meg for years."

"My pleasure. Meg is a good friend to Rebecca."

Mom rose from where she had been kneeling behind me. Mr. Fischer took her place, and my mother showed him where to put his hands about an inch away from my back to spot me just in case my core muscles grew tired of holding me upright in my cross-legged position. Kissing me on the head, she left the school.

My mother thought about the Fischers' kindness frequently that year. "Finally we have friends where you don't need to wait for me to be done with everything I need to do before you can go have fun with them," she often said.

She was just as disappointed as I was when, at the end of the school year, they announced their decision to move to Georgia that summer for a change of pace.

"Well," Mom said one day at home. "What if we add Georgia to the itinerary this summer? Go visit Rebecca's family?"

"Really? We can do that?"

"Yeah, we have to go through Georgia anyway. I'll give them a call to see what they think."

The Fischers were among the many out-of-state friends we visited along the way on our cross-country road trip.

Photo Credit: Anne Mulville Moore

My grandmother's death the previous year had marked the end of a twelve-year period in which my mother was constantly caring for a family member—first my maternal grandfather, then my father, and lastly my grandmother—during the final stages of their lives. She was ready for a break and had ideas for a suitable respite.

She and Da had always dreamed of taking us to Disney World. They had come close once, before he really declined. His doctor, Dr. Stanley Dudrick, had even agreed to come along in case medical complications arose, but Da quickly became too sick to travel. The trip remained on my mother's bucket list, and she gradually saved money.

"I figured I'd get you something small now," she said to us each birthday, "and put the rest of the money that would have gone into a bigger gift into the Disney fund."

I don't remember any of us minding. As a family who grew up on a steady regimen of Disney books and movies—everything from *The Lion King* to *The Jungle Book* to, my personal favorite, the princesses— the thought of being one step closer to a trip to Disney was exciting.

Finally having enough money saved, Mom mapped out a plan and route to take off a few days into the summer break of 2005. Along with visiting the most magical place on Earth, the vacation centered on getting together with our Uncle Joe, Mom's older brother, who lived on the gulf coast of Florida. With the trip to Joe's and Disney at the heart, Mom pieced together the edges of the vacation, creating a route that passed through areas where out-of-state friends lived, stops that gave us pleasant breaks from long stretches of the journey.

She decided to drive to Florida. Always a numbers person, she had calculated that the cost to fly there was far more than what it would be to drive. It seemed more economical all around—and driving gave us the freedom to see what turned out to be thirteen states.

When she drove home in a mini Coachman RV shortly before our departure, she had taken a lot into consideration. Traveling in a camper eliminated hotel expenses and carried beds on which she could rest her head when she needed a break from driving. Mom also didn't want the boys to go into men's rooms at rest stops by themselves and saw the RV as a safer option. Additionally, she had loved camping with Joe in Canada in their early adulthood and wanted to give us a similar experience.

"You guys up for a ride?" she asked one evening before the trip, bouncing a pile of keys and their green spiral wristlet in her hand. "I need to pick up a few last items at Kmart."

"We're taking the camper?" Brian asked, noting the keys.

"Yeah. I want to practice driving it more before we leave—get acclimated to the way it turns," she replied. "It's actually not that bad, though—it's just like the moving trucks I drove when we moved."

Mom timed our real departure so we could get a few states behind us in the low-traffic night and pulled the camper out onto the road just after twilight had set over Middlebury. As the night darkened, the boys fell asleep strapped into the two bench seats on either side of the small table. The TV had long been turned off, and I leaned against the cushioned back of my car seat, trying to fall asleep.

It was as if Christmas Eve had come six months early that year. Just as it did each December 24th, my mind remained energetic, too excited about the adventures ahead to drift off to sleep. Minutes passed of tossing and turning before I gave the attempts a rest for a while. Reaching up to click on the small spotlight above me, I pulled a book out of my small Girl Scout backpack that my family had helped me wedge between my car seat and the RV's olive-green plush armchair. My mind was soon engulfed in the plot of Laurie B. Friedman's *Mallory on the Move*—a novel that quickly became one of my childhood favorites.

The rustling of pages turning added a pleasant melody to the sound of the RV slicing over the road; after a few moments, Mom glanced in the rearview mirror.

"Can't sleep?" she asked.

"Nope."

"Well, at least you can keep me company until you can."

Mom and I talked for a while about the adventures we would have at Disney; with Uncle Joe, Aunt Sally, and our cousins; and all along the East Coast.

"Shoot," Mom said as p.m. turned to a.m. "These directions don't make sense—I don't know if I missed a turn or what, but I'm going to pull over up here and see where we have to go."

I watched her run a finger over the large map spread over the console as her eyes moved between the map and the printed MapQuest directions. She looked up, squinting to read the road signs before putting the directions down and getting back to driving.

"I still don't know what I did, but we're in luck—there's a state trooper barracks up ahead. I'll go ask for directions," she said. "See if you see a sign. I'm looking too."

"Is that it?" I asked, looking through the windshield from behind the passenger seat. "See the blue sign up there?"

"Yup, that's it. Nice job, Eyes Moore."

I remember drifting to sleep as she opened her window and flagged an officer down.

❧

Each morning, my eyes typically opened to take in the white walls of the tiny bedroom in the back of the camper. My family would help me hop off the twin bed and into the bathroom then into my wheelchair until it was time to get into the car seat for our departure. If we had been driving when I had fallen asleep, they carefully scooped me out of my car seat at the nearest rest stop and seat-belted me into the pullout that replaced the table and booth seats before getting back on the road. When she felt drowsiness creeping in, Mom found a rest stop or, as they welcomed campers to use their parking lot overnight, a Walmart and slid herself into the back bed until morning.

Once we were up and dressed, we gathered around the table for breakfast, overlooking the huge map as Mom showed us where we were and where she hoped to be by the day's end. She called her older brother Joe to let him know where we were before getting back on the road.

"Wanna say hi to the kids?" she always asked, taking her flip phone down from her ear and putting it on speaker. "Okay, you're on speaker."

"Hey, guys. How's life on the road?"

"Good," we replied almost in unison.

"That's good. You been listening to the music I sent you?"

"Yup, there's some pretty good stuff on there," Brian said, smiling at the thought of the cassette tapes Uncle Joe had mailed us beforehand. "John Denver and all them."

"Yup, the classics," Joe chuckled.

"And the recordings of the directions have been great too," Mom chimed in. "It's nice not having to pull over to read them on paper or have these guys read them to me all the time—you've certainly got us covered."

"Sure do. Well, let me know where you lay over next."

My mother had never driven cross-country in an RV before, but she had tremendous faith that she would find the support she needed along the way.

247

"How are we gonna know how to hook everything up?" Brian had asked before we left. "I mean, we've done it a couple times to practice, but still—there's a lot of steps."

"There'll be people around to ask," Mom had replied. "Seriously? Campgrounds in the summer? Those places are full of experienced campers."

My mother and brothers learned by flagging down the surrounding campers when a question arose as at least two of them—typically Mom and one brother while the other brother stayed inside with me—worked to dump the waste and refill the water. People were glad to help, showing them the ropes as my family grew more attuned to the process. Toward the midpoint of the trip down, they practically had it down to a science.

But no one in the family knew exactly what to do for a cable dragging along the road, leaving a shower of sparks beneath us as the RV rolled.

It all started with a biker sitting on a curb at a gas station.

As Mom placed the nozzle into the camper, he cocked his head sideways and then bent down to get a better glimpse.

"Excuse me, Miss? Do you know that you have a wire dragging the ground? It was sparking as you drove in."

Mom gasped and ran to the man, squatting next to him and discussing next steps. He brought out someone from the gas station, and they all talked about what we should do. Naturally, it was Fourth of July weekend, and no garages qualified to fix it were open.

Neither the biker nor the gas station employee could fix it, but they offered the most high-tech temporary solution possible—duct tape.

The camper's generator started to malfunction, causing the power to flicker. Uncertain that it would stay on, Mom booked a room at a nearby Holiday Inn, where we spent the weekend relaxing, swimming, and trying our hands at a nightly, restaurant-wide trivial pursuit at

Damon's, the eatery neighboring the hotel. Outside, we were able to catch vibrant fireworks bursting against the pitch-black night sky.

With a Monday-morning repair, we headed for clear roads.

Or so we thought.

It was during a pit stop at a Kampground of America in Maryland that we learned of it, unsure how it had escaped our eyes and ears when we listened to the radio or watched TV at night.

"Where are you guys headed?" a KOA staff member asked.

"Florida," Mom replied.

"No, you're not," he said, shaking his head with a straight face.

"W-what do you mean?" she asked.

"There's a massive hurricane heading there right now," he said. "Spots here are booking up like crazy. I only have two sites left."

"We'll take one," she said.

❧

At the time, we had heard they named the storm Hurricane Frances, but research later in my life disagreed, putting Frances on the map later in the season. While the way this mix-up emerged remains a mystery to me, there was definitely talk about Frances at the time, marking our memories because of the irony of it all.

"Seriously? Hurricane Frances is coming the week I'm driving down with the kids?" Mom laughed on the phone with Uncle Joe. "Is Mom trying to tell us something?"

My late grandmother, Frances, had been a very mild-mannered woman. It was uncharacteristic of her to storm in like this.

249

❧

The KOA only experienced a brief shower, with the sun shining afterward. I can still picture the scenery I overlooked as I sat outside under the camper's broad canopy and played with my Disney princess–themed paddleball set, swinging my right arm back and forth, winding up to hit the small pink ball at least once per swing. The site was a large, grassy clearing with one paved road and several dirt paths snaking through. In front of me was a dirt clearing, framed by large rocks for the firepit. My brothers were already walking along the untrimmed, grassy perimeter of the site, collecting sticks for that night's fire.

The KOA had been booked out for a family reunion that week. On our walks exploring the campground during our three- or four-day stay, we met some of the family members, and they invited us to join in some of their festivities.

"Well," Mom laughed as we prepared to meet up with them one night. "This is about as close as we've come to crashing somebody else's family event."

The evenings were filled with stories as we sat around the fire with them, rotating the host site of the campfire each time. As we roasted marshmallows—my mother and brothers helping me hand over hand to hold my marshmallow-laden stick to the heat of the brilliant orange flames until the marshmallow was golden brown enough to pair with a Hershey's chocolate bar and graham crackers—we swapped stories of where we had come from, where we were headed, and the experience or, for us, the prospects of being reunited with the family we hadn't seen in years.

❦

Mom's brother Joe, his wife Sally, and their two kids (already grown by the time of our trip) Brian and Mark had moved to Florida when our cousins were young. My brothers and I had met Joe and Sally for the first time we recalled a few years prior when they came back to Connecticut to visit. It had been a while, and phone calls had kept us connected in the meantime. We were excited to finally hang out with some familiar faces when the RV glided to a stop after one turbulent, though fun, journey.

With Sally's upbringing on a farm, my aunt and uncle's house was also home to four dogs, a parrot, and a ferret. To have our own space, we decided to visit in the house during the day and camp in the driveway overnight. Each morning brought Joe knocking on the door with a pair of steaming coffee mugs in hand.

"Wow, what service," Mom exclaimed on the first morning. "Just like Dad used to bring us."

"Yep," Joe replied, a smile appearing through the gray beard on his face as he stepped into the camper to greet us, looking at us through his glasses.

"You guys up for more beaches today?" he'd ask most days. "There are more I want to show you. Each of the beaches around here is known for something—one has the best seashells, the next is famous for being home to the most hermit crabs, and so on."

Along with other attractions, he guided us along the sandy shores of Florida, walking beside us as Mom and my brothers, supporting me with their hands under my armpits, helped me walk barefooted across the wet sand, my feet slapping on the squishy surface as the tide tickled my toes. We walked slowly, scouring the sand for seashells. My family sometimes helped me ease down to my knees as they bent forward. I dug the shell out, picking up fistfuls of sand and dropping them to the side before pulling the new treasure up and handing it to a family member to dust off and examine.

"Here's another one for you, Meg," Uncle Joe sometimes said, approaching with a shell balanced carefully in his open palm as I sat cross-legged on the sand, shoveling sand into my purple bucket in preparation of building a castle.

"Oh, that's a pretty one, Meg! What do you think?" Mom asked, sitting behind me and outstretching her hand to pick up the shell. "Souvenir-worthy?"

"Yeah," I exclaimed, looking closely as she turned it over in her hand, revealing a glossed, leopard-like pattern along its mini conch-like opening.

"You won't find anything like that in Connecticut, that's for sure," Joe smiled, sitting down on the sand.

"She's still amazed at the palm trees," Mom said.

"Probably the first time you've seen any in person, right?" he asked.

"Yup!" I smiled as the word popped out of my mouth.

***

Each evening, we met up with Sally after she got out of work, and with our cousins. Sally, who, as an EMT, couldn't get time off work to join us during the day, chatted amiably about how different the North was from the South.

"To-go box?" she laughed as my brother Brian asked for a to-go container at a restaurant one night. "What is that? I think you mean doggy bag. We're gonna teach you to talk like a Southerner while you're here."

Our cousins, Mark and Brian, sat by us, telling us about what they had been up to. Brian had a six-month-old firstborn son and bounced him proudly on his lap.

"So, Owen James?" Mom said; "after both your grandfathers."

"Yup," he said as the baby reached for Brian's hair and face. "Figured I'd give him the names of the wise ones."

Grinning, she told him how much our Grampy James would have liked that.

Mark told us stories of his experiences as a professional BMX biker, showing us videos and magazine spreads of him flipping in midair above huge ramps.

"Yup, just like your father," Mom laughed. "He always had to be on a bike or skateboard growing up, even breaking his leg once."

"Your dad said there's a cool skate park we could go to near here," my brother Brian piped up, dying to talk about anything having to do with skateboarding. "Have you been to it? Are the ramps nice?"

Uncle Joe had an adventure in mind that surpassed skateboarding, though. Our uncle rented a five-person bike to take us on a tour of the Gulf Coast. It was like the stretch limo of bicycles, with four seats and sets of pedals. The seats sat in pairs, forming two rows. While only one person steered with the front handlebars, all four people pedaled. With a strap and extra padding, my family secured me to enjoy the journey from the child seat in the front.

I looked out over my surroundings, the vibrant, sun-bathed world under the pure blue sky—the light khaki of the sizzling sidewalks; the faded green of the slightly dehydrated grass; the bell-bottomed, brown-gray trunks of the palm trees with the light green fronds bowing gently in the warm breeze; the rolling aqua waves swelling in the distance.

Uncle Joe narrated the significance of the various landmarks all along our route around Fort De Soto Park. Every few miles, we pulled to the side of the paved path to rotate drivers. With Sean's turn came laughter; the bike wavered, zigzagging as he cast quick glances to either side.

"Sean! I know you want to sightsee, pal," Mom called from behind. "But now would be a good time to keep looking straight ahead."

"Is Sean getting his license when he gets older?" Brian asked. "That is *not* a good idea."

"I'll be a great driver," Sean called. "Better than you will be, Brian!"

"Says the guy on a bike weaving in and out on the sidewalk," Brian quipped back.

"Crazy driver coming through," I began to shout.

"Hey, peanut gallery in front," Sean laughed. "Keep it down over there!"

"Sean, you're bringing this thing all over the place," I laughed. "People need to know you're coming."

I could hear him chuckle behind me.

***

After a week of visiting our family, we traveled northeast to the most magical place on Earth. Figuring it might provide a transportation advantage and a break from camping life, Mom had booked a room at Disney's Contemporary Hotel. All we had to do in the morning was take the elevator down to the hotel's indoor monorail station and board the rail line to the park of our choice.

Entering the Magic Kingdom through its grand, golden gates, our eyes raced across the sidewalk as we noticed our favorite characters—Mickey, Minnie, Goofy, Pluto among others—greeting the swarming crowds, posing for photos, and signing autographs. It was just as I had pictured, except even more thrilling.

"Alright, anybody see Guest Services?" Mom asked, looking up from her map when none of us responded. She laughed when she realized we were too mesmerized by the characters to acknowledge her question. "Come on, let's get the accessibility pass; then we can take as many pictures with those guys as you want. We can take pictures on the way too."

∾◦∽

I remember the smile on my mom's face in the Guest Services office as she turned from the desk to face us, her hand gripping the line hopper pass my disability qualified us for. She smirked as her eyes fell on me before she addressed the boys.

"You two can thank your sister for this. See? What did I tell you? Sometimes it pays to be disabled."

"Yeah, guys," I said, poking a finger at each boy's shoulder. "You're welcome."

"Thanks, Meg," Sean said, bringing his voice to a high pitch, a goofy look on his face to go with it.

"Thanks, Meg. Thanks a lot. Really, thanks, thanks a lot," Brian said in a similar distorted voice as Mom and I laughed.

∾◦∽

Our mother gave us jurisdiction over the ride choices, only reserving for herself the selection of the first we went on. Since her inaugural trip to Disney in college, it had been her tradition to go on It's a Small World first.

In its dim entryway, my family initiated a process that we would repeat for each ride. They rolled me to the row of vacant wheelchairs and strollers beside the ride operator's podium.

"Somebody is always in this area, right?" Mom asked the employees. "I know you guys know what you're doing—this chair is custom for my daughter, so I just want to make sure nothing will happen to it."

"Yes, ma'am," the attendants said each time, smiling in their multicolored, Mickey-print uniforms. "We'll be here the whole time. No need to worry."

"Great, thank you so much," she replied with a grin as she and the boys worked together to get me out of the chair, one of them sliding the tray off and unbuckling me as another one or two helped me stand and step off my footrest.

A family member stood holding me in a standing position until it was our turn to board. When the attendant gave us the go-ahead, my family helped me walk over and step onto our car. One family member got in first, sliding to the far end of the seat before turning and helping to slide me in next to them. With the ride's harness firmly across my torso, I grabbed hold of the safety bar in front of me or even to my harness, anchoring myself to keep my body upright. Sitting beside me, at least one family member put an arm around my shoulders to stabilize my balance for the duration of the ride.

With my weak core strength and trunk control, we had to be selective about what rides I went on. Those with abundant sudden twists and turns were not feasible, presenting the risk that I could slide into a position challenging for somebody to help me return to a proper one until the conclusion of the ride. Although aware that, unlike most people, we had to spend time watching and inquiring about the rides' movements before getting on, I don't remember this bothering me. At eight years old, I was too little and would still have had to merely observe as my brothers embarked on the Tower of Terror and other thrillers.

With Disney's seemingly infinite selection of rides, it was easy to find favorites among those I could go on. I loved The Haunted Mansion at Magic Kingdom and how our cart moved at a crawling pace, the chains of its conveyor belt chugging us through the cobweb-laden mansion almost peacefully while life-size figures of vampires, mummies, and ghosts popped out at us from various nooks.

I also loved Animal Kingdom's Kali River Rapids, sitting in the multi-person raft as it twirled us down the rushing river, laughing as it tipped just enough to allow cool waves to leap over the edge and splash my sandaled feet.

Epcot's Soarin' instantly became a favorite for the whole family. We waited in anticipation as the hang glider seats elevated themselves in the dark IMAX theater. When the room was lit up by the floor-to-ceiling screen, it was as if we had been transported into several different worlds. Aerial scenes of beaches, canyons, and golf courses appeared as our seats glided back and forth, making us feel like we were flying.

Brian was the first to laugh when Mom gasped and ducked as a bird flew in the center of the screen, growing larger as if it were swooping in and heading straight toward us. As our mother straightened up, smirking as she eyed us all, a virtual golf ball zoomed into the screen, sending a flinch through Brian's entire body.

"That's what you get for laughing at your mother," she exclaimed as another round of hysterics hit our family.

When we weren't off flying somewhere, we lined up for the character meet-and-greets around the parks. This was what I had been waiting for since I learned we were going to Disney. For some of them, I dressed the part, donning a red Minnie Mouse dress and a hat with black ears protruding from the sides so I could match Minnie for our photo shoot. I remember Minnie gesturing wildly at my outfit and then her own, giving me the thumbs-up before leaning in to pose.

The photo op I remember most, though, was the princesses.

Trembling with excitement, I peered around the snaking line, trying to get a glimpse of Cinderella, Belle, Snow White, and Ariel—characters I had absolutely adored all my life.

"Getting excited?" Mom asked, stroking my hair.

"Yeah!"

"Me too," she smiled at me before turning to the boys. "How about you guys? You excited to meet your favorite Disney princesses?"

"Yeah no," Brian scoffed.

"Just counting down the minutes till we can go ride the Tower of Terror again," Sean chuckled.

"Oh, come on," Mom laughed. "You know you love watching these movies with Meg."

When we reached the front, their royal highnesses greeted us warmly. Starstruck, a grin spread across my face as they complimented me on my smile, outfit, and overall beauty. They had begun to chat among themselves when they noticed the two strapping young lads behind me.

"And who might you princes be?"

My brothers, wearing mortified, I'm-only-here-for-my-sister expressions, sheepishly introduced themselves. The princesses flocked around them, immediately initiating a game of twenty questions.

"Do you have any princesses in your life? Any girlfriends?"

"Any fair maidens at school that you have your eyes on?"

The boys' faces reddened, as they were not yet old enough to be interested in girls. Mom and I watched as they tried inconspicuously to search for an escape from the circle of princesses, our laughter growing harder to suppress with each question. They looked like they wanted to run from the room.

It was Chip and Dale, Disney's famous chipmunk characters, who actually made my brothers sprint from our midst, though.

As we were on a tight budget, our mother had invested in Disney's meal package, calculating that it cost less than buying separate meals each day at the park restaurants and had the added benefit of letting us dine with different Disney characters at each meal.

We were having dinner at the Garden Grill in Epcot—a restaurant where the tables were situated in a huge ring that perpetually revolved around a large pillar. With each spin, a different exotic garden scene was visible.

The two chipmunks greeted us, signing autographs and posing for a picture. As they came out of their poses, their enormous, fuzzy heads angled downward, causing their giant, fixed eyes to point at the baseball caps on my brothers' heads. Pointing to their own heads and giving the thumbs-up, the chipmunks made my brothers grin and reach for their hats. Simultaneously, the chipmunks reached out and peeled the hats off their heads to try them on, first frontward, then backward, and finally sideways. We laughed as they admired each other's appearance.

They stopped gesturing abruptly, slowly nodding as if coming to some sort of agreement. Then they sprinted away, both holding the hats on their heads with one hand.

My brothers scrambled out of their seats and ran after them, belting out a nearly synchronized "HEY!" They chased the chipmunks around the restaurant's loop countless times.

Chip and Dale began to hide among the other families and spontaneously switch directions to trick my brothers before finally returning the hats. By the time the boys sat back down, fatigued and in disbelief, the whole restaurant had joined Mom and me in our laughter.

❧

Chip and Dale were running and hiding again a few days later—this time, with us.

All the Disney characters had sprinkled themselves along the courtyard just beyond Magic Kingdom's entry gate for photo ops.

"I wonder if they'd let us take one with all of them," Mom pondered aloud when we had posed individually with just about every character.

Curious to see if she could convince the man in charge, Sean, Brian, and I hung back a few feet, watching him think it over and make a few calls on his walkie-talkie.

"Quick, get behind that bus over there," Mom instructed, walking back to us. "He said yes, but we have to do it there. Otherwise, everybody will ask."

More than a dozen characters excused themselves from the crowds and initiated a mass exodus from their posts. They gathered around us, getting into the perfect pose without much effort. One click of the camera and a hundred high fives later, they all ran back to their posts, sending us home with the coolest picture ever.

The three-week time frame my mother had planned for the trip had been thrown out the window when the RV malfunctioned. Mom realized that we didn't have anything pressing to hurry back to—just leisure activities with friends. Not sure when we would ever have the opportunity to take a vacation like this again, she decided to extend the trip to the whole summer. As we made our way back up the East Coast, visiting friends all along the way, we stopped at a Walmart, picking up our school supplies. While Mom drove, the boys organized and put the supplies in the backpacks, helping me pack mine as well.

Our RV pulled into our driveway just before sunrise on the first day of school. We went straight from the RV to our buses an hour or two later.

Still buzzing from what I considered the best summer vacation ever, I watched the camper fall out of sight as the bus carried me away.

That wouldn't be the last of my experiences with unique wheels that year. A new set was ready to zoom onto the scene at school—this kind nothing short of life-changing.

Chapter 10

Get with the Times, Speedy!

She caught the sigh I never intended to release as I looked out the car window.

We watched as Long Meadow Elementary's third-grade teachers, students, and parents poured out of the school's front doors and flooded the sidewalk at the entrance, waiting to get on the coach buses snaked along the curved road before us. I could hear the buzz of innumerable conversations through the car's walls and stretched to see if I could spot my friends among the redbrick pillars that stood between the awning and the sidewalk for most of the building's length. There they were, chatting and laughing. I'd have to ask them to catch me up when we were reunited later that morning at Old Sturbridge Village, where we would spend the day at the living history museum seeing reenactments of New England's colonial times, which we had been studying all year.

"Someday they'll have coach buses that can accommodate wheelchairs," Mom remarked softly.

She and the school staff had spent weeks researching and contacting bus companies to see whether any had buses with wheelchair lifts, but vehicles of this nature simply didn't exist yet. They wouldn't until the following year, in time for the fourth-grade trip to Ellis Island.

"Yeah," I sighed again. "It's fine. At least you automatically got picked as a chaperone since you had to drive me. And all my friends are in your group, too, so that's cool."

"Yeah! Plus, I like to think you got the better ride. Aren't I better than any old bus?"

She had that look—that close-lipped smile and twinkle in her eyes indicating something humorous was brewing, just waiting for me to take the bait.

"Of course," I replied, my voice already turning to a giggle in anticipation.

"Good. You better say that. Or else you might have to roll yourself home tonight. They'll see you on the news—'Girl in Wheelchair Seen Motoring from Sturbridge to Middlebury.'"

The car filled with our laughter as hysterics overcame us both.

Years later, as I crafted the first draft of this narrative for this memoir, a mentor noted the irony. Here I was studying colonialism and encountering technology, like the bus, that was still behind the times accessibility-wise during a period of my life that centered on advancing through modern innovations more than ever before.

She called me Speedy.

Years before I entered her class, my third-grade teacher, Mrs. Duncan, had given me the affectionate nickname. Seeing an aide or therapist pushing my chair or watching me walk in my walker down the hall, she always greeted me with a "Hey, Speedy! How you doing?" or a "Looking good, Speedy!" Whether I was going fast or slow, "Speedy" was always mentioned, making me chuckle each time as I turned to wave to her as she leaned against her classroom doorway.

Photo Credit: Anne Mulville Moore

Perhaps fittingly, many memories from her class have my mobility at the heart.

Two moments come to mind immediately when thinking about third grade. It was 2005—the year Johnny Damon was traded from the Boston Red Sox to the New York Yankees. Mrs. Duncan had made it clear on the first day of school that, to her, the Red Sox were the best and the Yankees were good for nothing. I remember my best friend, Nikki, turning in her seat from across the room, her blonde curls bouncing as she moved, to smile and make eye contact. This was our second consecutive year with a teacher who passionately disliked our favorite team. We were going to have some fun with this.

On the morning after Damon's trade, Mrs. Duncan ushered the class into the classroom before entering herself, greeting everybody with a simple "hi" as she stood in front of the open door and gestured for us to come in. Leaving a moment's pause between the last student's entrance and her own, she swung the door shut with more force than usual, the emphatic boom silencing the melody of whispered conversations throughout the room and making each of us, now seated at our desks, turn to the door. She marched from the back of the room, a tiny smirk on her face, stomping with each step.

"As you may have heard," she said when she arrived at the front. "The Red Sox were victims of a traitor."

She gestured to the chalkboard as she described her disappointment. On the edge of the board, she had taped a picture of Damon in his Red Sox jersey up at bat. She had cut a thick red slash out of construction paper and had taped it diagonally across the picture. On the white space bordering the picture on the paper, she had written in black marker: "**TRAITOR!!!**" It remained posted for the duration of the year.

"So, my little chickadees, that's why Damon's name is now banned from my classroom," she said with a sigh, smirking as she watched us all laugh hysterically. "I suppose I should move on to your morning work now, huh?"

The screech of metal hangers sliding across the racks at Bob's Store accompanied my retelling of the story to my family. I stood in the center of my walker's horseshoe-shaped frame that came around my back and sides and gripped its red rubber handles, alternating between standing and pulling my legs up to my stomach, holding myself up with my arms so my legs could swing as if the walker was a jungle gym.

267

Nearly nine years' experience using assistive equipment had given me time to learn the balance between utilizing each piece of equipment for its intended purpose—in this case, helping me stand, walk, and run independently—and being a kid who enjoyed safely using it for acrobatics of sorts. My mother and brothers cracked up along with me as I gave the details of my teacher's reaction.

"It was a smart trade, though," Sean said, leafing through a rack of shirts. He and Brian, middle schoolers at the time, were stocking up on supplies for the start of their next season of sports—likely parks and rec basketball, given that Damon's trade was finalized in the winter. "I don't know if you guys have seen his stats, but he could really do a lot for the team. Hang on, I think I see something—"

He walked across the aisle, disappearing into the rows of clothes; soon Brian also wandered over to a different rack.

"Need anything while we're here?" Mom asked, still thumbing through the rack of boys' shirts.

"Nah, I think I'm g . . ." I trailed off, an idea dawning on me. "Actually, Mom, can I get a new Yankees shirt?"

It took my aide almost no time at all to see the joke that had come into school with me that next morning. Her chuckling began as she took my coat off in the hallway, gently guiding my arm out of the sleeve with one hand, helping me to bend my elbow as she pulled the purple material around my back and off the other arm.

"How about I roll you in backwards today? That way she'll see it right away," she said. "Maybe you should pretend to tie your shoe; she'll see it better if you lean over."

She waited until everybody else had filed into the classroom before bringing me in.

It seems silly, looking back. My teacher undoubtedly knew I didn't have the fine motor skills needed to tie my own shoes—she stooped down in front of me from time to time to tend to my undone laces. Perhaps that's why she was so quick to turn from the board to look at us. From the corner of my eye, I watched her eyes fall on me, taking in my appearance for a moment before releasing a gasp loud enough to turn the whole class's attention to me.

I wonder what she noticed first—the pinstriped jersey, the number 18 made of silky navy-blue material centered on the back, or, in the same material and stitched above the digits, the name Damon.

Still situating their folders and school supplies on their desks, my peers turned to me. Most burst into hysterics immediately. Some of my friends offered remarks such as "Of course. Of course you had to do that" and "You didn't waste any time with that one, did you, Meg?" Rumbling with laughter, I straightened up as my aide turned my chair around to face my teacher. Having left her mouth gaping for a prolonged moment, she closed it and cleared her throat, drawing everyone's attention to her. She left a tick of silence before speaking through an amused smirk. She glanced over at my wheeled computer table at the end of a row of regular desks, at the flat-screen monitor and adaptive keyboard occupying half of it and the empty space where my communication device would be placed in a matter of moments.

"I'm gonna unplug your computer, roll the table into the hall, and you can do your work out there all day," she said, beginning to laugh. "How dare you bring that filth into my classroom!"

What I remember most, though, aside from the jersey (which made countless reappearances at school throughout the year) and the comedy, is the sensation of riding in my chair that morning. As my aide spun the chair to face my teacher, the classroom became a blur of color, and I had the faint sensation of my stomach somersaulting inside me. It was like riding the teacups at an amusement park, though a much slower and tamer version. Trying to time it to coincide with my aide's movements in pivoting the chair, I straightened my torso up gradually, hoping to miss the curviest part of the turn, to avoid having gravity toss me into the back of the seat too roughly or too far to the side. Of course, that day, my ongoing laughter dulled my precision; my aim still got me where I needed to land but sent me leaning slightly against the cushioned lateral pad—a small square that jutted out from the chair back on either side and sat beneath each armpit, helping to keep my torso straight.

This routine seemed normal to me. I had grown up learning to intuit when others were getting ready to turn me, bring me to a stop, or change directions. Practically an automatic reflex, my body knew just when to put my arms down on the armrests or the seat to stabilize itself during wide turns, to lift my arms and place them on tables before I was rolled all the way up, to move my arms from the edges of the armrests when coming into close quarters with doorways, and more. I couldn't know the exact moment that I would be up against surfaces and bends of turns—my chauffeurs didn't call out directions like today's GPS units do (*In fifty feet, ease right onto the exit ramp*), but I learned to gauge it with fine accuracy. It was just a process running subconsciously in the back of my mind.

I suppose my limited ability to be independent in my mobility had always stood out to me. It was impossible not to notice that I had to rely on others to move my chair from one place to another—that when I saw a friend come in or an interesting event happening on the other side of the room, I had to ask and wait for someone to push me over to my desired location, hoping they could pause what they were doing quickly enough to get me there before the main part of the activity or conversation concluded. I tried to remember how nice it was that others were willing to help me, but a big part of me wondered what it would be like and how much more efficient it would be if I could get from one place to another on my own. I didn't know how or if this would ever be possible, but I couldn't help but ponder how much it would improve my life.

My mother was the first to help to make this my new reality. She didn't want me to have to wait for somebody to move my wheelchair to where I was looking to go. She wanted me to be able to do it myself. She knew I was ready—she could see it in the way I handled my equipment, being unafraid to goof around with my friends while taking care and ensuring that it all was set far away from the edge of the table and that, if someone outside of my family had to touch it, their fingers were tuned to its great delicacy.

"You hardly have to touch it at all," I'd say before granting my friends permission to push a few keys on my DynaVox. "Just use your fingertip, not your nail—my speech therapist said that could mess up the screen."

My mother saw the level of responsibility I had grown into even at eight years old—that I fully understood that it was a major hassle to have my equipment break and for me to be without it, unable to use my wheelchair and walker to assume the proper positioning and exercise regimen that helped me maintain good health or unable to speak to those outside of my family until communication device repairs could be arranged. She approached my therapists at school during my second-grade year, seeking guidance on how to initiate the process to get me my first motorized wheelchair.

"The team at Long Meadow was amazing," she told me years later. "They guided me through each detail. They made it so easy."

The memories of embarking on the process that first time blend with those that came later—every three to five years, when I grew out of the chairs and saw signs that they were wearing out beyond repair; electronic issues causing parts to move improperly; screws, pads, and

271

various control panels loosening and even falling off, no matter how many times they were tightened with tools; and simply seeing the chairs become outdated as new technology emerged.

I vaguely recall my first evaluation with the equipment vendor and my physical therapist. Lying on the school therapy room mat, I remember changing positions every few minutes at the vendor's request.

"Can you straighten your legs out as much as you can, Meg?" he asked, kneeling beside me as he smiled. "Yes, just like that. Hold still for a moment."

Wiggling slightly against the cool mat, as my athetoid cerebral palsy never allowed me to be completely motionless—at least not during my wakeful hours—I heard a measuring tape slide open, making a *sh* sound as the strip ejected from its thick black plastic case with a touch of a button. The highlighter-yellow tape rested atop my quads as the vendor wrote down the number of inches spanning the ends of my femur. He slid the tape down, keeping its case just above my kneecap and letting the strip descend to the edge of my heel. Having my mother and my physical therapist help me sit up—each taking a hand and guiding my shoulder as they lifted my torso from the mat—he measured from the top of my head to my shoulder, from my shoulder to my hip, and my shoulder and arm spans.

"You know, this would be a good opportunity to use those tummy muscles we've been working on. Instead of sitting like this," my therapist, Tina, said from beside me, slumping her posture, her chestnut hair hanging in front of her shoulders as she arched her back and neck, "you could be sitting like this; that would help get a better measurement of your back too."

She had straightened her body back up, taking extra care to put it as tall as it could go—almost as straight as a wood plank—and turned her head to watch me correct my posture. I pulled my stomach muscles to bring my upper body forward. My hands fell next to my hips, pushing against the mat to stabilize and uphold my body.

My arms burned slightly from the effort, and I put a little bend in my elbows to relieve some of the pressure. A small fire of exhaustion started in my abs as I kept them tight to stay upright.

"Good! You didn't think I'd let you come in here without making you do some therapy, did you?" she laughed as Mom and I began chuckling too.

"I can have her Shriners doctor write a letter," my mother said after the vendor began to talk about the medical documentation he would need to send to our insurance company to justify why they should cover this type of chair for me. "I could ask the pediatrician, too, but Shriners handles her orthopedics."

"I'll have my letter written within the next couple of weeks," Tina offered. "I'm planning to talk about how she is very bright and mainstreamed; that, with her getting older, she needs to have independence in her mobility in classroom and home settings; and how the seating system on a Permobil motorized wheelchair would be most beneficial for her posture."

"Yes, that would all be great," the vendor said. "You just want to be very specific on why she needs this exact chair and why a manual wheelchair is no longer adequate. The more information the better."

<hr />

For several weeks, I arrived home from school to find that Mom had taken a break from compiling paperwork to take me off the bus. Stacks of stapled pages sat neatly in a row on our marble dining room table.

"The letter from Shriners came today," she said, beginning her daily routine of updating me on the progress she had made while I was at school. "I've sent a copy to the vendor already. He has Tina's letter, too, so he's just about ready to send everything to the insurance company. Here, you can read what Dr. Masso wrote if you want."

273

She usually put a packet on my lap before returning to her sorting.

"Dys-kin-et—dyskinetic cerebral palsy?" I'd ask, stumbling over the medical terminology that seemed so foreign to my second-grader vocabulary. "What's dyskinetic? Is that like the kind of CP I have?"

"Yeah, it's just the name for the way your movements are unorganized and unsteady," she'd explain without hesitation. "Remember how I told you that when you were a baby, one of the doctors said CP is like a big umbrella? A general diagnosis with a lot of specific diagnoses underneath as the spokes? This is a spoke."

"Oh, makes sense," I said, giving the paper back to her with a very loose grip, knowing my CP would cause me to significantly wrinkle the page with a grip of any more strength (I had trouble regulating the intensity of my grip—it was often an all-or-nothing deal in which I could either grab onto something with full force or with a grip so weak that the items slipped through my fingers). "Can I watch TV or play something before homework and dinner?"

That was my mindset back then—a state between knowing at least the basics of what was happening with my medical care, flipping through the documentation's dense pages and asking my mother to explain it to me, and yet still in that child thought process—only able to lend my eyes to the not-so-kid-friendly paperwork for a few moments before returning to the simplicity of playing with dolls, creating shapes out of Play-Doh or Model Magic clay, or watching my favorite Disney Channel show, *Lizzie McGuire*. Mom continued to discuss the specifics with me, translating the foreign language of the medical jargon into something more manageable.

Each day she had new information to share with me, even if it was just an explanation of how she hadn't heard anything new from the insurance company or the equipment vendor but had placed a call to follow up. She told me of the approval process and how the insurance company could either approve or deny the claim.

"But there's always the appeals process if they deny it. We can submit more information from your medical records to show them more about why you really need this chair, and they will have to look at it and make a decision again with the new information," she explained. "But don't worry about that—if they deny it, I'm going to keep working until we get it covered. I already told people on the phone that I'm one of those annoying customers who doesn't go away until you have the chair you need."

I erupted into giggles. Beginning to chuckle, she assured me she had in fact done that on the phone. When I was home from school during the calls, she put the phone on speaker so I could witness it for myself.

⌘

I didn't realize the gift my mother had been so careful to give me as a child. When I started handling my own medical care at age eighteen about a decade later, I found it easier than I anticipated, discovering that I had absorbed quite a bit when she went over the documentation with me during childhood. At eighteen, reading the volumes of paperwork myself came almost naturally, the terminology familiar—I had, after all, grown up encountering it, thanks to my mom. It occurred to me that I knew how to have discussions with medical personnel and insurance companies with these terms, when to follow up with these individuals, and how to be a little firmer—to be the customer who won't go away until the equipment is in my possession and in working order—when necessary in correspondence with them. ("When we last spoke on October 25th, you estimated that the order would be fulfilled by November 26th. It is now December 16th, and I still do not have my part, which, as you had said, leaves me with a wheelchair that does not have the correct support due to

275

the need for repair. This could lead to health concerns if the repair is delayed much longer. Could you please provide me with your plan to have this issue rectified within the next week or so? Thank you.") My mother had sown the seed that enabled me to blossom into a fierce advocate for myself.

❧

Several months after submitting the claim, my mom received the good news that my chair would be partially covered.

"They're willing to cover $18,500," she told me. "And the chair is $26,000."

"So that's good, right?" I asked, trying to do the math in my non-numbers-person head. "That's like most of it."

"Good? This is amazing. There was a chance they wouldn't cover it at all."

I smiled, understanding that this was a major success.

❧

I didn't realize how much of a triumph this was, though, and I'm sure my mom didn't either. As technology progressed in later years, the price of Permobil motorized wheelchairs, and of motorized wheelchairs across the board, would skyrocket to $40,000, $50,000, and some even to $90,000. Insurance companies changed their policies, covering very little or nothing at all. We, along with innumerable other patients and their families, would eventually find ourselves in a quandary of how to secure the funding to get the new chairs before our current chairs became too small, uncomfortable, and worn out to use.

I personally experienced an insurance battle so extensive in intensity and length during college that I developed skeletal issues from growing out of my wheelchair and having to sit in it anyway for about a year until we could find a solution. Fortunately, this came at a time when my mother and I were surrounded by, to say the least, extremely compassionate people—peers, staff, community members, and especially Fairfield University alumni such as Bob Berchem and Bryan LeClerc of Berchem & Moses Law and Sergeant Rob Didato and his Fairfield University Department of Public Safety staff—who saw us struggling with denials and appeals that would never see approval and with a chair that was both structurally and mechanically failing. Out of the kindness of their hearts and their genuine desire to help, they started fundraisers and initiatives to arrange for the vendor to cut the commission markup and reduce the price to a more reasonable amount. They eventually gifted me the high-tech chair I needed—efforts I would never have expected or asked for and that still leaves me in incredibly grateful awe.

At seven or eight years old, though, I didn't have to worry about denials. My mind was free to ponder what it would be like to sit in a wheelchair that I could move myself. Back then, the standard timeline for the chair getting ordered, built, and delivered was three months from the time of the insurance approval. Of course, to a young kid, that seemed like an eternity.

I had never actually driven a motorized wheelchair, so I didn't really know what I was missing. I don't remember the wait seeming tremendously unbearable—I didn't have the experience of a trial to make me realize my independence before having to get back into a manual chair.

It was the curiosity that got to me—what would it be like? How would it feel to be at liberty to move across the room or playground at the exact moment my desire to do so emerged? The waiting was a lot like Christmas Eve—months of Christmas Eves, I suppose—knowing that something enthralling was under the wrapping paper, having an idea of the shape and size, but being prohibited from unwrapping it until Christmas morning.

I was always a kid who could never sleep on Christmas Eve, tossing and turning in bed as my mind unceasingly imagined what might be beneath the tree.

$\infty\!\!\oslash\!\!\sim$

A foggy memory resides in my mind from the day the chair arrived at school. Like looking through wax paper, the scene is blurred, but I can make out the figures of my mother, my physical therapist, and the equipment vendor standing beside me. I sat atop the new chair's cushy black leather seat as the vendor adjusted the hip guides—two rectangular pads made of dense foam encased in a perforated cloth beside each hip, keeping them centered and straight. With a socket wrench, he tightened screws that affixed the pads to the chair, emitting a *click, click, click* each time he wound the wrench in a half circle. He checked to make sure each pad sat at the appropriate level of my body, conferring with my physical therapist for confirmation.

I remember the vendor guiding me through the therapy room door, driving me with the glossy black joystick on my right as he walked beside me. Centering me in the deserted post-dismissal hallway, he showed me how the joystick worked, how even touching it gently made the chair move. He demonstrated the brakes, driving the wheelchair forward and then releasing the joystick to show how the chair stopped instantly.

278

Clicking a button labeled "Mode" on the control panel attached to the joystick, he pointed out how one click made a dot of green lights on the control panel flash repetitively.

"That's your speed," he explained. "Moving the joystick to the right will put more dots on there; left will put fewer. There are five dots—one is the slowest and five is the fastest."

"We want you on the slowest speed, at least for the first couple weeks," my physical therapist said from beside him. "So just leave it on one, please. We want you to get used to driving before trying any of the higher speeds, just so it's safer."

"Yeah, Meg," Mom said, breaking into a smirk in contrast to Tina's matter-of-fact, serious expression as she stood next to her. "No speeding. I hear Mr. Gusenburg is posting speed limits around the school as we speak."

"I won't," I said, laughing, imagining the principal stapling paper speed limit signs to bulletin boards in the hallways as the words popped out of my mouth.

"Meg, watch this," the vendor said, calling my attention back to the flashing dot. "Clicking 'Mode' twice will lock in the speed and bring you back to drive, but clicking it once will bring you to the seating mode."

Double-clicking the button, eliciting a soft *beep* (the chair beeped each time any button was depressed), he pointed to the cartoonish image of a wheelchair in the center of the control panel. About the size of a nickel, it was a simple line drawing—a white outline against the black background, two squares stacked on top of each other with a circle on either side. One red light shone on the bottom square—on the seat of the depicted wheelchair. He pushed the joystick forward, and the seat beneath me began to elevate, slowly raising to the height of the average counter.

It felt kind of like an amusement park ride, the motor vibrating gently from under the seat, creeping up as if building anticipation for the big surprise drop. I leaned to the side, peering over the black leather armrests to watch the floor grow further away as a smile spread across my face. The vendor kept talking about the benefits—how elevating the seat gave me a better vantage point of my surroundings and put me at eye level with my peers. Those were key factors that entered my eight-year-old mind as I gradually realized the new capabilities the chair afforded me. In the moment, though, I was simply fascinated by the sensation of rising and lowering. It was like the chair had a built-in drop-tower ride (without, of course, the sudden, plunging drop these attractions typically feature). As I grew up, I often found myself raising my seat just for the fun of it.

"Cool, huh?" he asked. "Well, wait till you see this. Let me bring you back down first."

The seat lowered, clicking into the tomato-red rectangular box that was the wheelchair's base covering the motor beneath the seat, protruding several inches from the seatback and also shielding the tops of the two large, smoky-gray front tires. He nudged the joystick to the right, then pushed and held it forward, and my seat suddenly began to slide outward, away from the base as it descended to the floor. The silver metal footrest met the ground, and suddenly I noticed the tiny roller-blade-like wheel under it. The footrest rolled itself until it was lying flat, leaving my legs outstretched.

I silently chuckled as I crossed my ankles and let my body scooch into a lounged position. It was just too cool that I got to do this and would be allowed to do it every day.

"What do you think of that, Meg?" Tina asked. "Isn't that awesome? You can sit on the floor with your friends now when you have assemblies and story time in class!"

"Yeah," I exclaimed, beaming as the words poured out of my mouth. "And at indoor recess and in library class and at Girl Scouts—"

"I think she has very big plans for this chair already," my mom laughed as my mind kept cranking out ideas. "And she's only had it for a matter of minutes."

❧

I vaguely remember test-driving the chair in the hallway as my therapist and the equipment vendor coached me, teaching me how my grip could be slightly relaxed for better flexibility of the wrist and, among other trials, testing how quickly I could release the joystick and stop the chair when they rolled a ball in front of me.

Mostly, though, the memory of my first real drive takes place on the quiet road of Dorothy Drive. I still remember how the sky was nothing more than an azure dome, housing only the golden sun that provided the summer heat. The equipment supply company's huge cargo van barreled up the deserted road, looking almost too big for our little neighborhood. I don't remember why the vendor took the chair back with him after my fitting at school—perhaps they had to adjust something back at the shop.

At the end of our driveway, my mother lifted me out of my old chair, standing me up on the small metal footplate and waiting for me to step down to the ground one foot at a time as she supported me, her arms under mine. She spun me around so that my back was to her and, wrapping her arms around my stomach, took steps that were nearly identical to mine until we were in front of the motorized wheelchair. Mom gently turned me around and helped me ease down into the seat, pushing her knees into mine to aid in scooching my hips to the back of the cushion. She leaned down by the side of the chair, her hands fishing for the half of the seat belt that had slid off the seat.

"How's it feel?" Brian asked as he and Sean stood nearby. "Like your own Hummer?"

281

"Yup," I replied as our mother clicked the seat belt's halves together and tugged on the belt once, then twice, the way all protective parents do when fastening their children into a vehicle. "Isn't it cool?"

"Yeah," he said. "It's like a racecar with the red."

"Imagine if it was street legal," Sean laughed. "You'd just see Meg tearing down the road to get to Long Meadow next to the buses."

"Yeah, you guys keep talking about getting your licenses when you're in high school," Mom said, turning to my brothers as the technician gave me a quick refresher on the chair controls. "But your little sister's got you beat. She's allowed to drive, *and* she has her own vehicle at the tail end of second grade."

"My car will be even cooler than that, though," Sean smiled, shaking his shaggy brunette hair out of his chocolate-colored eyes.

The technician, Dave, gave a small chuckle as he invited me to control the chair myself. My finger flew to the "Mode" button, clicking its papery surface twice. It almost came naturally, as if I had been doing it all my life. I held the joystick forward, feeling the squishy black gaiter—the rubber that sat in three circular accordion folds beneath the plastic tip and dome of the joystick, protecting the inner computer module from water and dust—crumple against the control panel's plastic. I was pushing it as far as it could go.

"But can whatever car you get do this?" I asked as my seat raised to its full countertop height before I lowered back down and began to descend to the pavement. "Or this?"

I watched my brothers' eyes widen in amazement as I landed on the ground, stretching my legs out across the footrest for added emphasis.

"I don't think so," I said with a prolonged gaze and grin.

"Oh, look at me, I'm Meg," Brian said in a goofily high tone, moving from side to side as his shoulder-length brunette hair swayed with him. "I'm so cool with my new motorized wheelchair. *Soooo fancy.*"

We all laughed, then Dave asked if I wanted to do a test drive before he left.

"Seems like she has the controls already down pat," he said to my mother as I brought my seat back into its normal position. "At least for the seat elevator."

"Yeah, she typically picks up on how to use her assistive technology right away," Mom replied. "You know kids and technology these days—they try it once and they already have it mastered."

Photo Credit: Anne Mulville Moore

The dead-end road of Dorothy Drive was still quiet, with little activity and traffic, so we decided that I could navigate between our driveway and the side of the road for a while, staying close so I could pop into the driveway or along the curb if a car approached.

The motor hummed beneath me, slightly vibrating with a quiet *sh* sound as I went—a sensation that never quite got old, even years later. The gentle summer breeze made my hair dance behind me as I continued down the length of our front yard. I drove straight and then turned, jerking the chair at first, making it move in short spurts as I tested to see how fast it would turn before I was confident enough to make one smooth motion. I learned by experimentation how to move the joystick in an arc from the right or left to redirect the chair.

The world seemed to spin in slow motion with each turn, the thick trees and my neighbors' houses parading in and out of my view at a gradual yet steady pace. Back and forth I went, my amusement at the sensation never dulling. My brothers ran at the edge of the grass beyond the curb alongside me, trying to match the pace of the chair. On the slowest speed, I was probably going only a little over half a mile per hour, but I felt like I was zooming along as fast as a racecar.

"Hey, Meg?" Mom called from in front of the driveway after a little while. She was standing with the technician. "Dave's gotta get going. Any last questions for him? Any last adjustments?"

"No, I think I'm good," I said, releasing the joystick and gliding to a stop in front of them, smiling at how precise my judgment had been in when to let go. "Wait, Mom, I know I can never do this inside, but I'm outside now with nothing around me. Can I try the fastest speed just to see what it's like? Please?"

"I had a feeling that was coming," she laughed. "Go ahead. Just make sure you're not right next to the curb so you have plenty of room to turn around without hitting it. What do you say to Dave?"

"Thank you," I called, already clicking "Mode" and holding the joystick to the right until the flashing green dots on the control panel numbered five.

After Dave's van reached the corner past our next-door neighbors' house, I began to drive again. The increased speed made every crack in the worn gray pavement feel prominent, causing my chair to dip down into the inch-or-two-wide crevices full of grass and weeds before it climbed back up and continued along the pebbly textured road. The breeze rushed over my face and through my hair, almost burning my cheeks as my mouth hung open, projecting laughter. I practically had my own personal teacup ride at my fingertips. I made several loops before stopping and allowing my body to rid itself of its sea legs–like dizziness. Sitting still, I let hysterical laughter wash over me as my family, all chortling too, caught up to me.

My brothers and I spent the rest of the day racing up and down the street and yard as our mother watched from the curb.

"Hey, Mom, who are you rooting for? Who do you want to win?" Brian asked as he ran, smirking slyly the way he always did when trying to trap someone in a prank. "Which one of us is your favorite?"

"Nice try, Bri," she said, shaking her head. "So not falling for it. I don't have a favorite—I love you all equally."

"She has to say that so you guys don't feel bad," he said, looking from Sean, who was beside him on one side, to me on the other. "But really I'm her favorite."

"Actually, Brian, you have it all wrong," Sean said in the goofy tone he always used when trying to sound jokingly superior in knowledge. "Everyone knows the firstborn is always the favorite. Get your facts straight, mm-kay?"

"I have my facts straight," Brian replied, "but you obviously don't."

"Didn't you guys hear it's the daughter that's always the mom's favorite?" I asked.

"Yeah, I don't think so, Meg," Sean said. "It's definitely the son and the oldest. Hate to break it to you."

"Brian's right—are you sure you have your facts straight?" I laughed as Mom and Brian cracked up.

Sean held his straight face for a moment, doing his best to look annoyed before bursting into laughter.

"A couple more minutes, guys," Mom called as we turned to take another lap down to the end opposite of where she was standing. "And then we have to start heading in for dinner, baths, and bed."

I tilted my head back to catch a glimpse of the rosy light beginning to appear over the street. My brothers and I took a few more laps and stopped at the far end, taking a moment to rest and enjoy a few more breaths of the summer air before turning for home. Brian stepped over the curb and onto the road, taking a close-up view of the heather-gray tires.

"Tires have some serious treads on them," he noted, tapping his sneaker against one in the front. "Are these like all-terrain? Think they can handle like curbs and stuff?"

"No idea," I said with a shrug.

"Can we try?" he asked. "I mean, the curb isn't that much bigger than a ramp, right?"

"I guess," I nodded. "Okay."

Sprinting down the short stretch that had separated us from her, our mother arrived behind us as the tires approached the edge of the curb.

"Meg! Brian! No," she cried, wedging herself between my brother and my chair. "Back up! Back up!"

I imagine my mother's mind was filled with images of the worst-case scenario: a three-hundred-something-pound motorized wheelchair tipped over, one or even two kids—depending on where Brian was standing—injured.

She sighed heavily, looking like the weight had been removed from her shoulders once a few inches lay between my tires and the curb.

"Motorized wheelchairs cannot go over curbs," she began, looking at us both. "It's just like how wheelchairs of any kind can't go down stairs—you guys have known that since you were really little, right? Well, a curb is just like a stair. It's just too much for the chair—this looks like an army tank, but it's really very delicate and could tip over."

"Yeah, sorry. It was my idea," Brian explained. "I just thought, with the bigger tires and the motor, it might be able to do more stuff."

"Yeah, Mom, I'm sorry. I didn't even think about all that," I sighed, shaking my head. I had been doing so well with the chair too.

"It's okay—I know it's the first day and it's exciting," she replied. "We just have to be careful. There are plenty of ways to have fun while being safe. And, Meg, this is something you are going to have to face with other people too. Your friends are probably going to ask you to try some crazy tricks, but you have to be the one that keeps safety in mind. It's a big responsibility, but I know you can do this. I know you're ready. I'm trusting you."

"Yeah, I'll be careful," I said, my mouth moving a mile a minute, my mind doing the same. "I don't want to go back to a manual chair. That's what would happen, right?"

"It's certainly a possibility," she replied, keeping a straight face for a moment before breaking into a smile and inspiring me to do the same. "But I *know* you can do this. I've been telling the school staff you're ready for the better part of a year now."

We learned to balance fun with safe driving, continuing with our races in the yard and in parks. Having a motorized wheelchair never got old. Each morning, I turned it on as my mother finished buckling me in, eager to begin zipping off to finish getting ready for school or to wherever the weekend brought us—sports, church, and playdates, among other activities.

Photo Credit: Anne Mulville Moore

287

"Why is this up to five? I never go this fast in the house, and I left it on the slowest last night," I said one morning before school, noticing that all the speed dots were glowing lime green.

Her close-lipped smile barely containing her laughter, Mom rested her hazel eyes on my face as if she was waiting for the answer to dawn on me.

The only person in the house that really likes the top speed all the time is—

"Wait. Did Brian really steal my chair while I was sleeping? Seriously?"

"And he was so careful to come and go so quietly so you didn't wake up and catch him," she laughed. "Although he was a little louder than usual last night, and he's slipping if he forgot to turn the speed back down."

"Usual? He does this all the time?" I asked, laughing in disbelief.

"Yup. They do it a few times a week."

"They *both* do it?" I gaped, giggling even harder now. "And you're okay with that?"

"I have to let them explore your equipment *somehow.* How else would they learn about it and be comfortable with helping you in it?" she replied. "But don't worry—I was on his tail the whole time last night, bugging him about the speed. I think he actually got annoyed with me for following him around and cut his ride short. But he figured out that thing you do where you only push the joystick lightly so the chair doesn't go the full power of whatever speed it's on. I would have been more on his case if he hadn't done that."

"I just can't believe they've been doing that and I haven't picked up on it until now," I exclaimed as her laughter grew to a roar. "I'm gonna get them! I don't know what I'm gonna do, but I'll get them."

Nobody was a stranger to pranks in our house; our mom was always making jokes, and our dad had been widely known as the prankster among family and friends. It was in our blood. I don't remember the prank I pulled as payback for the many counts of chairjacking, but knowing my mindset back then, it was probably along the lines of hiding one of their favorite toys or video games or switching their CDs in the car so that when they climbed in with their friends and clicked on the stereo after sports practice or a weekend outing—already talking about the new music they had just gotten—a high dose of Disney princess music serenaded them. A great blessing, my mother was always willing to be my accomplice, setting up whatever physical objects were needed for the payback—as long as it was good-natured—in a way that my hands couldn't, given my weak fine motor skills.

"I'm sure you'll come home today having thought of something while you're at school," she chuckled.

My chair didn't get delivered until the tail end of second grade, so I didn't begin to cruise through the school with it until the start of third grade. For the first few weeks, they only allowed me to use it in the hallways and areas like the library, music room, and gym—locations with the open space optimal for me to get accustomed to maneuvering. I continued to use my old manual chair in Mrs. Duncan's classroom. Of course, being infatuated with my chair, my eyes frequented the clock and the day's schedule on the whiteboard, looking to determine how much time had to elapse before I could take another spin (and perhaps trying to will it to pass faster).

Those weeks seemed so long to me back then, like it would never be time to use it as my primary chair. I remember, though, that transferring between chairs amused me almost as much as I longed to stay in my motorized wheelchair. It was like having my own car that I had to park. Having a couple extra minutes before the school day started one morning, I even taught myself how to parallel park, approaching the strip of wall between the doorways of Mrs. Duncan's room and the neighboring one from a diagonal, bringing the front tire next to the wall, and then moving the joystick in the opposite direction to get the back end of the chair in the same position.

My physical therapist gave me a more formal driver's education, setting up mini obstacle courses constructed of cones and therapy balls for me to zigzag through in the therapy room and the hall.

"See if you can start turning a little sooner when you go around the next cone," Tina said during one session. "Actually, wider, not sooner—your timing is fine. You're just a tiny bit too close to the cone on your turns. I want more space between you and the cones because, remember, the cones are standing in for the walls. You don't want to be right up against a wall. Can you try making a giant arc here? Just keep going straight when you see the turn coming, then make a really wide swing, almost making a half circle."

Advancing toward the pumpkin-colored cone, I watched the carpet, eyeballing the decreasing strip that sat between me and the cone. When there seemed to be only a few inches between the cone and me, I pulled the joystick slightly left, making the chair curve away from the cone. I gradually brought the joystick over to the right, keeping it pushed against the plastic of the control panel. Like a stencil acting as a guide for a pencil forming a precise curve, the plastic aided me in steering in a wide crescent shape.

"Yes, just like that," Tina exclaimed. "That's what I want you to do in the hall. How was that? Hard? Easy?"

"Not too hard," I said, stopping my chair as the words fell out of my mouth. "Kinda easy."

"Good! Just remember to do that for every corner."

⁓❧⁓

It wasn't always easy to gauge the exact second I should turn or the distance I should leave between my wheel and fixtures around me, though, especially in those first few months. I remember arriving home one day with a chip in my fender above my tire.

Eyeballing the inches between the chair and the door of the school restroom stall, it looked like I had just enough room to back out. I inched back as my aide, Mrs. Calzone, held the stall door open. The back of the chair had already made it through. It looked like . . . maybe . . . yes, it would! Half of the wheel was out, now a few inches left, and—

Crack!

It was like a truck backfiring, making me jump, making my hand fly away from the joystick as I leaned over to assess the damage. The middle of the fender was up against the metal edge of the stall. I moved the chair forward and turned to the left as I backed up again, now away from the edge.

What was that crack? I wondered, gliding past Mrs. Calzone.

Keeping one hand on the door, she bent down to pick something up off the tiled floor, her salt-and-pepper bob hanging in a curtain as she did.

"Oh, look at this," she said, showing me the shard of hard red plastic in her palm.

291

Her face tilted up to make eye contact with me, a small, amused smile appearing on her lips. "You had your first fender bender," she exclaimed.

I looked down at the fender. There it was, a chip only about the size of a fingertip, though my imagination inflated the size.

I wonder if my face looked as deer-in-the-headlights as I felt.

"Don't worry," she smiled. "It happens. I had one too when I started driving a car."

I nodded and tried to smile, sighing.

Photo Credit: Anne Mulville Moore

"I just can't believe it—I was doing so good," I said after school, sighing as I watched my mother bend down to assess the damage I had pointed out. "I was going slow. I looked to make sure I had room, and I hit it anyway."

"Well," she said, straightening up, "it sounds like you just misjudged it. It's fine—it's one little chip out of the fender, not the end of the world."

"I know," I sighed again. "But the chair was nice and new, and now it's got that chip—it's just disappointing. I was looking and going slow, and I hit it anyway."

"It happens to the best drivers. It's just an accident. You were doing everything you should have been doing." She smiled. "I don't think you and Mrs. Calzone were goofing off while you were backing up, were you?"

"What? No," I laughed.

"I didn't think so," she chuckled. "So, when you go to back up, wherever you may be, just look before you go, and then inch back."

She told me to keep looking the whole time and, after going back a little, to make a full stop and take a good look all around to see if I was near anything. She said to repeat the process until my chair was in the clear, no matter how long it took.

"You're doing a great job driving, so don't worry about this," Mom beamed. "Everybody at school has been telling me how impressed they are with how you handle the chair, even when your friends are around."

I grinned.

❧

I remember the distinct difference the chair made in my school routine. Suddenly I had the means to raise myself up so I could better see my teachers manipulating tools for tabletop demonstrations. For the first time, I had a bird's-eye view of the table. Like my standing classmates, I was able to see the objects—art supplies marking the canvas, page, or clay slab; science test tubes being filled; rulers measuring distances—from a little height rather than staring at the teacher's working hands at my eye level, unable to see much of what they were working on until the finished products were brought down to my lap afterward. I had often wondered whether my obstructed view was preventing me from catching a vital detail that couldn't be re-created later when I was at liberty to scrutinize the finished product. Now I could see it all—the moves involved in braiding together physical details to create the visual. It was like I had been given a new form of vision. Even as a child, it left me in awe.

What remains in my memory even more is the feeling that came from being able to lower down to the floor to sit among my friends for assemblies and class activities. They were fascinated by this feature, standing beside me to watch as I changed modes on the control panel and toggled the joystick before they sat themselves down. Some even made a dance out of it, lowering themselves at the same slow pace of my chair as it brought me down and looking forward while bobbing their necks back and forth like ostriches. By the time my footrest touched down to the floor, we were in stitches.

I could now witness my friends' real-time reactions to the speakers at the front of the room rather than being filled in later, when they could stretch up to kneeling during a momentary lull in the presentation and share their humorous observations.

Photo Credit: Anne Mulville Moore

"You guys see that thing moving closer to his face up there?" my friend Collen once asked during an assembly. "Look at him and look right. See it? Is that a spider? Or a microphone?"

"I don't know. I dare you to raise your hand and ask what it is," Gabby replied, a broad smile spreading across her mocha-colored face.

"No! You do it," Colleen exclaimed, twirling her chestnut hair around a pale finger.

"I'm not doing it. You're the one who brought it up."

"Meg, you do it. Just type it into the Dyna and ask," Colleen said. "It'll be less obvious who's asking."

"Uh, really?" I asked, looking at my communication device propped on a chair to my right as the words fell from my mouth in a whisper. "No."

"Yeah, Colleen, good one," Gabby chuckled as quiet laughter filled me and Colleen. "There's only one kid in our grade who uses a computer to talk. Someone's asking a question with a computer. Gee, I wonder who it is. Not obvious at all."

Mostly, though, I remember the thrill of simply riding down the hall with my friends beside me. Their hands always found their way to my armrests, sprawling their fingers out on the black leather as they matched their pace to mine and chattered away.

"How fast does this thing go anyway? Really fast?"

They were filled with questions about the chair in those first weeks. It amused me, bringing a smile to my face.

Many had been with me since kindergarten and had been around me enough to be able to understand my natural speech. Unable to use my communication device while driving—that would be just as distracting and potentially harmful as texting and driving a car—I spoke my responses with my natural voice in the hall.

"Yeah, really fast!"

"But you can't show us the fastest speed at school, right?" Gabby asked. "Not even in the hall or at recess?"

"Nope."

"What would happen if you did?" Colleen asked. "Your mom said they would put you back in your old one, didn't she?"

"Yup, and I'm not taking any chances. This one is so much more fun," I replied. "But maybe next time we have a playdate or something, I can show you. She usually lets me turn it up if I'm outside with nothing in the way."

The chatter continued as I proceeded down the hall alongside them, relishing my new ability to finally match their pace.

Photo Credit: Anne Mulville Moore

Chapter 11

When Agathokakological Words Strike

"Who can read what the cake says?" Dr. Shaw, one of my fourth-grade teachers, asked, holding the white cardboard box containing a sheet cake and surveying our forty-something-student class sitting before her on the classroom's massive white area rug. "John? How about you? Can you read this for everyone please?"

I remember it clearly. A grin illuminated her face as she peered through her glasses, her short brown hair falling just above the frames. A few feet away, our other teacher, Mrs. Bielert, stood smiling, looking between Dr. Shaw and the class. Beside the rug was the resource teacher, Mrs. Thorndike. I seem to remember that she appeared the way she did most days—laughing softly and clad in leopard-print clothing with a gold belt and sparkly jewelry to make the outfit pop. I always thought she looked fabulous.

They were both smiling, Mrs. T. and Mrs. Bielert. They knew Dr. Shaw had something up her sleeve and, sitting in the back corner of the rug with my chair lowered to the floor, I sensed that it wasn't the jokes and goofy gestures she often entertained us with throughout the day. No, something else was going on, something special.

❧

This was Long Meadow Elementary's Team Room. A wall had been removed between two classrooms in the fourth-grade wing, forming one cavernous classroom. For several years, Dr. Sue Shaw and Mrs. Stacey Bielert co-taught a class twice the size of the norm—forty to forty-five students instead of the typical twenty to twenty-five. The Team Room ran as a daily combination of whole-class and smaller-group activities, bringing everybody together on the rug to read a book aloud, have students share their work aloud, and give lessons suitable for large groups. At different intervals during the day, they divided the class in half so they could each teach a subject (for example, Mrs. Bielert might have taught a math lesson while Dr. Shaw did science) to half the class for a period before switching groups, watching as we paraded over the rug to the other side. Parents could request to have their children placed in the Team Room, or students could be enrolled randomly.

"What did you put on my form as a reason?" I asked my mother after she had submitted the request.

"Nothing. I put your name, signed it, and left the rest blank."

"N-nothing?" I gaped. "Why would you do that? Everybody's talking about how their parents wrote long reasons. What if they give everybody else a spot because of that?"

"Mr. Gusenburg knows me well enough by now to know why I want you in that class," she smiled. "I've been raving about those teachers for years. Don't worry. He'll know."

The Team Room had been a Moore family tradition since we moved to Middlebury in 2001. Sean, as most fourth graders new to LMES seemed to be, was placed in the class automatically. Seeing the teachers' amazing approaches and Sean's enjoyment of the class, Mom requested that Brian be in the Team Room the following year. At the end of Brian's fourth-grade year, she promised the teachers to return for Round 3 with me in a few years.

Photo Credit: Anne Mulville Moore

Photo Credit: Anne Mulville Moore

Many of my after-school memories in preschool and kindergarten took place in that classroom when Mom had to drop off paperwork or discuss something about the boys' fourth-grade happenings. The room, in its post-dismissal vacancy, had looked enormous. Yet, sitting in it as a fourth grader, the size looked just right.

❧

"John? How about you? Can you read this for everyone please?" Dr. Shaw asked, lowering the box so the cake could be seen by my peers in the front row.

In unison, he and Dr. Shaw read the saying aloud, a grin growing on the teacher's face as they voiced it.

"Hard work pays off."

"Hard work pays off," Dr. Shaw exclaimed a second time. "What do you think about that, ladies and gentlemen? Isn't that a nice saying? I finished my doctorate, so I thought we should all celebrate!"

"Getting your doctorate is a lot harder than doing fourth-grade assignments," Mrs. Bielert smiled. "Can we all give Mrs. Shaw, soon to be Dr. Shaw, a nice, big round of applause and say thank you for bringing in a celebration for us?"

The room instantly erupted into a burst of claps and cheers as Mrs. Shaw practically glowed before us.

It's something I always remembered—something I've taken with me ever since, like a relic from that year. That saying—those four words—they hit me, drew me in. I don't know why they struck me with such magnitude at nine or ten years old—perhaps the writer in me was already noting and collecting intriguing lines from my surroundings. They were so simple, yet so powerful.

I didn't know then that these words embodied so much of my fourth-grade experience and the life beyond it, or that I would be clutching onto words spoken by my teachers and family that year, a time when my life with a disability tested my strength unlike ever before.

~~~

It was early in the fall when my mother, coming home from the Parent Open House, delivered the news.

"The teachers are starting a math extra-help group after school once a week, so I signed you up," she said. "I talked to Mrs. Shaw and Mrs. Bielert, and we all think it will be good for you."

No surprises there. I had always struggled with math, performing well enough to pull out decent grades—though lower than my other subjects—but having to work long and hard to grasp mathematical concepts. I didn't have any learning disabilities—cognitive evaluations later ruled that out. Rather, as my mother and educators had figured out, my challenges with math stemmed from my fine motor skills. While my peers could manipulate base-ten blocks, rulers, scrap paper, and other objects to help them master the lessons, my weak fine motor skills prevented me from handling such resources. I, the epitome of butterfingers, had trouble picking them up without immediately dropping them. Back then, in the 2006–07 school year, technology was limited simply because the software and technological capabilities had not been invented yet. The most that could be provided was a computer program called IntelliTools MathPad, which allowed me to do longhand equations digitally. For most other equations and measuring activities, I relied on school staff and family members to follow my instructions on what object should go where as they moved the objects or marked my paper based on what I had said.

I regularly worked with a resource teacher—among them, Mrs. Thorndike, Mrs. Palios, Mrs. Bixler, and Mrs. Valentine—who came into class a few days a week and provided extra support during math lessons, and the regular classroom teachers made time to work with me one-on-one a couple times a week after setting the class up to work independently. They sat by me and watched me work, jumping in when they saw me beginning to take a wrong turn in the equations: "Hang on, Meg. Let's think about the steps again. What do you do with that fraction to make it an improper fraction? Do you add everything together or is there another step in there? Think about what the teacher did on the board.... Good, that's it! Remember to multiply when you move onto the next one."

Myself with one of my many wonderful
resource teachers, Mrs. Bixler.

My mom, the numbers fanatic that she was, also worked with me, explaining the concepts again and quizzing me on my math facts at home every chance she got—even as we waited at the end of our driveway for my bus in the morning as I, half-jokingly, made it known how crazy I thought it was: "I can see the bus coming up the hill and you're still making me do this? Come on! It's 81, by the way; 9 times 9 is 81." That always got her laughing as she gave me another equation.

I don't remember feeling embarrassed about working with a resource teacher or needing extra help. My friends were used to teachers, aides, and therapists coming into class to support me. They knew I was smart, and they never judged me for needing help. I remember, though, how I perceived my own challenges with math. Throughout childhood, I swore I detested it, but as I grew older, I understood that it was simply my weakest subject and that it was actually quite fascinating that a single number could emerge from a complex equation.

⌐◦⌐

"Okay," I replied when Mom told me about the group. "When is it?"

"That's the thing," she smirked as if bracing herself. "It's every Friday."

"You're making me do extra math? On Friday? After school? On *Friday*?"

Laughter crept into my voice as I watched her burst into hysterics.

"Fridays are for, like, playdates and fun stuff," I exclaimed. "Why would the teachers even pick that? They definitely have stuff to do outside school."

"That's just when it worked best for both of them," she said. "It's only an hour. You'll be done by 4:30, and there will still be plenty

303

of time to get together with friends. There's a whole group of your classmates doing this, so you're all in the same boat."

⁓❧⁓

The first session sticks with me. The dismissal bell sounded its long, monotone beep, and one of the teachers led the long line of students who were free to go home out of the room to the dismissal area as the other teacher began to gather supplies at the far end of the room.

"Your mom spring this on you too?" one of my classmates asked as the rest of the group made their way over to us.

"Yeah," my Dyna projected as I giggled.

"I get the point of us being here, but . . ." she trailed off just as my fingers finished typing on my communication device.

"Why it is on Friday?" I asked.

"Yeah! Like what's up with that? Out of all five school days, this is the day that got picked?"

"That's what I said! But at least it's—"

"Them," she said just as the Dyna spoke the same word to refer to our teachers. "Yeah, totally. They'll make it fun. Maybe they'll let us do some of our homework so there's less to do this weekend too."

"Alright, ladies and gentlemen," Mrs. Bielert called, moving in front of the desks with Dr. Shaw, each carrying supplies—calculators, stacks of loose-leaf paper, rulers, all in small plastic totes. "We know it's Friday. We know you would probably prefer to be getting on with all the fun you have coming up this weekend, but we both really appreciate you staying and working so hard. We are going to do our best to make this as fun as we can. Let's get started. Find a seat near Meg, please."

Those Fridays were full of laughter, with Mrs. Bielert and Dr. Shaw sliding in jokes as they gave us instructions and problems to solve:

"Let's say Erin has ten puppies. Meg coaxes eight of them away—maybe she puts some in her lap; maybe she has some extra seat belts to secure them in her chair. I'm sure you can get pretty creative where puppies are concerned, Meg. If Meg wanted to put the puppies into groups, what are all the possibilities for the number of groups and the number of puppies in the groups? Let's list them on our papers, then we'll share them on the board."

What later struck me, though, wasn't the humor that managed to give the whole group a good chuckle. It was the way the teachers managed to tend to my disability needs while also continuing to teach and work with the other students. I can't say it surprised me—this skill was what students and parents often noted while sharing our experiences as we gathered for social and extracurricular activities. It was astonishing that our teachers led a class of forty-something students each day with precise organization while also getting to know and satisfying the needs of each of us. It was their incredible trademark.

I don't know why it was decided that I didn't need an aide to stay with me—perhaps it was something with the budget or allowable work hours. Knowing my teachers, though, I imagine their "can do" attitude came into play, giving way to their willingness to support me without the extra set of hands.

Most sessions began with both teachers at the board, taking turns narrating the steps to solve equations as one of them wrote the math on the whiteboard. Reaching the solution, they asked us to try a similar problem they had assigned for homework that weekend. Taking turns as the other teacher made rounds around the room, one always took the seat next to me, picking up a pencil and my worksheet.

"Alright, Miss Meg," my teachers always said, calling me by the nickname they bestowed on me long ago—probably dating back to when my brothers were in the class. "What do I do first here?"

"You have to make a common denominator, so you have to multiply the two fractions by each other," the Dyna projected.

"Each other or is there a more specific step?"

"By the denominators? So you multiply the numerators and denominators by the denominator of the other fraction."

"Good! See if you can get the next one," the teacher always said after a while, standing up. "I'll be back—I see a hand up."

Seeing that her co-teacher was helping another student, she left to answer my peer's question. Since it took me a few moments to type directions into my communication device, I was busy the whole time she was gone and was done or close to it just as she was making her way back.

When the clock struck 4:30, they called for desks to be cleared and backpacks to be packed. It always amazed me how smoothly the teachers took care of this for me, assembling my belongings while holding conversations with the class.

"Anyone have special plans this weekend?" Dr. Shaw asked, smiling at the replies that came as she lifted folders into my purple backpack.

"The cord, Dr. Shaw," Mrs. Bielert once exclaimed in a tone hushed so as to not interrupt the conversation. She had unplugged my communication device battery charger from the wall and was handing it to Dr. Shaw. "Can't forget the cord—Miss Meg needs a way to gab with those friends of hers this weekend."

"Of course, of course," she replied. "And how about you, Meg? Have anything to share before we pack the Dyna? Doing anything fun with your friends or those brothers of yours?"

They never hesitated to bring me into the conversations or activities, giving me time to jump in as well as I was able to. They supported the needs my disability imposed while also looking beyond the cerebral palsy and the assistive technology to the girl that, on the inside, was no different than anybody else.

I didn't know in those early weeks of the school year how much I would have to hang on to my teachers' and family's attitude of positivity and acceptance. Their love and support were the remedy that soothed me as a fellow fourth grader tried to remind me of how, although they taught my peers and me that I was just like everybody else, my disability still set me apart from the norm.

∿

"Who's that?" Brian asked.

She appeared out of nowhere in a way—this girl I'll call Beatrice.

We were at my adaptive soccer practice, standing on the grassy field at Middlebury's Shepardson Community Center as the other players and their families began to leave. He had noticed her walk by, staring at me, the corners of her lips somewhat upturned as she kept her eyes on me while walking to the baseball diamond at the other end with her family, her little brother dressed in baseball gear. Her brown, shoulder-length hair cohered to her cheek as she turned to look at me.

"Beatrice," I replied. "She's in my class."

"Doesn't seem like you're friends, though."

He must have seen the way my hand had barely released the handle of my walker to wave to her, a stark contrast to the overexaggerated wave and laugh my friends and I usually exchanged. I didn't really know Beatrice yet, but something about her made me uneasy.

"I don't really know her," I told my brother.

"Yeah, but there's something about her. I don't know. It's just . . ."; he swallowed. "Something weird. I mean, she kept staring at you, then you waved, and she didn't wave back—she just kept staring."

"Yeah, I don't know," I replied. "It's probably nothing. She seems nice when she gets called on in class."

307

My apprehension dissipated when Beatrice joined my social circle a short time later, the two of us sharing mutual friends. She turned out to be nice. She was quiet—an observer almost the full time each day at recess. Six or seven of us girls would stow away in the cavernous space under the playscape slides, a fort we had claimed, one that offered enough space for me to lower my seat and sit among everybody else on the woodchips. The fort also allowed the aides to watch us but not hear us, so we didn't feel constantly eavesdropped on. It did strike me odd that she didn't really laugh at any of the jokes told. Heartily laughing but a few times, she usually stared at me until, laughing with everybody else, I looked over at her. She would leer at me for a moment before shaking her shoulder up and down as if laughing. I'd look away and, in my periphery, could see her stop. She kept her eyes on me the entire time.

The friendship progressed normally. We had playdates; she even joined my family on day and holiday break overnight trips around Connecticut and to Springfield, Massachusetts, where we made pit stops at the Basketball Hall of Fame and Yankee Candle Village following my semiannual neuromuscular appointments at Shriners Hospital for Children.

"Ed's on his way," Brian always announced, naming off friends we could expect at the door on days when Mom permitted us to bring friends along on outings.

"As is Jeff," Sean would call, walking around the house, collecting the items needed for the day—a favorite hat, a new CD for the car, all the prized possessions of a high school freshman boy. "Who'd you say you're bringing again, Meg?"

"Beatrice," I'd reply. "She should be on the way too."

"Ugh! No," my brothers would sigh almost in unison.

"You have so many good friends," Sean always said. "Why'd you have to pick her?"

"What's your problem with her?" I'd ask in a here-we-go-again sort of way. "She hasn't done anything to you. I don't tell you who to hang out with."

"It's not about me not liking her, Meg—I say hi and try to be nice to her and all that," he replied. "I just don't think she's really your friend. I get weird vibes when she's around you."

"Yeah, Meg," Brian piped in. "I have nothing against her either, but there's just something wrong there. I don't know what it is, but something's seriously weird with that friendship."

"Okay, well," I always exhaled. "I don't know what to tell you. She's coming, and I like hanging out with her. She hasn't done anything, so I'm gonna still be friends with her."

"She's a little eccentric—I don't have her figured out myself yet," Mom offered. "So we'll keep an eye on her and see what happens. Your big brothers are just trying to protect you, Meg."

She gave me that smile, and laughed as I smiled and rolled my eyes. *Brothers.*

In a matter of weeks, I'd be sobbing into their arms and expressing regret over ignoring their premonitions.

I suppose I watched it come about before my own eyes, but it seemed natural and normal at the time. When I saw her make her way around to my friends—those she wasn't already acquainted with—I just thought she was expanding her connections within the social circle. I saw her casually meander over to my friends at free moments during the school day when I was across the room or playground, still making my way over or detained by some obligation. I remember seeing her eyes shift to me as she whispered to them. I'm not sure if my friends' faces showed any clue of her words. Except for a brief flicker of an emotion that was hard to read afterward, most seemed indifferent, and I didn't ask them about it.

Maybe she just happened to look over when she was talking to them, I thought.

The mystery revealed its own answer a few days later at lunch. I had been the first person to get to our usual table in the back corner of the cafeteria. I watched as my aide carried my tray of food from the kitchen to the table; behind her, I could see my friends trickling out as though they were following her. She sat down beside me as I observed, befuddled, my friends avoiding the table and my eye contact. Some had started to move toward the table but then, nodding toward an unseen signal, swerved out of the way as if repelled by a magnetic field.

"Guys! What are you doing?" I called, bypassing the Dyna to save time and directing my voice to those I knew could understand my natural speech.

As if they couldn't hear or see me, they kept their gaze ahead, looking toward the table where Beatrice sat smiling.

"What's going on?" my aide asked.

"I have no idea," my Dyna read.

Concern washed over Mrs. Calzone's face as she glanced toward the table with everybody else and then to me.

"Doing anything fun this weekend?" she asked nervously.

The table had never felt as big as it did that day, and the lunch period never felt so long. I was used to a full table, with every seat taken and the time flying by, leaving us wishing for more minutes to get all the jokes and stories in before having to go back to class. I vaguely recall roaming the playground at recess afterward, trailing behind the pod of them as they kept moving away, stealing glances backward at me as they smirked. Beatrice laughed the entire time.

Mostly, though, the conversation I had with my aide as I ate sticks with me. We got along, and she had updated me on her high school– and college-age sons from time to time. On this day, though, the stories felt strained. I remember, too, having to work hard to listen and to come up with responses for her. She was sitting right next to me—her arm practically touching my chair's armrest as she lifted the fork to my mouth. Yet she felt far away, like she was talking to me from the opposite end of a tunnel as my mind whirled.

Mentally, I replayed the interactions I had with my friends that morning. Had I noticed anything strange? They all gave a wave, but class was starting, and we didn't really have a chance to chat between lessons; it was hard to tell if they had been acting weird then. Had I said something wrong? Had I offended them without knowing it the day before? But how could *all* of them be mad at once? It continued to nag at my brain as they gave me the cold shoulder for the rest of the day, hurriedly looking elsewhere when our eyes met.

"What do you mean no one sat with you?" Mom asked after school as I told my family what had happened. "They *boycotted* your table?!"

She blew me away with her use of the word "boycotted." It was a term they had taught us over the years as we studied the civil rights era. I had always associated it with those black-and-white videos we had to watch of people peacefully protesting an issue that hindered society's ability to provide equal and acceptable conditions. Why would my friends be protesting against me? The fact that I was the only one with a disability had not yet crossed my mind—I was too young to think like that. I'm not sure when it started to dawn on my mother and brothers that my disability might be the cause.

BOLD, BRAVE, and *Breathless*

I had gone home more confused than anything. Tears didn't come to me that day, and my bewilderment at the scenario had left me subdued. When recounting the day to my family, I was not compelled to do it so that a wrong could be righted. Rather, I felt like laying out all the clues and seeing what they saw in the puzzle I had spent all day working on without success.

"How were your close friends to you?" Sean inquired. "Nikki and all of them?"

"She was out sick. Most of them were—something's going around. I guess I'll see how they are tomorrow."

"Tell me again what went down," Brian said, looking as if he was focusing on turning something over in his mind. "You were cool with everyone when you left yesterday, you go in today, and they don't even acknowledge you?"

"Yeah, and I have no idea why," I replied.

"You said no one looked at you, or everybody avoided eye contact—whatever you wanna call it," he said. "Did you catch anybody's eye at all?"

"Just Beatrice's," I sighed. "She kept looking at me and laughing."

"There was always something about that girl," Sean said, shaking his head.

"I don't know if it was definitely her idea," I said. "But I did see her talking to all of them a lot over the last few weeks."

I told them about how Beatrice's eyes had lingered on me as she whispered words into my friends' ears. I noted that it could have been a coincidence but also explained the vibe that had chilled my spine each time. Everyone I had seen her talk to had ghosted me.

"I hate to say this, Meg, and I know you're not gonna want to hear this," Sean said. "But I really don't think that girl is your friend. Even if she wasn't totally responsible for this, anybody who sees something like this happening to you and thinks it's funny is not your friend."

"Yeah, I don't know," I sighed. "I was hoping it was like a joke, but they never stopped ignoring me, so I guess it wasn't a joke at all."

"I think I'll mention something to your teachers—maybe give them a call now or tomorrow morning before the class gets in," Mom said, shaking her head. "This really concerns me—I don't know what's going on, but it's something we have to nip in the bud."

❧

The next day, a small group of my friends greeted me as they normally did. Most were close friends I'd had since kindergarten who had been absent the day before.

"What up with them?" my best friend, Nikki, asked, sitting down at lunch and watching as the others ignored our table and went on to Beatrice's.

"Their new thing," I replied, relying on my own voice to explain since Nikki was already almost fluent in understanding it after almost five years of friendship. "They did this yesterday too."

"Oh," she said, growing quiet for a second before bouncing back to chatting. "Well, we'll just have our own party at this table. So you wanna know what happened yesterday? Super random thing to come up when I'm home sick . . ."

We'd be adults before she'd tell me that Beatrice had tried to recruit her too, framing it as a joke to be played for a few weeks, maybe longer, just because it would be funny to leave me by myself. Nikki refused, reminding her that we had been best friends since kindergarten and that she wanted it to stay that way. I couldn't find the words to respond to that at the time—all I could do was smile. Out of the worst moments of our lives, the most beautiful ones emerge.

My other friends, besides Beatrice, came back around in a matter of days, their sheepish greetings demonstrating their guilt without needing words to convey it. They sat down at our table almost simultaneously. Even at eight or nine years old, I knew I didn't have to talk to them. I could have ignored them as they had ignored me. I could have left to sit at a different spot, but I knew how I felt in those days without them, especially that first day—lonely, confused, sad, and disappointed. I had missed them terribly too, had missed the bonds and the jokes and laughter. I was tired of being without them, so I smiled when they returned and began to tell every comical sentiment I had been dying to tell them for days, picking up right where we had left off ahead of the silence. I had other, more pressing ball games in which to battle—I didn't need any more.

❧

The return of my friends came just before the small fire Beatrice had started grew to a wildfire—able to be extinguished eventually, but out of control at times. It began coming to a head at outdoor recess, in the middle of a game of catch between two of my friends and me. One, who I'll call Shannon, was able-bodied; the other, who I'll call Molly, was legally blind. We had figured out that by using a ball almost the size of a basketball and bright enough in its red hue that Molly could see it, I could leave my hands just above my lap and catch it on the soft toss that Shannon pitched. I then could roll the ball down my lap back to her before she lightly served it to Molly. Catching it, Molly could throw it back.

"Hey, Shannon," Beatrice called one day, walking up to us. "Recess is almost over. If you want to go hang out with your normal friends for a little, you can go. I've got these two."

"Normal friends?" Shannon asked, rolling the ball in her hands. "What do you mean 'normal friends'? These are my normal friends."

314

"But *that* one can't walk or talk," she said, jabbing a finger in my direction before doing the same to Molly. "And *that* one can't see."

My whole body burned as the shock settled in. So that was it. That was the backbone of it all—the disabilities. I think the question "Really?" slipped out of my mouth, but I don't know—my mind had gone numb by then. I looked at Molly beside me. She was shifting her weight between legs. Her emotions were unreadable except for the smile that had vanished into a poker face between the curtains of black hair. She looked how I felt—shell-shocked and uncomfortable.

"Like I said . . ." Shannon cleared her throat, her eyes still wide from the bombshell that had just dropped. "These *are* my normal friends. We're in the middle of a game. See you later."

Beatrice sighed as she walked off. I don't remember what exactly we said to one another after that, in the seconds before we resumed playing, but I recall finding something unrelated to laugh at, though my mind still felt frozen. The cadence of the game picked up again, holding steady until I noticed something flying down at me, falling into my face and then my lap.

"Oops," Beatrice laughed as one of my hands cradled the kickball she had thrown and as my other hand wiped off the dirt the ball had left on my face.

"Yeah, I'm sure you didn't," I said, surprised at how level my voice was as I rolled my eyes and gently sent the ball on a low bounce back to her feet.

"Are you okay?" Shannon asked. "Do you need to go to the nurse? Do you want your aide?"

"Nah, I'm good. It didn't even hurt that much. Let's just keep playing before they make us go in."

I was more prepared for the second attempt, seeing the ball coming back at me. Putting my hands in front of me just in time, I caught it before it neared my nose. I flung it over my armrest, watching it pound against the pavement on its way to the basketball court.

315

"Really?" I shouted as Beatrice looked at me and cackled.

"Oops! Guess I did it again," she said, turning to chase the ball.

I'm not sure how those incidents escaped my aide's notice. As she didn't have to be at my side every waking moment, she usually hung out with the recess monitors at the blacktop's edge. She must have been looking away, or maybe Beatrice had waited until she had taken her eyes off me for a moment.

Years later, it made me cringe to think that I let the rest of the day pass without delivering a word about it to my teachers or aide. My thought process back then sought to satisfy my craving for normalcy at a time when, thanks to my bully, my life at school was anything but. I wanted to go through the day tending to my assignments without having to deal with all the meetings and discussions bound to pull me out of what remained of normalcy once the news broke. I knew that the bullying eventually had to be addressed, but that could wait for a little while. Perhaps I was still too stunned to properly deal with it. It was like my mind was still frozen, stuck in the loop of thinking, *What just happened? Did that really just happen to me?*

❧

"So how was school today?" Mom asked as I rolled into our kitchen after my return home.

"Good. Well," I scoffed, "if you consider taking a ball to the face good."

"Wait, *what?!*" She looked absolutely horrified. "What did you just say? What happened?"

The story came with a deep exhale. As if I was on autopilot, the words spilled out of me automatically, without much thought or effort. I don't remember feeling sad or anything really as I told the ball story and the comments about my friend's and my disabilities. I was still so numb that emotions hadn't yet broken through. Watching my family's faces is what started to thaw me. My brothers had overheard the first few lines of the story from the other room and had silently stridden in to listen. The two of them and our mother looked as though they were watching a horror movie.

"I'm calling the Team Room—I'm calling them right now. Can one of you grab me the house phone?" Mom said as I finished, looking to my brothers. "I've got to hurry before they leave. This has to be addressed today."

"It didn't even really hurt, though, and I caught it the second time. Those balls are all deflated from being outside in the cold anyway. They're always like bags partly filled with air. Remember those from when you were there?" I asked Sean as Brian retrieved and handed the phone to Mom.

"Yeah," Sean said, the hint of a smirk touching his lips before a frown reclaimed its territory. "But, Meg, it doesn't matter if it didn't hurt. She threw a ball at your face—twice. We have to report it. The teachers will be nice about helping you through it, but it's just gotta stop. Now this girl's trying to hurt you physically. This is really serious."

"Yeah—yeah, I know," I sighed, already wondering when Dr. Shaw was going to pull me from class to talk privately the next day. "It's just annoying that I have to keep dealing with this. I just want to go to school like normal."

We soon found out that my mother's call was one of two complaints the teachers received that afternoon. Molly's mother informed mine that she, too, phoned after learning of the playground encounter.

Although that always remained vivid in mind because of the appalling notion that a child was capable of not only thinking of but executing such an action, the sting of the ball hitting my face was not the worst part of the encounter with my bully. No, it was not the worst of it. Rather, it was her words—those she used on the playground and others she slipped into my ears when passing by. The teachers did their best to keep us separate—had seated us in separate parts of the room, separate areas of the classroom rug, separate groups for activities—but she still found ways to put herself close to me, making comments to my friends or even just to me under her breath without catching the adults' ears.

My mind weighed these sentences like they were on a balance, seeing how wrong they were to have been said yet how parts of them—the terms she used—rang true. The word "cripple" did, after all, mean disability, which I did have. I had been exposed to the term at Shriners Hospital for Children. Sentiments like "Helping crippled children thrive for over 80 years" adorned the walls inside and outside. It was simply a descriptor for those with disabilities and, at Shriners, was often depicted alongside a picture of a child in a wheelchair or missing a limb playing a sport as an adult assisted them. There, "crippled" seemed to be used in a positive context.

Beatrice's tone, though, told me there could be a different interpretation of the term and those similar to it—how it didn't matter how the words I spoke and the activities I did resembled those my peers were taking on, and how it didn't even matter how much the teachers told and demonstrated to the class that I could and should be treated like everybody else. At the end of the day, as she reminded me, the physical difference was still at the forefront, and I could still be considered inferior.

And there I was, numb except for my ears that were unwillingly absorbing the words. It must have been a Friday or some special day, because I remember the teachers had ended the lessons early to give us time to socialize and do crafts or a few rounds of the games that were stowed in the classroom. With everybody moving around, trying to get their chosen activities from the cart in the middle of the classroom, my bully slid herself into my table of friends inconspicuously, waiting until all the adults in the room had their hands full with student requests. She sat there for a little while, just staring as we played.

"I'm gonna go get paper or something so we can draw," one of my friends, who I'll call Junie, said, rising from the table.

"I'll come with you," I said, pushing the power button on my chair as the words fell out of my mouth.

"Let's roll," she laughed. "I'm telling you; you need a sidecar for that thing so I can just ride along."

We made it by our table before I noticed Beatrice tailing us.

Oh, whatever, I thought. *She's not doing anything other than following us. It's fine.*

Junie lapped the cart, landing on the side opposite me and stooping down to get her items, becoming invisible to me. I did a big doughnut as I waited, surveying the room. Beatrice had stopped a few feet away, and I could see in my periphery that her eyes were locked on me. I turned, pretending to be captivated by something at the other end of the room.

"Got it," Junie called.

"Okay, guys! Time to clean up," Mrs. Bielert called. "Let's get everything back to where you found it and grab your stuff from your locker."

"Aw, man," Junie sighed, having stood up only to have to stoop back down to put the craft materials back.

"I'm gonna go back," I said.

"'Kay—I'm sure I'll see you before we go home."

I turned and began driving through the aisle between the first row of tables, passing Beatrice. She turned and began walking, keeping pace with my chair. She seemed to be putting herself closer and closer toward the side of my chair. The bubbles of personal space had been popped moments before.

Just ignore her and keep going, I thought. *You'll be fine. It's fine.*

The whispers seeped out seemingly effortlessly: "Hate," "you," "crippled"—all the words were making my mind swim. Surely I had heard wrong. Surely somebody my age couldn't string these words together in a sentence.

Her stern expression told me I had not imagined it.

I was frozen again—at least mentally, just like after the ball incident.

No, I thought. *No, you can't go home like this again. You have to say something before getting on the bus.*

I turned to look at my desk, still a ways off across the room. Maybe I could get there before—no, it was too late. My aide was already packing my communication device into its case. I sighed, my mind going a mile a minute. Should I try to signal that I needed it? Would she pick up on what I was saying? Would they hold my bus if I stopped to talk to whichever teacher could break away? What is the right thing to do? What is it that just happened?

"Ready, Meg? Your bus is probably here."

I nodded at my aide and followed her to the door. I think I even smiled and waved to the teachers. My body's autopilot had switched on, and I drove through the school as if it was any other day.

I don't remember much of the ride home, other than sitting and staring through the window, watching the world pass by without really seeing it. I was too deep in the tunnel of my mind to take it in.

When the wheelchair lift of the bus hit my driveway's pavement, I turned my chair on and drove off of it like I always had, smiling and waving to the aide as my mom said goodbye and picked up my bags from where the aide had left them on the ground. I zipped up the driveway, feeling my insides beginning to thaw all too quickly. If I could just duck inside, out of the view of the bus staff and any neighbor passing by, I'd be fine.

"I decided to get a jump on the day as soon as you left," Mom began, speed-walking to catch up. "I hopped in the car, went to the bank first . . ."

We arrived at the door, and Mom turned the knob, backing up to let me in before her. My wheels climbed over the threshold two at a time, sending me over a speed bump first from the front wheels and then the back. That's the last sensation I remember before the tears fell.

"Meg? Meg, what's wrong? What's the matter?" she asked, hurriedly setting my bags down on the floor and coming to my side. "Come on, tell me. What's wrong?"

"What's going on?" Brian asked as he and Sean crossed the living room to meet us in the foyer.

"I don't know," Mom replied. "She seemed fine getting off the bus, came in, and now this. Meg, what's wrong, hon? Did something happen today? Come on, can you tell us?"

"Can you tell me?" Brian asked, bending down in front of me, his hands on his knees. "I know you can, Meg."

"Yeah, Meg," Sean said. "We can't help you if we don't know what's bothering you. Can you tell us? You can do it."

"Beatrice," I began. Each word felt like it needed several breaths to precede it. My voice broke into sobs after I got "crippled" out.

"Do the teachers know any of this?" Mom asked, walking to the kitchen and appearing in the doorway with the phone in her hand.

"No," I breathed heavily. "It just happened at the end of the day. The Dyna was already going in the bag when I was going to tell them."

I watched her face crumple. She knew what this meant. That's the thing with relying on a communication device. You have to trust it to be your voice, yet you don't always have access to it when you need it the most. It has to be set up and packed by others who are on a specific schedule. It's always that one time when somebody puts it away quickly that an urgent need arises. It is a catch-22—you need the communication device to speak and report an issue, but you also need the communication device to tell somebody that you need the communication device to stay out so you can tell what happened. When you don't quite make it to the device in time to say something before it's stowed away, it's kind of like getting to a boat dock just as the ship has sailed away. You are stranded there without a means to get to your destination. You can't move forward on your own. You have to wait for another opportunity to board the ship, and all you can think about is how this delays the steps needed to move forward and how disappointing it is to have missed it by a few moments.

❧

"Hi, Mrs. Shaw? Hi, it's Anne Moore," Mom began, holding the phone up with her shoulder as she came to hug me before turning her attention to describing my state.

The boys came around me, wrapping me in a group hug. They enveloped me at just the right time, just as our mother was repeating my bully's words. They held me together as I fell apart again.

I began to wonder what it was about the words that stung so much. I knew that not everything somebody said was true, yet the words had hit me like a train. I suppose I knew the answer, even back then. When I had been introduced to writing about two years earlier, I had been amazed at the power of words. Words are agathokakolog-ical—they are composed of the good in the world, but also the bad. They can warm the heart and mind. They can also tear people down, reducing them to a stereotype or making them feel like an unwanted part of the world. Words never fail to stain the brain, making people remember how they are perceived even as the event moves into the past. The feeling that words invoke can never be forgotten.

322

❧

"They're addressing it as we speak," Mom said, hanging up the phone. "They may even call her family at home tonight to start to take care of it before tomorrow. Why don't we do something fun before home-work to take your mind off school for a while? What do you want to do? Go outside? Play a game? Paint the boys' nails?"

"Yeah, anything but the last one," Sean chuckled.

And suddenly I was laughing hysterically—we all were. It always amazed me how our mother could make us laugh so hard on our worst days, pulling humor out of thin air to help us forget the weight of our struggles, even if for just a little while.

❧

I remember my eyes feeling like sandpaper and like a fog shielded the clarity of my sight when I woke up the next morning.

Could all the crying do this? I wondered as I blinked away the fog and watched the details of my Tweety Bird wallpaper come into focus. There he was, striking various poses all over the wall, his little yellow arms on his hips in one; in another, his hands clasped to the side as he looked up bashfully amid purple, blue, and yellow flowers.

"Mego," Mom sang as she came into my room. "Meg—oh! You're awake! You beat me to it. Ready?"

"Yeah, I guess." I sighed, swinging my legs around to the edge of the bed as she took both of my hands and helped me sit up.

"It's going to be fine today, you know," she said as she stood me up and hugged me for a moment before turning me and supporting me under the arms to walk me to the bathroom. "It will be. They'll probably pull you out to talk to you, but that's nothing to worry

323

about. They all really want to help. And I'm only a phone call away. If you want me with you, just ask them to call and I'll come."

"Okay," I said, cocooned in my mom's arms, wanting to stay there.

Part of me wished I could have thought of a solid reason that would have convinced my mother to keep me home. I wasn't sick, though, and I knew she never let us take a sick day unless we presented legitimate symptoms.

"Your father got up and went to work every day even though he had cancer," she always said when any of us asked if we could take a day off because we didn't feel like dealing with the circumstances waiting for us. "He worked until the cancer got too bad. He took leaves of absence when he needed to, but he worked during much of the early phase. I think you can get up and take on the day, don't you?"

Of course my brothers and I never had a comeback to that, other than to silently get moving in preparation for the day before us. I figured she would tell me the same thing in this situation, brimming with compassion and gentleness, but reminding me that my father faced much worse than I had and still kept going. I imagine she would have pointed out that my problems would be waiting for me when I got back even if I was allowed to stay home too, so I didn't bother to ask.

I remember thinking all the way to school about how I'd still get to see my friends, laugh with them even. I wondered what lessons the teachers had in store for us, and what unique ways they would present the material—they always had comical examples to nail down the concepts. I tried my best to hold onto the thoughts about what would surely brighten my spirits, because I was not looking forward to being in the same space with my bully all day. The thought of having to face her when the wounds were still raw was like catching a preexisting cut on something—it stung uncontrollably. How was I going to make it through the day bypassing her completely? How was I going to ignore the stares and the comments she would surely try to deliver? I still felt so fragile, as if one word would sweep me away again with much less effort than the words had the day before.

My memory of that day is segmented, focused only on the key parts and blurring the rest. I vaguely remember saying hello to my friends as if nothing had happened—they would find out much later at gatherings outside of school, when the subject fell on the triumphs and trials of fourth grade. I remember, too, forcing my eyes to remain focused on the teachers even though Beatrice's eyes were practically burning my skin, as they rarely left me. I'm not sure if she and her family had already been spoken to at that point.

Mostly, though, I remember the trip to the hallway.

"I'm going to take the Dyna for a moment, Mrs. Calzone," Dr. Shaw said, approaching my desk after setting the other students up with an assignment. "Miss Meg and I are going to take a little walk."

"Oh, okay," my aide said. I couldn't tell if she had been told what had happened yet, but she didn't seem to expect this. "Do you want me to follow and set the device up?"

"No thanks. I think I can manage, and if something's not right, Meg will tell me how I can fix it—she's always good about that." Dr. Shaw beamed at me and took the Dyna in her hands. "You ready, Miss Meg? We'll only be a few minutes. Follow me, please."

We had done this each time Beatrice had come up with a new way to bother me. I knew the drill—I was not in trouble. She just wanted to hear what had happened in my own words and to reassure me that they were handling it, talking to my bully again, enforcing even stricter consequences and rules. Yet this one somehow felt different, even before it began. My palms began to sweat as I grasped my joystick and followed her out of the classroom. It was something about this incident and how much more severe it was compared to the others. I knew this would not be an easy discussion.

She brought me to the end of the hall and sat down on the bench there, setting my communication device down next to her.

"I hear you went home really upset yesterday," she began. "I can't tell you how bad we feel that you couldn't get to the Dyna before the bus. Hopefully you're not mad at us."

I shook my head, smiling slightly. It wasn't their fault—how could they know?

"Good, because if Miss Meg Moore was mad at us—I don't know—we'd have to do something about that, put ourselves in a doghouse, maybe."

We both laughed, shattering the tension that had loomed over me.

"Anything else you want to tell me about the incident? Anything more than your mom told us?"

"I don't think so. She told you everything I told her," my Dyna projected.

Dr. Shaw nodded, thanking me for having been so open so quickly after it happened. She then began to tell me that they were addressing the situation and how they would take extra care to make sure the two of us were separated at school without giving my bully any chance to come near me.

"And, Meg, I want you to know something," she said, beginning to divert from the topics we typically went over. "What I want you to know is this—you are so loved. *So* loved—here, at home—your family is crazy about you! I see it with your friends too—they're just over the moon when they see you. We love our Meg, more than I could ever tell you. Please know that, no matter what anybody else says, you are so unbelievably loved."

The best response I could think to give was a smile.

What I didn't know then was that some of the hardest work I'd have to complete in fourth grade was the task of looking past my bully each time the class gathered on the rug. She always took a seat a few rows directly in front of me, looking back as much as she could and mouthing "Are we still friends?" to me before the teachers reminded her to stay focused on the lessons. I never imagined how hard it could be to ignore her, to act as if she was not attracting attention in the corner of my eye, and I never anticipated that she would keep after me, occasionally trying to draw my new friends away from me each year until high school graduation separated us for good.

I didn't know as I sat in the hallway that they were a few days away from discovering the abusive household that might have been her motive. As I continued through my childhood, I'd see more incidents perpetrated by other kids who were neglected and abused at home. I quickly learned that these kids were agitated by the attention I received from adults because I needed help physically. These kids didn't even receive the attention they should have at home, and they watched me get extra. It saddened me to know this. All I had ever known was a home that overflowed with love and light. I couldn't even imagine what it was like to return each day to a home where love dripped intermittently, if at all. As I grew older, I hoped that, after receiving reports about my encounters with them, the school found ways to bring love into the children's lives as their raw realities were exposed.

I didn't know any of that as I talked to my teacher in that hallway. What I did know, though, was the power of love. Love is what elevated my spirits during that conversation and throughout that day and year. Love was the only thing that had consoled me when I arrived home the previous day. Love is what my mother sent me to school with and what she replenished when I got back. Love was what she had used as the groundbreaking cure.

❧

It escapes me now whether I saw the parallels between my in-school bullying and the discrimination that took place outside of school, or if too many months separated them for me to make the connection.

327

Since I joined Girl Scouts as a kindergartener—as a "Daisy"—my mom had been the troop leader almost from the beginning. She always made sure that all girls were included in every troop activity. Even at our end-of-year award ceremonies, when only about a quarter of the troop would be needed to perform a flag ceremony, she somehow managed to split up the parts so every girl had a role. All fourteen or so girls in the troop were always treated equally and fairly. I didn't think this was anything out of the ordinary, and I definitely didn't think there was an alternative way to run a troop. Looking back, I realize that I very much took it all for granted.

Mom made the decision at the start of my fourth-grade year to step down as leader. She loved this position and had received rave reviews from parents and girls for many years (in high school, some girls were still telling me about how much fun they had at events my mother had organized for us in elementary school), but she didn't get to spend as much time with me as we both had hoped. She was often tied up with trying to get parents to sign paperwork and with running the meeting, providing girls with craft supplies, and organizing ceremonies and events as I patiently waited until she was free to help me with the activities or, eventually, as I participated with the help of a high school student we knew. Although we enjoyed having this friend at the meetings, we wanted Girl Scouts to be more of a mother-daughter experience.

"Who will take over?" I asked when Mom told me she had officially made her decision to step down.

"They have an older woman lined up—she's supposed to be very good. They say she has abundant experience in scouting," Mom replied. "We're going to meet her in a few weeks."

There was something about her, this woman I will call Mrs. Arian, something underneath that wide, dimpled smile that did not sit well with me upon first meeting her. One look at her made me feel uneasy. I couldn't put my finger on what it was about her, though. As the number of interactions increased, however, her true colors grew more apparent—she began to exclude me from activities and separate me from the other girls.

The most memorable encounter was on our annual trip to the Middlebury Convalescent Home. Mom had started a troop tradition where we spent time with the residents doing crafts and hand-delivering holiday cards we had made the week before. That year, I strolled into the venue in my walker alongside the other girls and waited for them to occupy the chairs around a table before moving to stand in an empty space near it.

329

"Hey, Meg," Mrs. Arian called. "Why don't you come with me? I found a spot that is just perfect for you and your walker—it has tons of space. Come along."

I was too young to realize that I did not have to follow her just because she was an older, authoritative figure, that I did not have to literally walk right into the exclusive situation. I was too young to know that years later, one of my biggest inspirations would be Rosa Parks—a woman I had heard about in school but had not really grasped the true magnitude of her simple action of remaining in that bus seat. I was too young to realize that, just like Rosa, I could take a stand and go join everybody else even though the leader had told me not to.

Mrs. Arian had me follow her to a table on the opposite side of the room and told me this was the spot I was to sit in for the duration of the visit. "Someone will bring craft supplies over to you," she muttered as she pivoted and walked back to the rest of the group.

I used my foot to pull a chair out from the table, swinging it around backwards so I could sit on it without interfering with my walker. Sighing, I glanced at the chattering group of girls across the room. I had waited all day for this, had watched the clock throughout the school day, frustrated with the turtle-like movement of its hands, and now I wasn't even going to have fun with the other girls. I couldn't believe the leader could do this—*would* do this.

"Hello? Are you lost? Do I need to get your eyes checked? The girls are over there." My mother's easygoing voice, honeyed with humor, came from behind. "Why are you over here?"

I turned my upper body to face her. Her red hair fell gently onto her shoulders in thick, springlike curls, framing her fair-skinned face, hazel eyes, and that light-up-a-room smile.

"I tried going over there, but Mrs. Arian told me I have to sit over here for the whole thing. I don't know why—I didn't do anything to make her mad."

That easy smile instantly melted away, and her fair skin simmered into a fiery shade that almost matched her hair.

"No, I know you didn't. Why don't you, uh, go join the other girls? I'll be over in a few minutes."

Her voice had become sedate, nothing like the fun-loving tone from moments earlier. As I walked across the room, I eyed her curiously. She marched up to the leader with quick and purposeful steps.

"Let me ask you something. Have you met my daughter Meg? I know you have, several times. Meg has been in this troop since she was in kindergarten. Meg is part of this troop just like every other girl—"

Mom used to be shy. My brothers and I never knew that version of her, but she and her friends have told us that she used to be the quiet girl in school—the one who always did what she was told and never questioned authority. That all changed around the time my father was diagnosed with cancer. Suddenly, she became *that* woman, the one who was not afraid to speak her mind to whomever needed to know exactly what was on it. She became that persistent wife/mother/daughter/friend/superwoman who sought out the best opportunities and health care for her loved ones, no matter how hard she had to work to achieve them. She became the strong widow and fearless single mom who somehow found a way to raise three kids, care for her elderly parents, and serve on parent teacher organizations among other committees. Now *that* woman was showing me how to stand up for what is right, even if it means laying out the issue in the public eye and exposing why it is wrong at every level.

Mrs. Arian rejoined the girls looking as if she had just gotten stuck in an unforecast hurricane. She didn't bother me for the rest of the afternoon, leaving me free to participate in the festivities with everyone else. She went right back to exclusive behavior by the next event, though. Every week she took a different approach, and every week Mom countered it.

331

I loved Girl Scouts. Even after being treated so poorly by the leader, I loved the activities, the projects, and the people I got to meet. But it was in my weak moments—the moments during and after the occurrences—that I would seriously consider discontinuing my involvement.

We bridge to the next level of Scouts in June, I'd tell myself. *Maybe I'll quit after that.*

I don't recall telling my family, but somehow my mom seemed to know what I was thinking. Before and after meetings and events, she launched into little pep talks about not letting Mrs. Arian discourage me from doing what I loved and how I had to keep showing up to face her. Somehow I knew my mother was right and that everything would work out for the best. This is essentially why I kept going back every week, and at some point, her words clicked. It dawned on me: Why would I do all that work—the badge and patch requirements, the community service—just to throw it all away? I knew I needed to continue in Scouts, but I really didn't know how I would continue to deal with the intentional exclusion.

This was on Mom's mind too. I often heard her talking to my friends' parents about it as my friends and I ran by at playdates.

"We would never treat her like that in our troop," my friend's mother responded one day. "You're welcome to bring her to a meeting and see if she wants to join."

❦

We sat in the car the next Thursday, debating what to do. The school buses had rolled out of the school driveway, and I stared through the windshield at the empty traffic circle. The meeting would be beginning right around now. We could go check it out, but we didn't have to.

"It's entirely up to you." Mom said.

I was torn. My entire Scouting experience had been in my own troop. What would it be like to leave? On the other hand, a lot of my friends from school were in this other troop. My school friends had either quit because of scheduling conflicts or switched to this other troop because of the convenience of staying after school and going down the hall to meetings. They had all pretty much left my troop by the time the new leader came on board. With this departure came a new wave of girls that I never really got to know. Even after I overcame another round of exclusion and rejoined everybody else, they were standoffish, barely talking to me, as if they were torn between whether to be my friend or follow the leader's example. The more I thought about it, the more appealing the new troop sounded. Should I go check it out?

"I don't know, Mom. I don't know what to do," I sighed. "Part of me wants to go check it out; the other part wants to stay in my troop."

"Well, they are having a scavenger hunt at the mall on Saturday. Do you want to go to that instead?"

"That sounds like fun. Yeah, I'll do that, and maybe I can go to the next meeting? I have a lot of homework tonight. Can we go home now?"

"Okay."

◦◦◦

That Saturday, we met the troop in the lobby of the mall. Diverting from my mother as she went to greet the parents, I steered my walker toward my friends, sliding behind them before they spotted me.

"Boo!" I exclaimed, letting the word slide out of my mouth as I leaned forward into the space between two of my friends who were deep in conversation.

333

"Ah! Jeez, Mego, that's like the third time you've done that this week," Colleen sighed, whipping around to face me as I laughed. "Did you just randomly see us while you were shopping?"

"No, I'm here with you guys," I said, the words shaky from the laughter's tail end.

"Really?" she gasped, grinning. "Dude! Why didn't you tell me you were coming? We could have been talking about this at school."

"I wanted to surprise you. Show up out of nowhere."

"Aka be creepy and such."

Standing next to Colleen, the other girls began to note the conversation and join in our laughter.

"Oh, yeah," Colleen gasped, looking around the group. "Meg, this is Sarah—she's in the class across from the Team Room. And you know Nina, right? I know you know the rest of these goofs."

Exchanging greetings, we chatted there for a while before the parents began leading us through the mall, distributing papers listing items we needed to take pictures with. I remember how easy it was to join in with the group—they were so welcoming, including me in the activities and conversation just like everybody else, as if I was already part of the troop.

"Meg, you have to tell them that joke that you told at recess yesterday." Ali began to chuckle, a grin spreading over her face. "That was so funny."

The group turned to me in anticipation, and I told the joke—one that time later revealed was funny only to our fourth-grade selves.

"Why do you have to go to bed every night?" I asked as Ali repeated my words so that the girls who had just met me could understand.

"Why?" they asked as a chorus.

"Because it's not going to come to you—you have to go to it."

"That's—" Colleen began, chuckling.

"So dumb it's funny?" I asked. "I know! Alyssa told me it at snack time yesterday, and we both said that too."

A rumble of laughter shuddered through the crowd. When it eased, Colleen peered down at me from her basketball player–like height and asked if I would come to the meeting.

"Mom?" I called, looking toward my mother, who was chatting with the other parents. I giggled, knowing my next words were going to send my friends into hysterics. "Mother dear? Mommy dearest? Anne?"

Already smiling, she looked back at us as we laughed.

"Yes? Do I hear comments from the peanut gallery? And since when do you call me Anne?" she asked with a hearty chortle.

"Can I stay after school for the meeting on Thursday?"

"Yeah. Do you want to join the troop too?"

"Yes, she does," Colleen shouted.

"Is this an act of ventriloquism?" Mom laughed.

"Maybe," I laughed. "But, yeah, can you sign me up?"

"Yes, daughter dear," she said before turning to the other parents, chuckling. "See? I knew it was only a matter of time."

Cheering the word "yes," my friends filled me in on the little troop traditions and fun facts: "We meet in Mrs. Duncan's classroom. We meet in the cafeteria and then walk down there. We eat a snack first, and Mrs. Duncan's son, Patrick, comes and has snacks with us, since he always walks through at that time. What a coincidence, right? Not! We're trying to get him to join and wear the uniform! Can you imagine?"

Photo Credit: Anne Mulville Moore

About eight years later, I sat next to my old, discriminatory leader.

A senior in high school, I had been selected as a Girl Scout National Delegate. I was a few weeks away from traveling with Girl Scouts of Connecticut's delegation to the national convention and national council session in Salt Lake City, Utah, where I would vote on changes to Girl Scout policies and speak about an amendment in front of the national board and thousands of delegates hailing from the United States and its territories.

Sliding into the back of the service unit meeting for all the Girl Scout leaders in the region, I observed as the discussion got under way, turning to my mother and raising an eyebrow as my former leader stood before the audience to speak.

"They're looking for feedback on the proposals," she explained, studying a sheet in her hand. "Maybe you can send everything you have to me, and I'll get it to the nearest national delegate, or even to the council."

"Actually, we have a girl going from our service unit as the delegate," the service unit manager said. "I think I saw her scoot in here . . . ," she said, trailing off as she stood and surveyed the audience. "Meg, are you here?"

I finished typing the messages on my communication device just in time.

"Yes, I'm here. Do you mind if I jump in?"

"You have the floor," she smiled as I drove my chair to the front, my communication device mounted on a metal bar on the wheelchair.

As Mrs. Arian was standing front and center, I unintentionally stopped right next to her, her mouth slightly ajar as my device began to speak. Holding in a laugh, I looked out into the audience.

"The delegation is gathering any input that leaders provide; the last meeting before we leave for Utah is next week, and we will be compiling everything we have. I'll be sticking around a few minutes after this meeting. Please feel free to give me your feedback, and I can make my email address available if you have anything to submit after tonight. Thank you."

I returned to where I had been sitting with my mother.

"Her jaw is still wide open," Mom whispered as I laughed quietly. She then spoke the thought that had been on both our minds. "Well, what's the irony? The girl she excluded and almost made quit Girl Scouts is about to represent the Connecticut council on the national level."

‿❦⁀

As much as that fourth-grade year taught me about the prejudices I'd face throughout life, it also showed me how my disability could open doors to opportunities that would never have been available without my physical limitations.

I began to see the rays of this notion shine during our field trip to the Connecticut State Capitol. Surrounded by my classmates and friends, I traveled through the ornate first floor of the building, admiring the halls that all seemed to have their own luster as the light from the chandeliers reflected on the marble floors and the walls of balconies that overlooked us, framed by white ionic pillars. A tour guide had spent the day ushering us around. She reached the point of the tour where she invited everyone to follow her upstairs. I believe she was taking them to see some upper level in the senate chamber, though time has eroded my memory of the specific name and purpose of the space. Asking everybody to meet her by the stairs, she kept smiling at the class but appeared increasingly alarmed, glancing at me repeatedly.

"This part of the tour is not wheelchair accessible," she said, coming over to Mrs. Bielert and my aide, Mrs. Calzone, who stood next to me.

"I'm surprised nobody mentioned that on the phone," Mrs. Bielert replied. "Sue and I called several times to verify that everything was accessible."

"I'm sorry about that," the guide said, her eyes darting around rapidly. "A total oversight on our part—b-but we do have an alternative! I'll tell my assistant to take over for me upstairs and will be right back to get you."

Watching the guide hurry away, Mrs. Bielert turned to my aide. "If you want to see upstairs," she said. "I'll stay with Meg."

"Okay," my aide replied. "Sure you don't want to be with the class?"

"No, that's okay. You can kind of see it from down here anyway," she said, turning to exchange a smile with me. "Plus, I'll get to spend some extra time with this young lady."

As Mrs. Calzone went to join the group, I could see my friends filing up the stairs, looking back at me as if they couldn't decide whether to keep going or ask to stay with me. I grinned and waved, though I hated the thought of missing time on the tour with them. I wasn't sure what to make of being diverted to an alternative activity.

The guide took us down to a vast, circular room with rows of glossy, wooden desks framing the perimeter. An oval area rug depicting the Connecticut state flag was placed directly in the center of the white marble floor—an object, the guide told us, that no one was allowed to tread on it, symbolizing a conscientious upholding of respect for the state. Milling about were countless senators in formal business attire. The guide excused herself for a moment and walked over to some of them.

"Hey, Meg," Mrs. Bielert said. "Look up—look who it is!"

My class had assembled at the balcony's railing and was waving down at us, my friends giving the most dramatic gestures. I laughed and mirrored the wave.

"I've arranged for Meg to have a quick meet-and-greet with a senator," the guide said from behind.

"Wow, thank you very much! That's so nice," my teacher exclaimed. "Did you hear that, Meg? Your friends are going to wish they could have borrowed your chair so they could have done this!"

I giggled, turning to follow the guide.

❧

"So you were the only one who got to meet a senator because they messed up on accessibility?" Mom asked as I described the trip after arriving home.

"Yeah, I guess." I shrugged, smiling. "It was so cool. He was nice too."

"Like I've always said," she laughed, "sometimes it pays to be disabled."

Chuckling along with her, I didn't know then that, both because of and despite my disability, I was heading toward places even more magnificent than this.

Chapter 12

Learning to Fly with GRACE

Until that moment, I had never understood what it meant to hear yourself scream.

My ears filled with this sharp, high-pitched tone. My mouth hung open as I whizzed through the balmy Virginia air. It took me a moment to realize it was my own scream I was hearing as my limbs flailed wildly.

For the first time in my life, I was moving on my own—without somebody else, a piece of furniture or equipment, or even the floor to support me.

It seemed like a great idea at the time, but the bird's-eye view of Water Country USA, the mid-Atlantic states' largest water park, was beginning to make me rethink the decision my brother and I had made to encourage Mom to stop standing in the opening of our huge two-person water tube and walking through the lazy river and jump up into a sitting position.

"I've got Meg," Sean had said, reaching over from his single tube to firmly grip my hand and shoulder. "Just hop up."

"Yeah," I had called from the rubber seat in the front of the tube. "Come on, Mom. It will be more fun for you if you ride instead of walk."

I felt the tube shudder before anybody else saw it coming. "Uh-oh" was the last thing I uttered before my end of the tube swung upward, dumping Mom into the water and launching me into the air. I plunged into the waves, a grand splash erupting all around me. As the world became a blur of color, I felt something grab and pull me up. Sean sat me on his knee as he squatted, gently patting my back as I coughed up the residue of the waves and began to panic.

"Oh my gosh! I just . . . I could have . . . *oh my gosh!* What if—"

"Dude, chill," Sean said calmly. "I caught you before you even hit the water. You were fine. You *are* fine."

"Yeah," Mom panted, swimming up from behind. "And I'm fine, too, in case anyone's wondering."

For a moment, stunned expressions took the place of words. I don't remember who started first, but laughter overcame us all, shattering the silence, leaving my body rumbling as Sean held me and waited for our mother to situate herself in the tube before putting me back in my seat.

"Did he even—" I trailed off, my hand gesturing to the lifeguard perched on his seat almost directly above us.

"Nope! Didn't even faze him," Sean scoffed. "He took his sunglasses off and looked over at us after you and Mom stopped splashing around. Missed the event itself."

"Great. Nice lifeguarding," I laughed.

❧

As she drove us back to our hotel hours later, Mom asked what our favorite ride had been. I listened to my family rattle off names of roller coasters and tried to swallow my laughter to keep my reply a total surprise.

"How about you, Megatha?" Mom asked.

"You were," I exclaimed, giggling as the boys broke into hysterics.

"Wait, what?" Mom asked, trying to piece together the joke.

"You were my favorite ride, Mom," I laughed. "We just gotta work on the landing."

"Yes, yes, very funny," she snickered. "They say there's one in every crowd, but I've got three of you!"

"I'm gonna tell my friends I learned to fly on vacation," I said. "No plane, no harness, just flying myself."

As the car filled with our chortling, I didn't know my joke was about to become my reality—that this summer would leave me flying to heights I had never anticipated reaching.

∽❧∼

The blueprints for this summer had begun to materialize a year earlier. My brothers' friend Brandon Traver and his family had invited us to join them for a few weeks in their Hilton Head, South Carolina condos. Driving down in our bronze Ford Excursion with my mother and brothers, I didn't expect this to be anything other than a fun stay with opportunities for swimming, beachgoing, and exploring the island.

"We were thinking of taking you guys kayaking tomorrow," Paula, Brandon's mom, said as my mother and I sat on the couch one of our first nights there.

Paula sat across from us. A broad grin spread across her face but began to fade as she said this.

By nine years old, I knew this look well, had seen it many times from people who had just started to get acquainted with my family and me. She was at the point where she didn't know whether to proceed with her intended question, given my disability. She was too far into the question to avoid it now, and she didn't know what to expect.

"But if that's not something Meg can take part in, I'm more than happy to hang back. The three of us can do something else while Jack takes the boys and Jill."

"I'm assuming there are life jackets involved?" Mom asked.

I smiled. I could see that glint in her eyes that told me the gears were turning in her mind.

"Oh, yes, of course," Paula nodded. "The boys will be safe. We have life vests ready to go."

"Of everyone going kayaking, who's the most experienced?" Mom asked.

"Probably Louie," Paula replied, naming the friend of her husband, Jack. "He's like a bodybuilder—he's into all the athletic stuff."

"All Meg really needs is back support, so if she could go in somebody else's kayak and maybe lean against them, we can probably make it work," Mom said. "I'd say the boys or I could take her in one of ours, but I'd feel better if somebody with a lot of experience took her."

"Oh—oh, okay, great," Paula replied, appearing to breathe a sigh of relief. "I just wasn't sure if she could do anything like that."

"A lot of people are concerned when they invite us to do anything out of the ordinary—which is really nice; we appreciate it when people are mindful of that," Mom smiled. "But we try to treat Meg like a normal kid and give her an opportunity to try everything we are doing as long as it's safe. You're interested in going, right, Meg?"

"Yeah," I exclaimed. "That sounds awesome!"

"Why did I bother asking when I already knew what you would say?" she chuckled.

It seemed like the greatest adventure in which I'd find myself in South Carolina. Sitting cross-legged in the kayak cockpit as Louie created a border on either side of me with his legs, I looked out at the marsh our caravan of boats was gliding through. I had never seen anything quite like it. The water glimmered softly as its waves surrounded us like a blanket that stretched beyond the range of the eye's vision, rocking the boat gently as Louie paddled on. Popping up through the water's surface were the chartreuse stems of cattails with their cylindrical sepia heads. Dangling my arm over the side of the boat and letting my fingertips graze the warm waves, I peered around, not wanting to miss a glimpse of the beauty.

It seems funny now that of all the spectacular sights our surroundings offered that summer, a billboard was most memorable.

"You guys see that billboard over there?" Sean asked as our mother drove us across the island. "The GRACE Center?"

"What does it say?" Mom asked. "I don't want to take my eyes off of the road."

"It's some center that specializes in CP—some special kind of therapy or something," Sean replied. "We should check that out for Meg."

By their early teens, my brothers had long been in the habit of noting opportunities that might improve my functionality. I don't remember our parents explicitly telling them to keep their eyes peeled for unique endeavors that may help me. They seemed to have picked up on it simply by observing our parents. I believe, too, that the boys had developed at a very young age a genuine desire to see me progress. Beginning in my early childhood, I found myself filled with appreciation and amazement at the way their findings turned into some of my life's most transformative endeavors.

❧

What Sean had seen was an advertisement for conductive education—a multidisciplinary approach to education, development, and training specifically designed for individuals with cerebral palsy and similar motor disabilities. It works to establish a daily series of tasks that emphasize learning the appropriate physical movements associated with activities of daily life, such as feeding, dressing, and tending to personal hygiene. Applied in real-life scenarios (as opposed to traditional clinic-based therapy) perpetually throughout the day, this system has proven to provoke the brain to develop new connections and map out actions for the body to take to complete tasks once inhibited by the disability. The goal of conductive education is to help the patient gain the skills to live as independently as possible, relaxing their dependence on assistive technology and other people.

Owners Stephanie and Andy Reed discovered the Hungarian therapy in their travels and had brought two therapists back to the United States for their daughter, Hannah Grace, who had CP and was around preschool-age at the time of my family's vacation. Named for Hannah Grace, the center's title, GRACE, was an acronym that stood for Growing, Rising, Achieving through Conductive Education. From Mom's research, it was one of the most effective treatment options available. She phoned the center, arranging for an evaluation during our vacation.

In some ways, it mirrored the traditional therapy evaluations I'd had throughout my life. The therapist, Erika Bartos, checked the flexibility of my muscles, placing a hand behind my heel and another on my knee, pushing down on the kneecap to see how straight my hamstrings could extend. I tried to resist the urge to squirm as I lay on the cool mat and felt the burning sensation run potently down the back of my leg.

"Okay, nice, Meg," she smiled, setting my leg down. "You can rest for a minute. Your hamstrings are pretty tight—have they done much with them in the therapy at home?"

"Well, that's one thing I haven't been too thrilled with," Mom sighed.

Though I'm not sure if my nine-year-old brain fully comprehended the concept, the reason for her sigh was something we often discussed among ourselves as well as with my doctors and therapists. There is a period in child development when muscles are able to be stretched to gain sustainable flexibility. When the child begins to hit growth spurts, the muscles' limberness, as in my case, often does not expand as the muscles themselves are growing. Although continued stretching throughout life enables minor gains in flexibility, the muscles largely lock at the pre-growth-spurt tightness level, and the leg will be limited in flexibility unless surgical intervention occurs.

One of my therapists at home was affiliated with a surgeon specializing in the hamstring-release operation. It was a point that Mom consistently had to work to counter through in-person and phone conversations as I grew up. Adamant that I would eventually go under the knife anyway, this one PT, who I'll call Gwendolyn, had reduced the intensity and frequency that she stretched my hamstrings. She explained to my mother and me that stretching would be more effective after the procedure, so rigorous stretching beforehand didn't make sense. My memory flags six years old as the age I was when Gwendolyn started to describe her theory directly to me as she stretched me.

"The surgery will take care of this, you know," she said for years. "It's only a matter of time before your Shriners doctor recommends it. It's not that bad, though—all he's going to do is make a little slice in each of your hamstrings to relieve the tension."

I'd lie there, trying to keep a straight face as my horrified mind produced images of a knife slicing my skin and muscles. I couldn't find any words to interject, but I'd talk to my mother about it later. She'd tell me not to worry, that it was not up to the therapist and that, even if the doctors did make the recommendation, it was really her decision whether to go through with it. She talked to Gwendolyn about how inappropriate her remarks to me were, but Gwendolyn continued making them until I graduated to the next therapy age group and left her care. I panicked each time my neuromuscular checkup approached, hoping to escape the potential surgery recommendation by asking my family to help me stretch more frequently and stretching myself as I grew older and obtained motorized wheelchairs with standing features that enabled me to do so independently.

It wasn't until my college years that my medical team mentioned that I would never be a candidate for the procedure because of the nature of my cerebral palsy. Modifying my hamstrings would cause other muscles to increase in tightness and tone. Though relieved that the possibility of surgery was eliminated, I couldn't believe I had spent most of my childhood and adolescence worrying that my PT's prediction would become my reality.

❧

"I'd like to see her keep going the natural way and try to avoid surgery," Mom explained at the GRACE Center, having described the philosophy of my therapist back home.

I couldn't quite read Erika's expression as I peered up at her face. It was stoic, unrevealing of emotion. Part of me wondered whether she was about to launch into a spiel about the benefits of the operation.

Erika's response stunned me.

"We don't typically recommend surgery—that procedure only gets kids so far, and they have to redo it when they grow," she said. "A big part of conductive education is finding ways to naturally release the muscles' tightness. If you enroll Meg here, I would do some intensive stretching."

I smiled, breathing a sigh of relief.

Of all the equipment that Erika had me try that day—benches I had to balance on, therapy tables I lay on while she stretched my muscles, and more—it was the parallel bars that were the most astonishing.

Parallel bars are two wooden poles equal in length that resemble two ballet barres set next to each other at about a three-foot distance. They sit on an adjustable base, allowing them to be raised or lowered to meet the height of each patient. They are used to help people learn or, in the case of an injury, relearn to walk.

I had grown up seeing this type of equipment in the Shriners Hospital Orthotics and Prosthetics clinic. Several times a year from the time I was six, I'd sit in the waiting room as my braces were being adjusted—heated and molded into a new shape to relieve pressure points caused by my foot growing and landing in a different part of the plastic. Stealing little glances, but careful not to stare—I knew how annoying it could be to have bystanders staring as I used my own assistive technology—I'd watch as children missing their legs were rolled into the exam rooms in wheelchairs. Moments later, they reappeared, wearing new legs of titanium or, as innovations developed over the years, with silicone covering to make them look like natural legs in color, shape, and width. The patients stood and entered the aisle of the parallel bars, gripping them as they slowly tested their ability to take steps while the prosthetist observed. I always considered it a miracle.

I never imagined, though, being able to use parallel bars. Everybody I saw doing so had stellar trunk control and could hold their upper bodies straight upward. I was just the opposite, relying heavily on the chest prompt of my walker to hold me up. I don't remember being particularly disappointed by this—I had learned very early on that we all have our own ways that work best for us in navigating the world. I was content with running around in my walker—it was one of my favorite activities. A small part of me, however, wondered what it would be like to walk supported by only two bars.

⌘

"What you need to do is take a step, let go very briefly with one hand—usually the hand on the same side you just took the step with—grab the bar a little further down, and then do the same with the other hand and leg."

I nodded at Erika's instructions as I stood between the bars, gripping them with all my might. Erika stood behind me with her arms outstretched, spotting me, ready to catch me if things didn't go as planned. I moved my leg forward, but my fingers were reluctant to let go. Growing up with the inability to stand and walk on my own had instilled in me a "never let go" rule that I religiously followed—the idea of a face-plant (which I never experienced) was not appealing. What I was being asked to do with the parallel bars went against everything I had known. Finally, I unclenched my fingers, sliding my hand forward without breaking its contact with the smooth wood of the bar.

My body soon found the rhythm, and the process became more automatic, giving me confidence and speed. Seeing that I could hold myself up and move without falling, I allowed myself to pick up my hands, letting them briefly break contact with the bars as I reached further down the bars' length. As I pulled my body forward, my biceps burned. I could feel a smile growing on my face as I traveled further along, astonished at my ability to walk like this.

The ends of the bars were connected by wooden frames that had rungs between them. They reminded me of ladders that came to about my eye level in height.

"Now that you are at the end," Erika called from behind when I was a step or two away from the rungs. "Keep your right hand where it is. Take your left hand and put it on the nearest rung. Inch it toward the left, and then move it to the regular bar."

I could feel my body naturally pivot as I stood with one hand on the rung and the other on the regular bar. As I removed my hand from the rung, my body seemed to speed up its motions, wanting to reduce the seconds that my body was supported by only one hand. I grabbed the regular bar and reached across the aisle to latch my right hand onto its bar. Now fully turned, I began to make my way back to the other end, smiling and making a funny face when I noticed my mother filming me, grinning from behind her phone as she slowly walked backward to keep me in the camera's shot as I advanced.

It was a video that she showed off to a great number of friends and family when we got home. Her face lit up each time she told somebody about discovering the GRACE Center, and she slid her hand into her pocket to retrieve her flip phone to play the video. It became part of her normal routine.

A trip to Goshen, Connecticut, though, is the instance that most stands out in my memory.

Mom had driven Sean and me to pick up Brian after his stay at his friend's lake house, and his friend's family invited us to Goshen's Woodridge Clubhouse, the area's community center. I remember sitting on the heather-gray deck overlooking Woodridge Lake, its vast blanket of waves sparkling in the sun. Out of the corner of my eye, I saw two familiar faces approaching, beaming from ear to ear. My brothers' cross-country coaches, Ron and Kathi Peck, a husband-and-wife duo from the area, had been at the clubhouse and happened to see us.

We had known the Pecks since Sean joined our middle school cross country team as a sixth grader when I was six years old. Brian joined when he reached sixth grade the following year, and both my brothers served as team captains. Seeing me sitting in my chair or standing in my walker with my mother at each meet and award ceremony, they had introduced themselves, getting to know us over the years. Known for their positivity and their "no kid on the team is benched—anybody who wants to run is welcome to run" philosophy, they had told me that when it came time for me to enter middle school, they would have a spot on the team for me and would adapt a course I could run in my walker. They kept their word, putting me on the team and even encouraging me to become a team captain for two of the first few years of what turned into a running career that lasted through adulthood.

At the time we were seeing them in Goshen, though, I was still about two years away from middle school. The conversation turned to our summer adventures. Mom pulled out her phone, telling them about finding the GRACE Center as she found the video to play.

"See? Parallel bars," Mom exclaimed, smiling as she held the phone so that everybody could see. "All the therapy she's had, and no one has ever tried anything like that with her."

"Wow, Meg! Look at you go!" Mrs. Peck turned to me with a wide smile spreading across her face.

"That's amazing," Mr. Peck agreed, a broad, dimpled smile appearing on his face. "Are you going to go back and do the program?"

"Yes," Mom exclaimed. "I'm in the process of figuring out the logistics."

"How much does something like that cost?"

"The tuition is through the roof," Mom sighed. "I still have to figure out the financial piece, but I *have* to get her in there. They were having her do exercises and stretches that nobody had ever shown her before. It was unbelievable."

"It would be great if you guys could get back there," Mr. Peck said. "It sounds like it would really help her."

We were always on a budget. Mom considered returning to work to be able to live a little more comfortably. With her unsalaried full-time job of tending to three kids, my medical care, and the household all on her own, she knew it wasn't feasible. She looked into different part-time opportunities but never found anything offering the flexibility she needed. We received monthly checks from my father's Social Security survivor benefits. She knew how to budget and save, pooling the Social Security checks and the savings that she and my father had put away and price shopping all our grocery orders and clothing to make sure we had what we needed without going into the bank accounts' red zone. Vacations required gradual saving, cutting costs by buying smaller birthday and Christmas presents so she could put something away for a trip she wanted to take us on in a few years.

I don't remember noticing the budget constraints too heavily growing up—we had what we needed to be healthy and happy. Mom began teaching us how important it was to save at a very young age and how, little by little, we could raise enough for the extravagant toys and trips we wanted by putting the money enclosed in birthday cards away and letting it accumulate over the years and by doing chores around the house that she could reward with a few dollars.

Looking back, I'm not sure if we would have been able to return to South Carolina so soon after that first vacation. Tuition to the GRACE Center was several thousand dollars and would have taken many seasons of saving. In a way, there was a time limit too—the program's age cutoff. I was about six years away from it, but especially since I'd have to attend when school broke for the summer, Mom must have felt the finite boundary of time. My mother had this tremendous faith that if she talked to enough people about our goals in life, she would eventually find the support we needed to execute them.

A few weeks after our trip to Goshen, Mr. Peck extended an invitation to a social organized by the Litchfield Village Striders—a running group the Pecks were part of. The Striders often initiated charity events to support local individuals in need of extraordinary medical treatment and those who were initiating service projects to benefit people in poor health and poverty conditions. The social gave donors a chance to mingle with potential candidates and decide whether to offer their support.

I don't remember feeling the pressure of needing to impress donors. I understood that the evening could help me get back to the GRACE Center, but attending the event in the fall of my fourth-grade school year, I was too young to know how the revolutionary approach to therapy needed to be articulated to demonstrate the magnitudinous impact it would have in my life. My mother's mind must have been whirling at how much was riding on this one night. She seemed to know just how to phrase the account of my evaluation at the center to emphasize the leaps she saw me inching toward in the few hours that I was with the therapist.

"This therapist had her sitting on all sorts of benches and stools without back support. Meg has always needed full trunk support, but the therapist was starting to show her how to hold herself up in ways no one ever has," she said as we stood—me in my walker—in a half circle of people. "They'll work on helping her do some dressing and feeding herself too. It's a very comprehensive program."

"Meg's gonna be one of our runners at the middle school in a few years," Mr. Peck said, smiling. "We're already planning to adapt a course for her."

"Looks like you're already getting ready, Meg," Mrs. Peck exclaimed, pointing to my lavender Nike sneakers as I beamed. "Look at those shoes!"

"But this program—this center that Anne's trying to get her into—there's nothing like it in this part of the country," Mr. Peck explained before turning to my mom. "Why don't you show them the video of her on the parallel bars?"

I watched the group cluster together to see my mother's cell phone screen. Eyebrows raised as people watched the recording, and I couldn't help but wonder what they were thinking.

☙

"Mr. Peck just called," Mom told me one afternoon following the social. "They want to sponsor you! The Striders raised enough money to help a few people, and you were selected as one of them! We're going to the program this summer!"

"Really?" I gasped. "They want to cover all of it? Isn't that, like, a lot of money?"

"Yes! That's why I want you to write a thank-you note before you do anything else this weekend. Write one now and one after we go. I'm going to call Erika then make reservations at a hotel. Oh, and they want you to make a speech about the experience at another social in the fall."

I sat there grinning, contemplating how best to describe my gratitude and imagining what treasures the five-week program might hold.

My GRACE Center days fell into a comfortable routine. Erika met us at the door of my mother's van each weekday with a walker that belonged to the center. This walker had no straps or supports for under the arms and around the torso. It was one where the users stand behind and push as opposed to mine, where I had wraparound padding and harnesses securing me.

My first stroll in that walker was a perfect mixture of excitement and terror.

My body leaned forward as much as it could to rest my forearms over the frame. It wasn't that I couldn't get my body upright. Ten years of knowing that I couldn't balance myself while walking and standing had instilled in me a fear of falling. It was like an automatic reflex, leaning forward for support, my body clinging onto anything sturdy that might hold me up as my feet took little steps beneath me.

"Hey, Meg. Can you stop for a second?" Erika asked from behind me. "What if we tried to get you to stand a little straighter? Can you hold onto the walker but make your arms straight? Bend your elbows a little so they are not stressed. Good! I'm keeping my hands so close that I'm literally almost touching your shirt, so don't worry about falling. I've got you."

I took a deep breath and started to walk again. I suddenly felt free in a way I never had before. The only parts of me that were attached to the walker were my hands gripping the foamy handlebars. Once I gained momentum, it was like nothing could hinder my rhythm. I had never known what it was like to walk independently, but I was sure this was the closest I had come to it. I walked faster on my way in and out of the center as the weeks went on, loving how free I was to push this walker without toppling over. My body learned to stand

356

to attention more quickly and automatically, growing in strength and confidence.

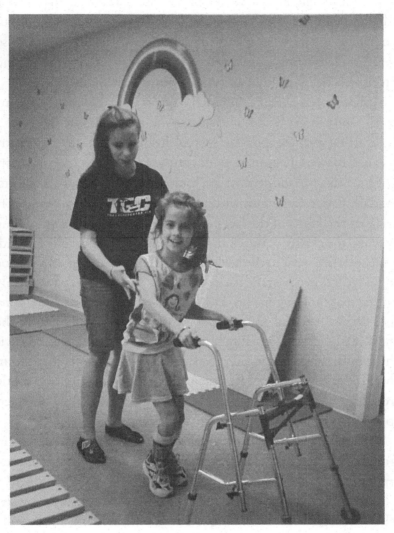

Photo Credit: Anne Mulville Moore

357

Walking through the cavernous lobby, we arrived at the therapy room. Aligning the back of my body with the mat against the wall, Erika put her hands under my arms and eased me down. Turning both legs so that I landed sitting cross-legged, I placed my hands on the ground on either side of my hips, getting my bearings with my balance.

"Shoes, please," Erika said each day just before I reached for my feet. "Don't forget to use one hand to stabilize yourself."

Starting with the foot that was on the outskirts of the pretzel my legs had formed, I began to work out the knots in my laces with my fingers. Erika had me do this with multiple types of shoes—sneakers, sandals, Crocs. Suited up with my sneakers and braces, my fingers released the knots of the laces, poking into the middle and pulling through the cluster of the cloth until a single strand was in my hand. My hand then went to the heel, pushing on the back edge of the shoe to nudge it down past the back of the foot. My other hand sat firmly on the mat, holding me up. Leaning on it a little more, I lifted my foot off the mat and grabbed the toe of the shoe, pulling until the sneaker was off my foot. Pinching my fingers together around their thin width, I peeled the violet Velcro straps of my brace away from their white counterparts. Removing the plastic, calf-to-toe orthotic from the back of my leg and foot, I put my foot down and prepared to switch positions.

"Okay, remember, this is the tricky part," Erika coached from in front of me. "Put both hands on the mat and keep your arms locked straight so you don't lose your balance when you move your legs."

My hands fell to the mat, pressing into its spongy surface as my elbows straightened, beginning to burn as I shifted my weight fully to my arms. I uncurled one leg, bringing it a few inches away from where it had been lying in front of its twin. Beginning to straighten my other leg, I lifted it into the air slightly and put it on the other side of my opposite ankle. I pulled both legs toward me, regaining my balance enough to release the weight from my arms. Then I started on the other shoe.

I had never been able to remove my own shoes—not properly anyway. The most I could manage was to run my heel along my opposite big toe, using my toe to nudge the shoes down before kicking them off with a flick of my foot. I relied on somebody else to take my braces off. I could never even get the Velcro undone most of the times I tried—I had a hard time getting my fingers coordinated enough to hold material of such a slim width. I marveled at how this task suddenly became possible for me and how, over the weeks, it grew into an easy and almost automatic process.

It seems silly now that such a small, ordinary task amazed me so deeply. This, though, is a prominent phenomenon in life with a disability. Throughout my life, my family always reminded me of how momentous it was that I was achieving small victories in doing everyday activities I had never been able to do before. As an adult, I often laughed when they, buzzing with excitement, pointed out that I was taking off my own shoes or coat. I told them it was not that great of an accomplishment, reminding them that it was just a simple little action and that we had all had achievements in academics, athletics, and careers that should be the real celebration. Their exuberant enthusiasm over my small acts, however, always inspired me to appreciate my capabilities.

Some gains, though, never faded in their novelty. When I began my conductive education journey, I had minimal trunk control. Like a ragdoll, my body began to teeter backward after only a few moments of sitting up with no support behind me. The small fire of exhaustion in my abs grew rapidly, and people or pillows had to catch me when I inevitably couldn't hold myself up any longer. Within minutes of starting the program, I was thrown into a balancing act with nothing to back me. Erika sat me on a small, square bench. With wood legs and wooden slats for its seat, it was no more than a foot or two tall, but that first time, it felt like a skyscraper.

"Have you done much sitting in anything without a back, Meg?" Erika asked, looking from me to my mother, who had automatically raised her arms toward me, spotting me as Erika did the same.

I shook my head as Mom explained that I had needed full trunk support since birth. I tried to stay as still as my constant, spastic movements caused by cerebral palsy would allow. My eyes crept to the edge of the bench, calculating the distance between it and the floor as my breath quickened.

"I have a handlebar that screws into the table for when we work there if that would make you more comfortable," Erika offered. "But know that this will get a lot easier for you in a matter of days. Would you like the bar for the table?"

I nodded. As she walked me to one of the many therapy tables lined up in a row occupying the middle of the room, she carried with her a bar a little thicker than the width of a drumstick and shaped like a rectangular arch. Matching the table in its maple wood hue, it had thick, black knobs on either side. As the tabletops were composed of three-fingers-wide wood slats, the bar screwed into the space between.

For the first few days, I clung to that bar for dear life. My left hand never broke contact with it, even as my right hand held a thickened pencil and worked to write my name or, at my mother's insistence, the answers to math facts.

It didn't occur to me until a week or more had passed that I was no longer gripping the bar for support. Erika continued to put it in front of me throughout my time there, but I suddenly realized I was only using it when I did my sit-to-stands—exercises in which I had to pull myself out of sitting into a standing position for several repetitive sets. It had become second nature to sit unsupported. Even as years passed, it stuck in my memory that I had entered the center unable to sit on my own and left with the permanent ability to do so. It always amazed me how this one five-week program made such a remarkable difference in my capabilities and in my life.

It must have been strange for my family to see this transformation. They were thrilled to see how much more I could do. I spent many evenings demonstrating my new skills for them, watching their jaws drop as I sat at the edge of a couch cushion without resting my back against anything. or showed them how I could crawl, write, and take a jacket off myself much faster, smoother, and easier than ever before.

I also remember how it took them a while to get used to me being so self-sufficient. It is in these moments—at the expense of, I admit, my poor mother's nerves—that I had my fun.

Once I had gotten into a comfortable routine at the center, Mom began to come and go throughout the day, leaving to do errands, check on the boys at their chosen adventure of the day—minigolf, the beach, a trip to the movies—or even to get together with the grandmother of the boy, Kingsley, who shared the afternoon session at the center with me.

"Hey, Meg," she always called, walking back into the room after making some trips to the car to bring in the rest of my stuff.

Erika usually had me sitting on the bench at this point, asking me to balance without putting my hands down on anything.

"Kingsley's grandma and I are gonna run to the store."

I'd time it so that she was in the room, looking at me.

"Are you good? Do you need anything before I—oh my gosh!"

Seeing my body abruptly lurch forward, she always ran toward me, looking as if she was about ready to dive to save me from falling. I'd pull my body back up, laughing, just as she really started to panic.

361

Erika, her husband, Peter, Kingsley, and I always burst into hysterics as Mom smirked, shaking her head at us.

"Yes, *very* funny. You guys are just *so* funny," she said. "Goodbye, I'm leaving now. I'll be back to pick you up—unless you want to keep laughing at your mother and just go home with Erika and Peter instead."

"I love you, Mother dear," I said, still laughing.

"Yeah, yeah, yeah," she replied, walking out the door before popping her head back in. "I love you too."

"You've done that how many times?" Peter said, shaking his mop of chocolate curls as a smile lingered on his lean, bronze face. "But I don't think it will ever get old."

"Probably not," I said, pushing the words out of my mouth and laughing. Part of the conductive education involved communicating without my speech device while at the center.

"Poor Anne," Erika chuckled.

❧

It's my brother Brian's expression, too, that I remember most.

My family members had seen me perform the actions I had learned each day, grinning as I lowered my wheelchair seat to the floor to demonstrate the way I had been taught to get myself out. Having them unbuckle me since my poor fine motor skills did not permit me to click my seat belt's button independently, I put both legs to one side and inched my upper body in the opposite direction, putting myself at a diagonal. Bringing my hands to the ground, I began to lean my upper body forward, putting my weight on my hands. Walking my hands forward, I moved away from the chair and pulled my knees under me as soon as my legs were clear of the footrest. I crawled over to the couch in our hotel room, leaning against it as I brought my hands to one side and held myself up while bringing my legs out in front of me, folding them into a cross-legged position. Both brothers were amazed, beaming as they watched me and listened to our mom explain the muscles that Erika had said I was using and how Erika had devised the process.

Each day, my brothers listened to the technicalities of the exercises I had done and bits of humor that emerged during the day. The conversations, I later realized, were clinical, though in a casual sense, the language much less formal than a medical report.

"It's fun for you, though, right?" Brian asked with a face full of worry, swimming next to me as I lounged in my floaty in the hotel pool one afternoon—my daily post-therapy ritual before we went sightseeing. "I know it's hard work, but do they at least make it fun for you? Do you like it?"

"Oh yeah, I love it," I exclaimed, giggling. "We spend most of the day laughing because we all joke around as we're working. And that kid that's in the afternoon session just like me, Kingsley, is so funny. This is his last week; we're going out for burgers with him and his grandma in a few days, so you'll get to meet him. But the kid's hilarious."

A blond-haired, bright-eyed boy around six years old, Kingsley filled the room with chatter and provoked laughter from us all throughout the afternoons.

"Grandma and I went to the store yesterday," he'd say, "and this funny thing happened—"

"Kingsley, Kingsley, Kingsley," Peter once said as he stood behind him, spotting him as he rose from his bench and prepared to climb up on the table for his hamstring stretching. "Keep telling us the story, but keep moving too—every time you talk, you stop moving. Meg's already ten steps ahead of you. Let's go, Grampa!"

"Yeah, Grampa," I laughed. "You don't want me to get to my spot first, do you?"

"Did you just call him . . ." Erika trailed off into laughter as I crawled onto the table.

"Who ya calling Grampa, you grandma?" Kingsley laughed, beginning the first of many grandpa-grandma banter sessions that occurred throughout our days together.

❧

Peter's humor came in many forms. I always caught him stealing glances at the logo on my T-shirt, looking for that Hershey Park cast of characters—cartoon versions of packs of Reese's cups, Hershey bars and kisses, and KitKats, complete with big eyes and smiles— that adorned the hot pink T-shirt I had gotten on the way to South Carolina that summer.

Our real reason for the detour to Hershey, Pennsylvania, was to see my neurologist, Dr. Charles Nichter, who had recently transferred to Hershey Medical Center. Unable to find somebody else with the same ingenious mind and caring bedside manner as Dr. Nichter by the time I was due for a follow-up, Mom had added Hershey to the driving route, securing a medical rate at the Hershey Lodge, a family package for a day or two at the park (touched that we had made the trip to see him, Dr. Nichter and his wife dropped off tickets at the hotel's front desk as a surprise, granting us an extra day at the park), and so much complimentary chocolate that none of us touched the stuff for a month after.

The T-shirt was my chosen souvenir purchase at the gift shop, and thanks to the laundry facilities at our South Carolina hotel, I wore it a few times during my five weeks at the center.

"Meg, you brought me chock-o-lat today so I don't go hungry looking at your shirt all day, right?" Peter asked when he first saw the shirt, his accent coming through thickly on the word "chocolate."

"No, sorry," I giggled.

"Ah, come *on*, Meg!"

"Peter, you do realize that Meg is ten years old," Erika laughed. "So when you ask Meg to go get you chock-o-lat you are really asking Anne to go buy you chock-o-lat, as Meg goes with her."

"I just want chock-o-lat," he shrugged as a smirk crossed his face.

On the eve of our departure for home, my family and I rang Erika and Peter's doorbell, a gift bag dangling from my hand as I stood with my mother's arms under mine.

Inside, we sat on the couch and watched them tear through the tissue paper together.

"Ah, yes! Yes, yes, yes," Peter exclaimed, opening one of the packages of Hershey's chocolate in the bag and popping some into his mouth. "Finally you brought me chock-o-lat, Meg!"

"I can't believe you actually did that. Thank you! Hang on, we have something for you too," Erika said, standing, pausing to look at her husband—still munching on his candy bar—before she disappeared into the other room. "Save some for me. They gave that to both of us, you know."

He shrugged, smiling as he took another bite.

She returned with a pile of Hungarian chocolate bars wrapped in metallic gold foil with white paper jackets. We all sat there for a little while, enjoying treats from a culture different from our own.

Erika knelt in front of the couch as my family began to make moves to leave. Taking both of my hands and helping me stand up, she wrapped me in a bear hug.

"You work very hard, Meg. Thank you so much for working so hard this summer," she said. "You are going to do big things in life because of all your hard work."

I grinned as I returned the embrace, already beginning to miss our routine at the center.

❧

As Connecticut's leaves transformed into autumn's fiery hues, I found myself sitting before a room full of Village Striders at the Litchfield Community Center. Lined up in numerous rows, they created a border around the empty part of the room where the fundraiser beneficiaries had assembled near the microphone. Moving to the center with my DynaVox secured to my wheelchair, I looked out into the audience, my grin widening as I spotted my family, Mrs. Peck, and Berta, a prominent Strider with whom we had become friends, all standing in the front row. Beside me, Mr. Peck knelt, holding the wireless microphone up to my Dyna speakers. He turned to me and beamed as the device began to read my speech.

I described my routine at the center, explaining the main exercises that made up my days. Sharing how I had relied heavily on the bar to hold onto at the table the first few days, I told of my surprise that I subconsciously stopped gripping it after a little while and of my astonishment that I could now sit up without support: "I could never sit up by myself for more than a few minutes, but that's so easy for me to do now."

I could see the audience's eyes and smiles widen as I shared how, for the first time in my life, I could get out of my wheelchair and sit myself up against the couch or wall. They laughed as I told some of the jokes that my therapists, Kingsley, and I invented during our days together, and beamed even brighter as I detailed some of the equipment—the modified, thickened writing instruments, the feeding utensils with the curved handles that allowed me to lift food to my mouth without having to reposition my hand to turn them, the walker, parallel bars, and benches—that I had succeeded in using.

"We even ordered some of the smaller equipment, like the curved spoon and fork, so that I can keep working with them at home," my Dyna announced.

I could feel my smile spread even broader as my communication device read my last few lines. I had incorporated the center's motto as the conclusion—an approach that, even at ten years old, the writer in me considered artful.

"I can't thank you enough for helping me get to the GRACE Center. I was definitely Growing, Rising, Achieving through Conductive Education. Thank you!"

Fireworks of applause burst throughout the room. I spent the rest of the evening receiving congratulations for making such gains in the program.

My brother Sean and me with Striders Mr. and Mrs. Peck,
Mr. Oneglia, and Berta Andrulis Mette
Photo Credit: Anne Mulville Moore

367

I didn't realize then that this was just the beginning of a season of tremendous heights I'd reach.

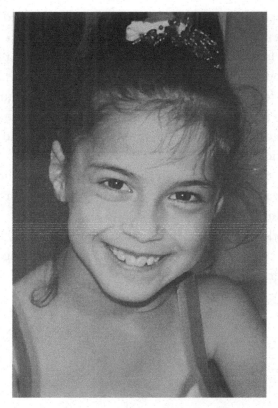

Photo Credit: Stephanie Reed

Chapter 13

Flourishing Blossoms

Ms. Kelly stood smiling from her lofty height, occasionally brushing the blonde bangs of her bob out of her blue eyes, but I couldn't yet tell what she thought of me.

Brian had studied under Ms. Kelly when he was my age, entering her class daily for a period, then returning to Mr. Vesneski's class (fifth graders switched classes for one subject to get a taste of the routine of changing classes throughout the day in middle school and high school). My brother hadn't revealed much about Ms. Joan Kelly, though, other than saying that she was strict but very nice.

I remember sitting there on the first day of school, stealing little glances of her out of the corner of my eye and wondering what was running through her mind as I sat at my desk, decorating the introduction activity page that each student had been assigned. Feeling the edges of the hexagonal Number 2 pencil between my index and middle fingers—the position that, as I had discovered with my occupational therapist years earlier, allowed me to drag a writing instrument across a page with as much precision as the rigidity of my muscle movements permitted—I remember grinning as I scratched my name onto the page. My marking still appeared as squiggly lines, but they had become refined at the GRACE Center that summer—the mountains of the "M" were a little sharper in their peaks, and the curves of the "E" and the "G" were smoother.

"That *does* look clearer, Meg," my physical therapist, Tina, exclaimed, leaning over my shoulder. "Your mom said you worked hard this summer—I can't wait to have you show me everything you learned when I steal you for therapy."

I smiled. Ms. Kelly caught my eye as she beamed and told me I was doing a nice job. Still, I wondered about the thoughts that were going through her mind. I wondered what she was thinking as she looked at the squiggly lines my therapist and I were celebrating and what she expected from a student whose handwriting and doodling were essentially one and the same.

"I always knew you would do great things," she told me years later. "I always knew you were destined to make positive changes in the world."

As a freshly minted fifth grader, I didn't realize that my teacher's vision would begin to blossom into my reality so abundantly and vibrantly during my final days at Long Meadow Elementary School.

Photo Credit: Anne Mulville Moore

From first grade on, I attended regular weekly art classes with my peers. A few times a month, my occupational therapist came with me, observing how I manipulated art supplies. Bringing thickened pencil grips and paintbrushes with a ball at the non-bristled end, she helped me arrange my fingers around both conventional and adaptive art supplies before giving me the okay to put them to the page, canvas, or slab of clay. She studied my movements and markings and made adjustments to my position as I worked. Placing her hand over mine, she stabilized me, weighing down my hand to calm my muscle spasticity and allow me to make smoother, less jagged lines. My therapist often gave tutorials to show my aides how they needed to support my limbs on the weeks when she would not be in my class.

"She's doing the work, dictating the shape she makes and where it's placed. All I'm doing is applying a little pressure to the top of her wrist to make her movements more controlled," she'd say. "And see how I have my other hand next to her elbow? I'm using it as a border so that her arm stays there and limits how far her wrist brings the pencil. That lets her keep working the range of the page without accidentally trailing off onto the table. Would you like to try while I'm here? Is that okay with you, Meg?"

There were times when, so engrossed in creating and contemplating what color or design was to come next, I almost forgot to let the word "yes" slip out of my mouth.

What I remember most, though, is working with Long Meadow's art teacher, Mrs. Porter-Hahn. Having worked at a facility for special needs children in a past career, Mrs. P. H. was familiar with cerebral palsy and made time to work one-on-one with me each class that my occupational therapist did not attend. First distributing supplies and instructions to the rest of the class, she always found her way to my table, standing next to my chair as her paint-smattered, blue button-down smock hung open on her slim body.

"Alright my dear," she'd say. "What color is first?"

I'd reach over to my Dyna, sitting off to the side on the table, and, finding my "Color" page—a screen in which forty square keys showed the name of a color in black font and had the color itself as a background surrounding the label—I'd select and speak the name of my chosen hue. Holding the paintbrush vertically by its tip, she waited for me to secure it between my right hand's first two fingers. I let my hand slide down the smooth wood, stopping just as my fingertips began to graze the metallic silver ferrule. She pushed a small paint palette toward me with my chosen color in the crater nearest to me. I slowly moved to dip my bristles into the paint; then, to beat any looming drips, I quickly brought my brush to the surface I was to paint.

"Remember," Mrs. P. H. always said, "slow, purposeful movements."

She gently enveloped my hand in hers as I made my first stroke, spreading thick paint or glaze on canvases and clay objects I'd sculpted in previous classes.

"Hang on," she sometimes said after a while, when the range of my strokes grew substantially and unintentionally shorter. "Your arm is getting tight. Let me stretch you."

Removing the brush from my hand, she guided my arm into an outstretched position and gradually lifted it up, down, and to each side, igniting twinges of burning sensations in my muscles. After having me spread my fingers wide for a moment, she returned my brush and allowed me to resume my work.

"One of your fellow chickadees is summoning me," she often said as she surveyed the room and noticed a hand raised, gesturing to my aide to switch places with her. "Keep going with the painting and I'll be back. Remember, slow, purposeful movements."

◦◦◦

I always loved art, always found myself drawing or playing with Model Magic clay and Play-Doh at home. I loved making scenes full of any shape and color I could think of. Art class was one that I couldn't wait to get to each week.

The difference between my art and my peers', though, was abundantly clear. Mine had stray lines of color sweeping through the figures illustrated or the negative space around it, giving the people I depicted unintentional flyaway hair or running mascara. I could look at the collection of my class's art at a distance on a drying rack or at the annual regionwide art show and pick out mine right away. I was proud of my work and always had a blast crafting it. Yet there was always a sense of melancholy within me—my friends' work looked almost museum-worthy, while mine looked worthy of a kindergarten bulletin board. I don't remember saying this out loud, but my teacher seemed to intuit it.

"I've seen work from many artists with disabilities, Meg," she always said. "And their work is so beautiful because it is so unique. It's not like anybody else's work, and that is one of the best things about it. Your work is phenomenal, my dear."

I always grinned, turning back to my work with new eyes, noticing how there was beauty in my designs and knowing how both my teacher and my family would celebrate it upon its completion, wanting to showcase it at the Region 15 School District's annual art show and on the walls at school and at home.

Mrs. Porter-Hahn and me with my pottery piece at the
2008 Region 15 art show.
Photo Credit: Anne Mulville Moore

I don't think I realized, though, the extent that my teacher believed this.

"I'm glad I caught you both because I've been wanting to talk to you," she said one day as my mother and I were leaving school during my third-grade year. "I'm about to make selections for next year's art enrichment, and I wanted to see if you'd be interested. I don't typically tell students ahead of time, but I figured I'd get your thoughts, Anne, since we meet an hour before school once a week."

"Oh, yes, that's doable; I'm willing to stay and be Meg's one-on-one, since it's before school hours," my mother replied before turning to me. "What do you think?"

I was stunned. Art enrichment was known as the class for students who exhibit exceptional talent. It was a program that ran from fourth through fifth grade and offered a curriculum, in addition to the regular weekly classes everyone at school had, that taught students more intricate drawing, painting, and sculpting skills. Each year, students in art enrichment had an opportunity to spend the day touring the Yale Museum of Art.

"Yeah," I finally said, still astonished. I looked at my mother, feeling a grin start to appear as the words came out of my mouth. "That'd be awesome!"

"I knew you'd say that," Mom exclaimed as she turned to my teacher. "She's a yes!"

I spent the next two years in a class of fifteen or so fourth and fifth graders to learn to sketch, shade, paint, and sculpt with refined precision. Even years later, I could never quite get my hands around the fact that I was chosen to be part of this group.

❧

I suppose Mrs. P. H.'s vision for developing and promoting my art unveiled itself before art enrichment, though. Late in my third-grade year, she had announced that the Yale Center for British Art had agreed to put up an exhibit of the finest art produced by LMES students. As she did with the Region 15 Art Show, she made her selections of student work quietly, reviewing and choosing from the pile of recently handed-in projects without telling us that our work was being considered until after she returned graded assignments. Those who did not receive their work back were then told that their art was being exhibited.

I remember the ink print assignment she gave around then. Drawing clusters of circles—a landscape of stemless flowers—on tracing paper in pencil and watching my teacher place the page on a Styrofoam rectangle, I retraced my flowers, pushing the pencil down hard into the foam. When the foam showed etchings of the shapes—some presenting as merely blank outlines, while others had tracks of graphite—my teacher replaced the pencil in my hand with a mini paint roller. Driving it back and forth, I began to cover the Styrofoam with violet and rose-pink inks. When the Styrofoam was sufficiently dyed, Mrs. P. H. flipped it and put it face down on a piece of sky-blue construction paper. With the heel of my hand, I rubbed the back of the page. As Mrs. P. H. peeled the page away from the construction paper, I saw that my flowers appeared as sky-blue outlines filled with purple and pink paint. We later mounted it on black construction paper.

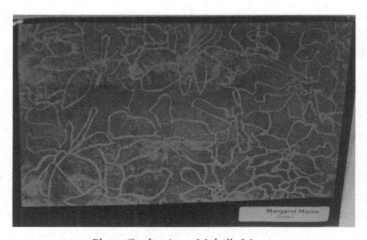

Photo Credit: Anne Mulville Moore

I lingered at the end of the class that followed, watching the teacher hand my classmates their finished pieces. Most of the class had taken their work and lined up at the door. With only a few of us left, she smiled and showed her empty hands.

"As for the rest of you," she said, "your work is off to Yale. I hope you and your parents can go to see the exhibit."

My jaw must have dropped. My work, the flowers with the petals that were anything but even and identical in shape, was up at Yale? My work was at Yale!

❧

I remember wearing my yellow dress to school the day I went to see the exhibit. Finely checkered with daffodil-yellow and white and falling past the knee, its sleeveless material was trimmed in green and had orange and red flowers across the waist.

"You look extra pretty today, Meg," friends, faculty, and staff members remarked throughout the day. "Do you have anything special going on?"

"I'm going to see my artwork at Yale," I exclaimed through my Dyna, smiling a little broader each time.

"Wow! That's amazing! Congratulations!"

My eyes couldn't help but fly to the clock throughout those hours of school. My mother had permission to pick me up a little early, since the museum was only open until late afternoon and since, without traffic, it took around forty minutes to get there. The clock seemed to stand still all day, but finally it was time to go down to the office to meet my family. Since high school let out in the early afternoon, Sean was able to come with us; Brian, still in middle school, had to stay in class and meet up with friends after school while we drove back.

I can still picture walking across the polished hardwood floor of the museum in my walker, mazing through the wax sculptures of men, the benches before each display, and the pop-up walls that were stark white to contrast with the multitude of colors of the artwork that hung on them.

"There's LMES! Come on," I exclaimed, quickening my pace. "Look, mine's in the top row—the purple and pink one. See it?"

"It's beautiful," my mother beamed, moving in to take a picture of it.

"That's cool! What's the blue? Chalk?" Sean asked. "No, wait, it's too bold to be chalk. What is it?"

I began to detail the materials and process I had used to make it, giving my mother and brother short glances, not wanting to lose time to see my work on Yale's wall. I remember walking up to see my work on a granular level and then backing away to admire the whole wall. What my teacher had been telling me suddenly leapt out. Each piece on the wall had its own style, its own curvature of lines. At a distance, some looked similar. Those that stood out were distinguished by their unique color patterns, even their squiggly lines. They didn't look bad next to the ones with the perfect angles and refined color schemes. No, they stood out because of their unprecedented beauty. And each of them, it was easy to see, deserved its place under the spotlights that shone brightly from above.

⤜◦⤏

This theme of showcasing my talents in the arts despite my disability making the performance a little abstract became prevalent in fifth grade.

Fourth and fifth graders at LMES are required to participate in their grade-level chorus, meeting once a week during school hours and putting on an annual concert. I remember an aide expressing concern while walking beside me on the way to the first fourth-grade rehearsal.

"I suppose we have to let you participate, but I don't know what they expect you to do," she sighed. "You won't sing of course. That's not something you can do with your communication device."

I tried not to scoff audibly. This was the type of attitude my family had taught me to ignore, reminding me that I was entitled to participate in every activity my peers were doing. Of course I would be in the chorus. Of course I'd sing. I could move my vocal cords up and down to the melodies just like everybody else. Would I solo? No, I didn't see myself going as far as to even remotely consider it given my speech impediment, but I would certainly sing as part of the group.

I don't remember feeling particularly disappointed or embarrassed by my inability to solo—at least not for more than a few moments. Unbeknownst to her, my best friend provided solace.

"Did you see how many people flooded the front of the room when Mrs. Odoardi announced solo audition sign-ups?" she asked during a playdate one day. "And I'm just sitting down on the riser like 'Yeah, I don't think so. No one needs to hear me sing on my own.'"

"Same," I laughed as I released the words from my mouth. Knowing me for over five years had trained her in understanding my natural speech. "Put me in a group and I'll sing along, but do not give me a solo. Spare the audience."

As she laughed, I realized we were in the same boat, just coming from different angles. She wouldn't dream of auditioning to solo because she didn't believe she was good at singing (though, knowing her, she was probably better than she thought). I didn't have any interest in soloing, both because of my speech impediment and because I didn't feel that I was good at singing either. As we talked to more of our friends, we learned that many shied away from the solos because of their perceived inability to carrying a good tune. In a way, it was a laughable, shared experience that prevented me from bearing the brunt of feeling incapable because of my disability.

∾⦰◠

There were other opportunities, though, to engage with the music. Perhaps stemming from memories of watching the joy light my mother's face as she performed in her Irish step dancing troupe, I was drawn to chances to become more immersed in music.

I still remember the day they asked for students to volunteer to be dancers in the fifth-grade concert.

Our theme that year was *American Bandstand*, and the set list featured everything from the Beatles to the Beach Boys. The gym teacher, Mrs. McVerry, who choreographed all the shows, stood in front of the music room's risers with the music teacher, Mrs. Odoardi.

"Okay, kids," Mrs. McVerry called, picking up a pencil from the music stand they stood behind. "Next, we'll do volunteers for the Beach Boys' 'Surfin' U. S. A.' Who would like to dance for that?"

A year earlier, I had volunteered to ring the jingle bells in our cultural-themed concert. I met my classmate at center stage and accepted the set of jingle bells she had picked up backstage for me along with her own. Sliding the looped strap between my thumb and forefinger, she mouthed *Got it?* and waited for my nod before taking her place in the line of students beside me. Shaking the strap in each hand to ring the attached circular silver bells as a flute melody began to play from the stereo backstage, I grinned at the audience as the class sang the chorus: "Follow the leader, winding around, earth untraveled, O hollow ground." The golden spotlights above made the bells sparkle as they played their sweet tune. I remember how beautiful it all felt during the song and after, as my family and other audience members complimented my playing. I craved another chance to be more actively involved in the music and didn't hesitate to raise my hand when Mrs. McVerry requested dancers for "Surfin' U. S. A." the next year. It was a number I enjoyed because of its catchy tune and cool lyrics.

"They asked for dancers, Meg," my aide whispered from beside me. "Are you sure *that's* what you want to volunteer for?"

I nodded, smirking, knowing from years of experience exactly where this was headed.

"*You're* going to *dance*?"

She was new around school, and I could tell she hadn't understood the full meaning behind my teachers' and therapists' briefing that I liked to be treated like everybody else, having access to all the same opportunities. She often tried to dissuade me from my actions—everything from using a pencil to independently draw lines on a craft to playing capture the flag in my chair with friends at recess—even though I had permission to participate from my mother and other staff. Hearing my frustration after school, Mom had suggested that I ignore her if what I was doing was safe and permitted by other adults.

I nodded in response to the aide's question, keeping my hands raised.

"How are *you* going to dance?" she asked.

"I've done stuff like this before," I explained, letting her read the words on my Dyna screen rather than having my device broadcast them to the whole room (though, later in life, I wondered whether it would have been better to draw attention to the conversation).

She wasn't too suave in the words she chose for her response—she never was, and I often found myself having discussions with my mother and teachers about gibes she had made.

381

"I'd take a moment to think about whether you really want to be center stage in your chair while everyone else is dancing."

I don't remember reporting this one—I don't think I did, other than to make a joke to family and friends later about how she had discouraged me, and yet the performance had gone off without a hitch. In the moment, I recall wincing at the remark and turning my options over in my mind. She had just heightened my awareness that I would have to dance differently than my peers, that I would be seated rather than standing and walking, that this would be an obvious difference in the eyes of the audience, and that, as her tone indicated, this was not a positive way to stand out. Something made me consider, though, how I might feel if I put my hand down before I was noticed by the teachers, whose eyes were still fixed on the other side of the room as they slowly marked down the names of the students with raised hands, and how I might feel at the show if I didn't volunteer and then watched others doing the dance without me. Knowing I would regret not being involved, I left my hand up.

I knew I didn't have anything to worry about with the teachers. They had always found ways to fully include me while balancing the needs of my disability.

"Meg Moore." A smile appeared on Mrs. Odoardi's face.

"Nice, Meg," Mrs. McVerry exclaimed, scrawling my name on the page before her. "That'll be awesome."

This is one of the things I loved about LMES—when I put myself out there and volunteered for unique roles and activities just like my peers, the staff smiled back at me, marked me down for my desired role, and found ways to accommodate my needs.

Taking place in a vast, square area downstairs where stairways, doors to the kindergarten playground, and halls all met, that first dance rehearsal remains in my memory. With "Surfin' U.S.A." playing softly on a portable radio seated on the jade carpet, Mrs. McVerry guided us through the choreography, showing us how she wanted us to come forward from the middle of the stage together before striking our best surfer positions. Everyone hopped and pivoted, bending their knees as they threw their arms out to either side, moving them up and down as if trying to balance while riding a wave. Observing the movements of their upper bodies, I made the same arm motions, flinging them out to the side and tilting slightly to the right and to the left as if attempting to maintain balance.

"That's perfect, Meg. Good," Mrs. McVerry exclaimed, switching her surfing motions to swimming movements. "Okay guys, now swim . . . swim . . . swim . . . swim!"

She led us through the front stroke before having us transition into the backstroke. As we paddled into the chorus ("Everybody's gone surfin', surfin' U. S. A. . . ."), our teacher stopped us, taking a moment to contemplate our next step.

"Meg," she finally said, looking to be deep in thought. "Can you show me how you do a circle with your chair?"

Moving forward out of the semicircle of dancers, I spun around, holding my joystick to the side and stopping when I was facing her again.

"Good! I want you to do that when you guys sing 'inside outside U. S. A.' Come forward at 'Everybody's gone surfin'.' I'll cue you too."

I loved this move. It was unique, and I was the only one with the means to do it. Perhaps it was my teacher's way of celebrating my disability, showing the audience that, yes, my dance moves differed from everyone else's but that this could be a positive attribute. Each time I twirled during the show, the audience roared louder, reaching an apex as I straightened the chair out and drove into the opening of the semicircle the other dancers had formed during my last loop. Throwing my hands up in the air as those surrounding me struck surfer poses, I beamed as thunderous applause filled my ears.

"I loved your doughnuts," audience members exclaimed after the show.

I smiled, amused at the way they had worded my onstage claim to fame.

Photo Credit: Anne Mulville Moore

384

This would only be one of my signature moves on stage, though. Late in fourth grade, students attended an assembly where the band and orchestra conductors showcased the instruments the school offered to teach fifth graders. Joining either of the two groups was not required, but the option was typically popular among the students.

As I watched the teachers play a few notes on each instrument, I tried to envision myself producing melodies on them. It was not a question of whether I was joining one of the ensembles. I wanted to know the foreign language of music—to be literate in notes and to be able to translate them into the beautiful sounds I always loved listening to.

The question was which instrument would best suit me. As I watched the teachers' demonstrations, I began to weed out the instruments that didn't seem to fit. I started with the wind instruments, since I had trouble coordinating my muscles to produce elongated breaths—an effect of my cerebral palsy that I continuously worked on improving in my occupational and speech therapies. I knew that with practice and the help of my therapists, playing a wind instrument was possible and would become easier after a while. It would take time to reach that point, though, and I wanted my experience of learning to play an instrument to be focused on the music, not on working toward producing the breath needed to play each note.

Although I wasn't completely sold on playing them, I decided to list the drums as my first choice since they only required hand movements. Also, as a lot of my friends were requesting to play the drums, I would get to have my lessons with them. Unable to think of any other instruments of the same nature, I went to class prepared to request to play the cymbals and the triangle, even though they were technically not presented as options at the assembly.

"Are you sure you want to sign up for drums, Meg?" one of my aides—a different one than the aide who accompanied me to chorus—asked. "I mean, I know you could do it, but just remember that the whole band would be following your beat."

By then, I had learned to block out the naysayers and their words of discouragement to keep moving toward my goals. At the same time, my mother had always taught my brothers and me to go with our instincts when making a decision. Something was still telling me that the drums were not what I was looking to play, so I asked my aide to only put down the cymbals and the triangle.

I think the summer passed before my instrument choices were brought up for discussion again, because I recall there only being a few days before lessons began when Mom popped up in the hallway at dismissal, explaining that the band teacher, Mr. West, had requested that the three of us meet after school. We found him sitting at his desk. As his rolling office chair swiveled to face us, a wide grin spread across his face.

"Now, Meg, I was reviewing your instrument choices—cymbals and the triangle? Those are very good choices." He paused to smile. "But I'm concerned that they would get boring for you—they don't require much effort, and you would only have a short part in each song. I think you would like playing something a little more involved, so I did some thinking and wanted to show you these."

Reaching behind him, he lifted a keyboard with metal keys onto his lap. It was an instrument that hadn't been shown at the assembly. Each engraved with small capital letters at the bottom, the silver keys glittered under the fluorescent light. Introducing them as the orchestra bells—a member of the xylophone family—he gently struck a key with a rubber-headed mallet, releasing a stunning sound an octave lower than a wind chime. As the note echoed, I stared at the instrument in awe.

"And," Mr. West said, smiling at my reaction, "we ordered a special mallet with a strap for you, so you don't have to worry about losing your grip while you play. Would you like me to put it on now so you can try?"

I nodded, extending my hand and allowing him to fasten the mallet on it.

The mallet itself was a thin white stick with a small wood ball at the end. It had been slid into a white cloth tube. One side of the tube was simply the white cloth sleeve clinging to the shape of the stick. The other, where my palm was to rest, had dark gray cushioning. Attached to either end of the mallet holder was a Velcro strap that looped around the back of the hand and pulled tight with its tail. As I slipped my first four fingers through the loop and joined them with my thumb to enclose the mallet in my fist, he fastened the strap so it was just tight enough to stay on.

Looking back, it amazes me how prepared he was. I hadn't had much interaction with Mr. West before this. Brian had played the violin in the orchestra when he was my age, so I had watched the band perform during their section of the two-group concert. Most of our other interactions were simply passing each other in the hallway. I imagine he initiated a collaboration between Mrs. Odoardi to see what I had done in music class (she often had me play the xylophone as the other students played the recorder or other woodwinds) and perhaps even my occupational therapist. I always appreciated the steps they took to ensure that I had an all-access pass to Band; it immediately became a favorite activity of mine.

"Now, watch how I strike a key," Mr. West said, picking up a mallet, tapping a key, and leaving the mallet head on the key. The note came out choked, making a soft clang that lasted only a second. "See how it didn't make the sound right? The trick is to strike the key and then lift the mallet up right away. Let it bounce up like the end of the mallet is a bouncy ball."

He struck the key again, immediately moving the mallet away from it. A deep tone emitted from the instrument, echoing for a moment. I smiled as he invited me to try, and I gently hit the head of my mallet against the nearest key.

Photo Credit: Anne Mulville Moore

"Excellent! Well done," he exclaimed. "You can hit the key a little harder if you'd like—not too hard, but a little more will give you a stronger sound. Let's try this. Can you hit E, D, C?"

The notes rang out beautifully in the small office as Mom and Mr. West beamed.

"Good! Now how about D, E, E, E?" he continued, pausing for me to play. "E, E, E? And finally, D, D, C, D, E?"

"Excellent! Can you try putting it all together now?"

My mom and Mr. West applauded and cheered as the final notes of "Mary Had a Little Lamb" rang out.

I loved the way the mallet almost seemed to vibrate as I moved it from one key to the next, as if the music was transferring from the keys to my body. I couldn't wait to hit the next note and had to work hard to refrain from doing so as my mother and teacher began to speak.

"What do you think?" Mom asked.

"They're awesome," I said as she chuckled and repeated the words that had passed through my lips.

Mr. West smiled. "The real question is, would you like to play the bells for Band? I could loan you these so you can practice at home; we have another set here, so you wouldn't have to lug them back and forth to school each week."

I nodded, already looking forward to the next year in the band. As Mr. West packed the bells into their black case, he encouraged me to practice until my first official lesson. Excitedly telling him that I would, we accepted the bells and departed for home, where, after Mom set up the bells in the living room, I began to practice immediately.

"Can I try?" Brian asked as he and Sean stood by watching.

"Yeah, just don't hit the keys too hard," I said, gesturing to the regular mallets in the case nearby. Amused, I often caught them playing my instrument as I entered the room.

A few days later I found myself on stage, behind the blue velvet curtain, ready to begin my first official lesson. I was the only bell player in the band, and as the two instruments were in the same key signature, I shared my weekly lessons with the flutes. After teaching us to hold our instruments (in my case, the mallet) on our knees in concert rest while waiting for his cue to lift them just before playing, Mr. West turned to me and asked me to wait patiently while he worked with the flutes. Sitting in concert rest, I watched amazed as he transformed my friends from producing nothing but the sound of breath moving slowly down the silver flute to playing sweet tunes.

"Okay, Meg," Mr. West finally said. "Why don't you show us what you have been working on at home?"

My mallet flew across the keys at his request. I played "Mary Had a Little Lamb" followed by "Hot Crossed Buns," concluding by running the mallet across the bottom row of keys and finally tapping the high C key—the highest key. My hand and mallet dropped almost naturally into concert rest on my lap, and I smiled as the rest of the group applauded along with Mr. West, who commended me on the progress made since he saw me last.

⁓⊙∿

The small group lessons went like clockwork—Mr. West essentially split each one into sections: teaching us all how to read sheet music, working with the flutes and teaching them to play selections from the book; working with me on the bell version of the selections, conducting as I played, taking a mallet and demonstrating the melodies before I tried myself; and talking me through my notes and rhythms before having everyone try to play simultaneously. We also met weekly as an entire band.

Playing the bells with my CP was a learning curve. At home, I experimented with two-handed playing. I had trouble coordinating my movements so that both hands hit notes simultaneously—the right hand hit keys when I wanted to, but the left straggled behind, struggling to reach the keys and often striking them much later than I intended because of the heightened muscle tightness in that hand. My bells-playing career became a single-handed one.

Between the one-handed playing and the way my muscle coordination made my hand move to strike the keys slower than average, Mr. West had me play only the first note in each measure. I don't think I minded too much—as long as I got to play, I was happy.

With months and years of practice, I eventually managed to play every note in a song.

We performed winter and spring concerts. Dressed in white blouses or shirts and black skirts or slacks, everybody streamed up the stairs of the stage while I, using the ramp, traveled to my spot from backstage. Mr. West met me there, fastening my mallet onto my hand and making sure that my sheet music was situated correctly on the stand and that the student nearest to me was prepared to turn the pages for me. As he stepped in front of the band, butterflies fluttered in my stomach.

"You're going to do great, guys," he whispered, beaming at the sea of nervous band members. "And remember, don't forget to bow and wob at the end! I want to see some serious bowing and wobbing!"

Mr. West's playful word "wob" and the fun memory of everyone at rehearsal taking turns guessing its definition (which, according to our teacher, was the act of bending the body back to its upright position after taking a bow—hence the term "wob": "bow" spelled backward) sent chuckles across the stage. We moved out of concert rest at his cue and began to play (holiday-themed selections for the winter concert and springtime selections for the one at the end of the school year). The stage spotlights shone down on me and my bells like the warm sun, practically illuminating them. Even more gorgeous was their sound blending with other instruments into one melody. Briefly interrupting the thunderous applause following the last song, Mr. West closed the show by expressing to our families what a delight it was to work with us, motioning us to take our bows and wobs and telling us how beautifully we had played.

Photo Credit: Anne Mulville Moore

"You were great," Mom exclaimed when I joined her and my brothers afterward. "I remember when you guys were just starting at the beginning of the year, and it was mostly squeaking. Now you're little professionals!"

"It was awesome, dude!" Sean grinned.

"Rock star!" Brian high-fived me.

I thanked them, asking about their favorite parts of the concert. I could hardly wait until I performed again.

Our last two lessons of the year remain in my memory, but not just because of the concert praise our teacher offered and the fun, "last hurrah" selections he had us play.

"Hey, Meg?" he called at the end of the second-to-last lesson, gesturing for me to stay after the last student had departed. "I hear you're quite the writer. I was wondering if you would write something for me about your experience in Band this year. It won't be graded, and it can be however long you want, but I'd be curious to read your response. Can you do that for me for next time?"

I gladly agreed and, a week later, passed him a typed page at the end of rehearsal. He read it on the spot. I watched his eyes scroll over my words about how joining the band, learning to read and play music, and sharing this experience with my friends was a major highlight of my year and one of the best decisions I had made. His grin grew when he reached the middle of the page, where I described my thoughts about how the bells were the most beautiful instrument and how I promised to continue playing (a promise I upheld through middle and high school, college, and beyond). His laughter echoed as he read my last line aloud: "Rock on, Mr. West, rock on!" With a hug goodbye, he told me he hoped that I would keep that promise, that he enjoyed teaching me, and that he knew I would continue to thrive in my musical and life endeavors. I left grinning.

As the year neared its end, I found myself center stage before the school's population, no instrument in hand—just words about my writing and its recent publication. It was something I always dreamed would happen but never anticipated having it occur so soon.

I suppose, though, that it was a year in the making, as I had written a poem entitled "The Meaning of Life" in fourth grade. Time has eroded my memory of how the idea came to me, but I imagine it stemmed from the thought that my birth always inspires. Even at an early age, almost losing my life at birth has always made me stop every so often, not only to reflect on how fortunate I am to be here, surrounded by such love and getting to experience incredible blessings, but also to consider the purpose of my life, the reason for my survival, and whether I am living in a way that fulfills its purpose.

The memory of crafting the poem at eight or nine years old, though, still remains clear in my mind. I remember approaching my communication device on our kitchen table one weekend and my fingers beginning to drum on the screen, typing the lines bouncing around my mind: *The meaning of life is a beautiful thing...*

Long Meadow introduced students to the main genres of writing—fiction, nonfiction, and poetry—right from the beginning of their writing studies, so I had learned the basics of rhyming and creating line breaks from lessons taught in the last two going on three years. This wasn't a school assignment, though. It was just an idea that came to me in my free time, and I decided to get it onto a page as a weekend leisure activity just as I had ever since second grade.

It kind of hits you with a ping...

Time seemed to fall away as my fingertips danced over the glossy screen. I remember finishing the concluding line—*And that is the meaning of life*—and rereading the poem with a surge of positive energy and excitement within me. It was the first of countless times this sensation would come over me. Later in life, I'd recognize it as the inkling telling me I was onto something—that I had written a piece that should be shared widely and that would do well if sent out for publication.

"Check out this poem I just wrote," I said as my mother strode into the kitchen.

"Let's see," she said, coming over to read my screen. "Is this for school?"

"No, it's just an idea I had."

She fell silent for a moment as her hazel eyes took in my lines.

❧

The Meaning of Life
By Meg Moore

The meaning of life is a beautiful thing!
It kind of hits you with a ping.
But what is the meaning of life?
It comes with every husband and wife and every child in the world,
The meaning of life is God put us on this planet for a reason,
To love, to learn from our mistakes, to learn about our history,
I'm so glad he put us on this planet, and you should be too!
And every night when I go to bed, I thank him,
Because things happen for a reason,
Like people dying and people crying.
And that is the meaning of life.

❧

"Wow," she exclaimed. "This is amazing! This is really good. You should do something special with this one. Put it at the beginning of your book maybe."

"Really?" I gasped. "You really think it's that good?"

"Yeah, and it would go with the theme of your book. People would love it if they opened the book and saw this."

"That's a good idea," I said. "Maybe that could be, like, my signature as an author—have a poem at the beginning of every book."

"You're welcome," she said, making us both laugh.

I could never quite get the thought of seeing this poem in a book out of my mind. It was one of the pieces I was most proud of, and I couldn't wait to see it bound between covers.

The poem's title is the first thought to come to me a year later, when Ms. Kelly announced a poetry contest for students in kindergarten through ninth grade sponsored by Creative Communications—a company that worked with language arts teachers nationwide to promote the composition and appreciation of student poetry. Chosen poems would be published in the anthology for the specific geographic area (in our case, the Northeast). I immediately decided that I would enter—that I *had* to enter. Later in life, I realized that this was the first appearance of my "writer's instinct." Throughout my writing career, I would find that when an opportunity to publish or present my work in some fashion arose, I had the urge to jump at it, especially if I had a piece I was particularly excited about. Following that instinct often led to success.

For the next few weeks, curiosity about my submission's outcome practically haunted me, nagging at my mind while daydreaming or working on other writing.

"Hey, guys," Ms. Kelly finally said, holding up a thick pile of white envelopes a few weeks later. "The contest notifications arrived today. Congratulations to . . ."

As she began to read the names and distribute the envelopes to those whose poems had been chosen, I began to fidget, picking up pencils, rolling them between my fingers, trying to be inconspicuous in my attempts to reduce my nervous energy.

"Meg," she finally called, placing my envelope in front of me.

I don't think I stopped grinning as I left school and rode the bus home.

"Guys," I practically screamed as soon as I was off the bus. "My poem got picked to be in that book! Look in my backpack! Look! Look!"

"Nice," Brian exclaimed, high-fiving me.

"Good going," Sean exclaimed as Mom read the letter.

"Can we get one, Mom?" I asked when she noticed the book order form in the envelope. "Please?"

"No," she said. "We'll get two—one to leave out to show people and one to preserve and keep nice!"

◦◦◦

The novelty of getting accepted for publication had not worn off (nor would it ever really) when an unexpected visitor showed up at the classroom door a few weeks later.

"Hey, Meg?" Ms. Kelly called from the doorway. "Dr. Shaw is here. She has a question for you. Could you just zip out into the hall for a minute, please?"

Nodding, I backed away from my desk and made my way to the door as my aide followed with my Dyna. As I crossed the room, my friends' curious expressions caught my eye. Shrugging back at them as I passed, I began to mentally chip away at the puzzle before me: What would my fourth-grade teacher want to ask me?

Dr. Shaw played multiple roles at school—from dressing up as the leopard mascot at events to serving as the host of *L.M.E.S. Live!*

Photo Credit: Anne Mulville Moore

Each month the faculty, staff, and student body gathered and celebrated student achievements, song and dance numbers performed by the class chosen to be on stage that month, and art presentations, among other festivities, at an assembly known as Leopard's Pride. A popular segment of Leopard's Pride was *L.M.E.S. Live!*—a talk show in which Dr. Shaw and her student co-host interviewed students who had reached extraordinary success in their academics, school activities, and community service.

With this notion, I had narrowed Dr. Shaw's request down to two possibilities: Either she was going to ask me to be her student co-host, or she was interested in interviewing me when the staff and student body gathered for the next Leopard's Pride.

"Hello, my dear!" Dr. Shaw, standing with another female student, greeted me warmly in the hall. "You're looking marvelous as usual! It looks like fifth grade is treating you well!"

I beamed, and as we made our way to the bench at the end of the hall, she introduced me to the other girl, the *L.M.E.S. Live* co-host for the following week's Leopard's Pride.

"So," Dr. Shaw said, taking a seat on one side of the bench as my aide set up the Dyna on the other. "We heard your poem was chosen to be published in *The Celebration of Young Poets*. Congratulations—although I'm not surprised! You were always a fabulous writer!"

I couldn't help but grin in response.

"We're wondering if you would be interested in being interviewed on *L.M.E.S. Live!* about getting your poem published. What do you think?"

I couldn't push the "yes" button on my Dyna fast enough. Unsurprised, she thanked me and shared her plan of dropping off the interview questions to me a few days in advance to give me time to program my responses into my communication device.

After the preceding days had passed at a snail's pace, I found myself waiting backstage, trying to stop fidgeting with my purple dress. They had rolled the *L.M.E.S. Live* desk—a wooden desk decorated with a huge black banner that read "L.M.E.S. Live!" in light gray lettering—to center stage with my Dyna sitting on top. Once the student hosts of Leopard's Pride had announced her, Dr. Shaw made her glamorous entrance to the tune of the 20th Century Fox theme song as she always did. Greeting the applauding audience and calling her co-host up, she began to make small talk, chatting about how there were so many wonderful things happening around the school. Segueing into the subject of writing, she talked about how Long Meadow had an abundance of brilliant student writers.

"And we have one of those talented writers joining us today, don't we?" she asked the co-host.

"We do, Dr. Shaw."

"And who might this fabulous writer be?"

"Meg Moore from Ms. Kelly's fifth-grade class."

Dr. Shaw's request for me to join them on stage was nearly drowned by thunderous applause and shrill screams. As my chair glided over the stage's hardwood floor, the cheers amplified. A grin stretched across my face as I parked next to the hostesses.

"Welcome, Meg!" Dr. Shaw beamed.

"Thanks for being here," her co-host exclaimed. "So we hear you wrote a poem. Can you tell us about it?"

"Yes, it's called 'The Meaning of Life.'"

Over the next several minutes, I answered their inquiries, describing how the idea popped into my mind one day and attempting to convey my excitement at having the poem published in a book. They encouraged me to elaborate on how writing was my favorite subject in school and that my dream was to keep publishing my work and to write books.

"Will you share your poem with us?" the student asked.

"Sure," my device projected before reading the piece. "The meaning of life is a beautiful thing . . ."

I peered out into the sea of faces, wondering whether I could tell the audience's reaction to the poem by their expressions. Those in the front rows smiled at me as they listened. I couldn't make out the expressions of those further back, though. I spotted a few teachers rise from their seats and hurry to the front to consult the principal, Mr. Gusenburg, and the music and gym teachers, Mrs. Odoardi and Mrs. McVerry.

"Can't hear her in the back," I heard one of the teachers say.

"Is it the mic?"

"That or the DynaVox."

Slight disappointment settled in. Of course the one time I'm speaking to a big audience, the communication device fades in clarity. I think they did a sound check before the show, as my mother and school technology consultants showed Dr. Shaw and the music and gym teachers where to put the microphone so it was in range of the Dyna's speakers.

The technology malfunctioned anyway—the story that often comes with using assistive technology. I don't remember this incident dampening my spirits too much, though. I kept smiling as the poem neared its conclusion, finding myself grinning broadly again when everybody burst into applause at the end. The hostesses thanked me and, returning the sentiment, I turned to depart for the ramp backstage as the applause ignited again.

"And," Mr. Gusenburg said into the microphone from in front of the stage as I passed through the door leading back to the cafeteria. "Just to make sure that everybody has the chance to hear Meg's poem, she will be reading it on the morning announcements next week. See you in my office on Monday morning, Meg!"

Photo Credit: Anne Mulville Moore

The crowd cheered once more, and I turned to smile at him in gratitude. It occurred to me later that all of this—the interview, the

401

readings of my work, the praise—was a taste of what it would be like to be a published author. The Long Meadow staff had given me the opportunity to share my work with a large group of people in multiple ways, and I was always grateful for their encouragement and support in all my endeavors.

❧

In the latter part of my time at LMES, I found myself speaking to an audience of a different caliber. By fourth grade, my speech pathologists had identified me as a "model Assistive and Augmentative Communication device user." I had become independent in programming sentiments needed for future speaking opportunities, navigating the settings menus and operations unaided by my mother and speech therapists. They also noticed how swiftly I moved through the word prediction dictionary, keeping my eyes on the strip of everchanging words between my onscreen keyboard and message window as I typed letters and immediately spotting and selecting the words I had been looking for. They told me the way I manipulated the DynaVox was exemplary.

Jill Laudati, the Long Meadow fourth- and fifth-grade speech therapist, was the first to ask if I could participate in a live demonstration as part of a guest lecture she was giving to Southern Connecticut State University students studying to be speech therapists.

I remember entering the university building with my mother and Mrs. Laudati, rolling myself through the hall that, with a tasteful color scheme of grays and other reserved tones, looked starkly different from the elementary school's green-carpeted corridor, where vibrant artwork by students and renowned artists adorned most of the white walls. At SCSU, an occasional image of a royal blue owl—the school mascot—stared at us from the wall, and notices for academic opportunities hung like wallpaper. Each person that passed by looked decades older than I was. Butterflies took flight in my stomach, and my left hand crinkled and un-crinkled my purple plaid skirt repeatedly as my right continued to control my joystick.

"And here we are—the elevator," Mrs. Laudati smiled, pushing the button and turning to face me. "Are you ready, Meg? They'll love you!"

"Y-yeah," I smiled, trying to mask my nerves as the word slid through my lips.

She stepped into the now-open elevator, turning to make sure I got on okay. The door began to clatter shut before I even approached the threshold. Emitting a loud gasp, she dove for the door, stretching her arm forward and leaning toward the opening. It almost seemed like it was happening in slow motion, like one of those action movie scenes where the character makes a heroic dive to save a loved one. The door retracted again, revealing my speech therapist's chuckle as she watched me dissolve into hysterics.

"I don't know why I was so freaked out," she laughed. "Your mom was still with you."

"She may never let you live this down, you know," Mom chortled as I imitated the arm movement my speech therapist had used in her dive.

By the next school year, I had nicknamed her Ella Vator.

I soon found myself in front of a classroom full of future speech therapists, showing how I spoke my name and age through my device as Mrs. Laudati explained the programming I had.

"She used to have to do everything letter by letter. We just put in word prediction for her last school year, and that has really optimized her response time," Mrs. Laudati said before turning to me. "Do you have anything to say that you can type on the spot? Ooh—how about you tell them the elevator story? Do you mind if I let them come up behind you to watch?"

"No, they can. I'm good with that," I said quietly with my natural speech as my finger poked the Dyna's "Clear" button to make room for a new message.

It was always a strange feeling—one I had grown not to mind but nonetheless still felt the oddity—to have people watching over my shoulder as I typed. I began worrying that I was taking too long to produce my message, but a deep breath washed the feeling out of my system and cleared my mind enough for me to realize that they didn't care how long it took; they were just interested in seeing my process and hearing what I had to say.

As I left the class that afternoon, my ten-year-old brain ranked making the whole class, including the professor, laugh hysterically at my elevator story as my most profound accomplishment of the presentation. Later on, though, I realized the real highlight was delivering a demonstration that had the potential to help those future speech therapists treat patients with communication devices. Knowing that hearing about my triumphs and obstacles in using this assistive technology might help them to help others was the greatest reward of all.

⌒◯⌒

Mrs. Laudati and I had more than enough material to use to depict not just the victories but also the challenges of using a communication device. At the end of third grade, I had received the new model of my device after about five years of using my first one. The manufacturer later admitted that the entire product line for this model was defective, causing abundant freezing issues—which I experienced so frequently that I was sure my fourth- and fifth-grade teachers had Mrs. Laudati's phone extension memorized. Quietly padding into my classroom and to my desk, my speech therapist scooped up my device and returned to her office, parting with whispered words about having it back to me soon.

Those not involved in the maintenance of assistive technology often underestimate the severity of having it malfunction. As it is specialized, it can only be fixed by specialists rather than the average IT person (although many of Region 15's IT staff members were instrumental in helping implement solutions throughout my childhood and adolescence). If my speech therapists could not fix my device through their own remedies or over-the-phone instructions from the manufacturer in the early 2000s, it had to be shipped to their headquarters in California. The company did not provide loaners back then, so depending on the nature of the repair, this could leave me without a device for several weeks.

I don't remember feeling unbearably disappointed when this happened, although it was frustrating to need to tell somebody something, to try to slowly verbalize my words to people who were unfamiliar with my natural speech, and have them assume I was saying something completely different.

L.M.E.S. staff made this as easy to deal with as possible, though, framing the experience as an opportunity for me to work on my speaking more in the classroom in addition to my speech therapy sessions.

"Can I have the blue binder please?" I might have asked staff members, knowing that my "b" sound had been almost nonexistent because of my poor muscle coordination.

"Bear with me here," some replied. "I got the 'can I have the,' but I don't think I got the rest. Are you asking for the math book?"

I shook my head, searching my surroundings for some object of the same color and pointing to it.

"Pen?" they said as I pointed to a blue one nearby.

I shook my head but kept my hand angled toward it.

"Okay, not the pen, but something about the pen? Ink? No. It's blue. Blue!"

I nodded and moved my gesture to my binders.

"Binder? Blue binder! Got it, Meg! I swear I'll get better before the Dyna gets back."

We always ended up laughing at our little game of charades.

Some glitches themselves were cause enough for laughter. My assistive technology always seemed to be prone not only to conventional bugs; it was also susceptible to the unusual, the unprecedented, and the strange.

The "strange" came in fourth grade. My mother had picked up my friend, Ali, and me up from school and brought us back to our house one Friday for a sleepover.

I parked myself at the dining room table and pushed the power button of my Dyna as Ali slid into the seat next to me.

"So, what do you wanna do first?" I asked verbally.

Ali and I had known each other since kindergarten, and she was able to pick up on some of what I said without the device.

"Oh, I don't know. We could play, uh . . ."

She trailed off as a faint movement visible from the corner of our eyes distracted us. We slowly turned to face the device. All I had done was push the power button—neither I nor Ali had laid a finger on the screen, yet lines of letters were appearing across the message window.

"You, uh—you see that too, right?" I inquired, although Ali's expression had already provided the answer.

"Y-yeah?"

I poked the "Clear" button, but the letters remained and continued to accumulate. I held the power button down, allowing the device a moment to reset itself before turning it on again. The alphabet buttons continued to push themselves, and now a paragraph's worth of letters filled the message window.

"*Mom?*" I called.

"Yeah? I'm just about to get dinner started. Any requests?" she asked, appearing in the doorway.

"I don't know, but there's something wrong with the Dyna. All I did was turn it on—we didn't touch the screen—and it's . . . it's typing by itself."

"What do you mean it's typing by itself?" she asked, beginning to chuckle as she walked up and peered down at the screen. "Is this a prank you're trying to pull on me?"

"No—although it would be a good one if I could figure out how to do that," I laughed as Ali did the same. "But watch what happens when I turn it off and back on."

"Oh, wow," Mom laughed as the device came back on and resumed typing. "I don't know, Megatha, you and this equipment—crazy stuff happens. I'll call Jill Laudati."

My wonderful LMES speech therapists viewed my ability to communicate as being so important that they gave us their personal contact information in case any major glitches came up after school hours. Some, like Mrs. Laudati and, from kindergarten through third grade, Mrs. Moreira, made house calls if they felt the glitch was too disruptive to my communication to wait until the next school day. I always knew that was out of the ordinary—most people would not go out of their way for their patients like this—but the magnitude of it didn't occur to me until adulthood. They were taking time out of their personal lives to help us on hours probably not compensated. As an adult looking back, I wished every special needs individual could have therapists like this.

Mom narrated what we were seeing over the phone to Mrs. Laudati as the three of us stared disbelievingly at the screen.

"I know this must sound crazy," Mom laughed into the phone.

When she had followed Mrs. Laudati's instructions for a hard power reset—putting the tip of a paper clip into a pinpoint-size hole near the power button—and reported that the device was still typing by itself, Mrs. Laudati decided she wanted to see and attempt to fix this outlandish glitch herself.

As the huge gold chimes bellowed their deep, beautiful song from the center of the house a short time later, I glanced down at the screen. The typing was still going strong. The click of the deadbolt unlocking and the sound of Mom's and Mrs. Laudati's greetings had become audible as Ali and I watched the device type. We could hear their footsteps crossing the slate floor of the foyer and the three steps into the dining room. As we looked up to greet her, I could see the typing continue out of the corner of my eye.

They came around to our side of the table, and we all turned to the screen. I did a double take—in the second I had looked away, in the time it had taken them to walk around the table, the device had stopped typing, the message window had cleared itself, and everything had gone back to working normally.

"But it was typing," I said incredulously, the words projected by the device as my jaw dropped. "There were paragraphs of 'Z's and other letters. It was doing it a second ago!"

"It was! I saw it too," Ali agreed.

Mrs. Laudati laughed and did a thorough check of the device, making sure the settings were normal, typing a few messages in an attempt to trigger the device to start typing again, and restarting it to clear any quirks. When the Dyna had checked out with no technical issues, she stood up to leave.

"Well, I'm at a loss," she sighed. "If it happens again, call me, and Meg, if it does it at school, make sure they call or find me."

The next few weeks were filled with similar occurrences at school. I would be sitting at my desk, typing out my work or a thought to share with the class, when it would start up. My friends rapidly grew accustomed to glancing at me, mirroring my rolled eyes, and, if my aide had stepped out for a minute, they raised their hands, saying, "Mrs. Shaw? Mrs. Bielert? The Dyna's doing it again." After a brief phone call or after somebody had run across the hall to her office, Mrs. Laudati would come running in, only for the device to stop typing as she arrived at my desk.

"I'll catch it one of these days," she always exclaimed as we both laughed.

She finally caught it weeks later.

✺

This peculiar DynaVox experience was floating through my head when my teachers asked everyone to write a poem on a topic of our choice. Before my computer could beat me to it, I began typing, documenting my accounts, thoughts, and feelings on the matter.

"So," one of the teachers said as the forty of us assembled on the rug in the center of the room afterward. "Who would like to share?"

Everybody began to play the old "avoid the teachers' eye contact to get out of having to go first" game. Seconds passed as the teachers surveyed the class, looking for the slightest elevation of a hand. Finally, looking at the poem sprawled across my Dyna's message window, I raised my hand.

"Thank you, Meg. Go ahead."

Giggling as I pressed the message window, I looked out at my friends as the Dyna read my poem entitled "Dyna Is Driving Me Nuts!!!"

✺

Dyna Is Driving Me Nuts!!!
By Meg Moore

Dyna is driving me nuts, it is typing by it's self, I think there is a little evil elf in it.

Mrs. LaDottie called the company, the guy says Dyna's fine. Well, it's not! Not even a line that's fine!

410

I think I might punch that guy and say, I
love you a bunch!

Mrs. LaDottie, please **HELP ME
AND DYNA!!!!!!!**

Or else you'll hear me yelp! I might throw
Dyna out the window.

And if the guy still won't take it back, I'll
find a way to take away his voice.

Its his choice. Either fix the dyna or I'll
take his voice!

My classmates rumbled with laughter as the device read the comical
lines, and the adults looked at each other in awe of my overarching
"please don't take away my voice" message. Mrs. Laudati, finally
catching the Dyna in the act, placed a copy of the poem in the box
before shipping it back for repair.

Fourteen years later, my speech therapist sent the poem back to
me. Opening the file on my smartphone, I thought it would be the
poem preserved in my memory as the funny poem that had made
the whole class laugh.

What I saw through my adult eyes, though, amid the abundant
typos and sometimes-nonsensical lines, is a raw depiction of the experience of having trouble with a communication device. The poem shows
how nine-year-old me had fully grasped the idea that this computer
was my voice, my way to reveal to the world my thoughts, my intelligence, and my needs. Layers of frustration shine through, thoroughly
illustrating the challenge of not having a reliable communication

system or a timely solution. It was humbling to see this, to have these sentiments set in ink.

I also couldn't help but wonder what on earth the manufacturer must have thought when opening the box containing my device and finding an ultimatum written by a nine-year-old.

⁓∾⁓

Though it no longer typed unless my fingers drummed across the screen, the device continued to freeze throughout fifth grade. This inspired Ms. Kelly and my resource teacher, Mrs. Palios, to order my new device. It arrived at the conclusion of the year.

"We ordered it months ago," Mrs. Palios said with a broad smile as I sat in her office astonished at the monitor on the table before me. "We wanted it to be a surprise. I could have gotten purple, but I went with pink just to tease you."

"Pink is my second favorite color," the new device projected for me. "I love it!"

I looked at the screen bordered by black papery material. Beyond the black frame, rose pink–painted metal made up the thick frame, interrupted only by the black box that sat on top as the speaker.

This was my first communication device that had a built-in Windows computer—with the touch of a button, my speech software minimized to reveal a normal Windows XP operating system. With access to the internet, a scientific calculator, a second language (Spanish) in the speech software, and Microsoft Office, it replaced my need for a desktop computer at school and later enabled me to travel easily from class to class in middle and high school with everything I needed at my fingertips.

"What do you think?" Mom asked, smiling as she watched from beside me as I continued to explore the new Dyna's features.

412

"It's, like, got everything," I exclaimed, beaming as the words passed through my lips. "It's the coolest one I've had!"

"We thought it would help you keep doing all your amazing work and chitchatting with all those friends of yours," Ms. Kelly said from next to Mrs. Palios. "Can't wait to see how far you go with this one, honey!"

✑

Fifth grade turned out to be a time of new horizons for writing and talking myself into opportunities I had never anticipated.

It began with a coffee table.

Hours before some family friends were due to arrive one weekend, I wandered through our living room, absentmindedly observing the decorations—most family pictures, artwork, and awards my brothers and I had brought home over the years—that beautified the rectangular space. It all looked so cozy and kid-friendly, yet it had an elegant quality with our pastel-yellow, daisy-covered plush couches and chairs and our glass-topped coffee table with its thick, triangular sheet of glass balanced on the rough white base. Something appeared to be missing, though—something to complete the contrast.

"Hey, Mom?" I called. "Do we have any magazines?"

"I don't know," she replied from the other room. "We can check the mail pile if you want."

Wait, I thought. *I'm a writer. I can take care of this myself.*

"Never mind! I've got it."

Pulling up to the computer, I conducted a quick Google search on the most recent news events. Having absorbed the major details of the stories, I began to write, elaborating on them in a way that was my own. I organized my work into different sections and added pictures to them like a real newspaper. At the time, I had envisioned a future in

413

journalism for myself. Later on, though, I realized I preferred a style in which I had more liberty to choose my topic, angles, and genres, and I eventually fell in love with the field of creative writing. Finding a solution to the coffee table issue was my first step in exploring what it might be like to be a journalist.

After my articles were in order, I sat back for a moment, looking at the white space left at the top of the first page. I contemplated an appropriate title, one that was catchy and completely unique. What words had never been used for a newspaper title? Four letters suddenly popped into my head: "swax." Of course! It was perfect! "Swax" was a word I had accidentally invented during a science experiment a few days prior. Mr. Vesneski, our science teacher, had placed us in small groups and had given an assignment that involved observing the movement of the string of an old-fashioned tin-can telephone when sound was produced at one end. Confident in my classmates' ability to comprehend my simple words, I verbally asked them to refrain from moving onto the next question on our worksheet while I finished typing an idea for a worksheet response with my DynaVox.

"Wait," I said as I typed. "Hold on."

In my attempt to speedily compose my response, I misspelled "sway," putting an "x" instead of the "y" and only realizing when my device read it aloud. Laughter shook our bodies, and through a series of retellings in the style of the telephone game down the length of the hall, it quickly spread to the whole class.

"So what does 'swax' actually mean?" my friend pondered as the class traveled back to Ms. Kelly's room. "I mean, it has to have a definition."

"Sounds like an expression," one of the boys began. "Like 'aw, swax! Not again!'"

The crowd erupted into a fresh bout of laughter as others offered similar ideas.

"Guys," my friend Gabby interrupted. "This is Meg we're talking about here—swax is obviously what purple monkeys eat!"

My friends had thought to morph my favorite color and my favorite animal at the beginning of the year, and now the idea of associating purple monkeys with swax buzzed through the crowd as we approached Ms. Kelly at her classroom door.

"Hey, guys," she greeted us. "What's all the chitchat about?"

"Swax," the class practically sang in unison.

"It's a word Meg accidentally made up in Science," Colleen explained. "And now it's—"

"Purple monkey food," Gabby exclaimed, restarting the class's outpouring of ideas.

When everyone had finished, Ms. Kelly turned to me and simply raised the question, "Meg?"

I shrugged and nodded, giggling. She bobbed her head as if she completely understood our logic and began to laugh—and continued to do so when swax-related jokes were worked into ordinary conversations and class discussions throughout the year.

Thus, the swax inside joke was born, and stemming from it was *The Swax Report*. My makeshift newspaper, with its fancy WordArt headlines in eye-catching colors—purples, blues, and oranges—only remained on the coffee table until the end of the weekend before Mom whisked it off the glass surface. I hadn't even realized she had done so until I saw her slip it out of her purse at school. She had come in to volunteer in my classroom one afternoon, and even after Ms. Kelly had escorted everybody else to the dismissal areas, she and I stayed in the room.

"Why did you bring that?" I asked, watching her pull the pages out.

"I want to show Ms. Kelly."

"But I just did that for home. It's not an assignment or anything."

"So? It's good writing."

I responded with my best "you're such a mom" sigh.

❧

Ms. Kelly was somebody my mother and I had both grown close to, talking to her about what accommodations were helping in my schooling and which ones needed improvement, the adventures that occurred beyond school, and even sharing inside jokes that had solidified throughout the year. I always considered her a great mentor.

❧

Ms. Kelly echoed my mom's sentiments as she flipped through my pages.

"This is great, Meg! Hey, can I keep this and hang it up so everybody can look at it tomorrow?"

"Sure," I replied with my Dyna, beaming as she hung it on the chalkboard with a magnet.

She announced it at the start of the next day, smiling as she shared the title as if already anticipating the wave of laughter soon to follow. In the minutes of transition between lessons, my classmates flocked to the chalkboard to read my pages. By the end of the day, it seemed as though everybody was voicing the same inquiry: "When's the next issue coming out?"

"I don't know," I said through my Dyna, not having thought about the next issue—or even future issues in general. "I guess I could do it this weekend."

"Yeah!" my friends exclaimed.

"Sounds good! We can't wait to read it," Ms. Kelly exclaimed. "And Megster? When you have it done, bring it to me; I'll put it right up."

"Okay!"

This rapidly became my routine every week. Having created a new issue over the weekend, I brought it to school on Monday and gave it to Ms. Kelly, who took a moment to read it before posting it. The class made their way to the board throughout the day and week, and my friends and I often sat at lunch and recess brainstorming for the next issue.

I began to hunt for methods to incorporate more of my classmates' thoughts. I always loved leading discussions about literary issues with my peers. A year earlier, I had started a book club. Meeting at a local public library, I led weekly discussions about Connecticut's Nutmeg Nominees, using the page my speech therapist had helped me program into the Dyna containing conversation starters such as "What did you think of the plot twist where the character . . . ?" I was later struck by the respect that club members showed me at our meetings. The sign-up sheet I brought to school had solicited a tableful of people—probably about ten—and they never hesitated to give me the floor, continuing to talk while I typed thoughts into my communication device and stopping when they knew I was ready. They always waited for me to officially open the meetings and to suggest a plan for the following week at the end. I craved a way to bring this kind of community to the paper. The ultimate solution would appear on the last page of an issue released toward the end of the year—a colorful ad that announced an unlimited number of openings for reporters and called for a simple note to be placed on my desk with the name of the interested individual.

"So, who signed up?" Mom and the boys asked when I had gotten off the bus after school.

"Quite a few people!" I showed them the stack of sticky notes in my pocket. "All girls. A bunch of my friends."

"Wow, that's awesome!" my brothers beamed.

"All girls?" Mom asked. "So how are you doing this? Do you need to get together with them outside of school?"

"I don't know." I shrugged. "We're getting together for a few minutes at recess to brainstorm in a few days. That's as far as we've got."

"Well," she began, "you can have them over here too if you want. Do a sleepover or something."

"Really?" I gasped. "That would be awesome! Thanks Mom!"

After a night of hard work (and perhaps more fun and games than work) at our sleepover weeks later, we printed off the finished *Swax Report*. A five-person team sitting around my family's laptop, we had each chosen a section to write. The sections were each one news story, letter, or poem speaking to a school or world news event that an individual *Swax* reporter had been passionate about.

What I remember most, though, is seeing the paper up on Ms. Kelly's board, our names in bold, black fonts under the vibrant purple WordArt we had picked for the newspaper title.

It had never been my intention to start a class newspaper. Sitting there looking at the product of my one little idea that had flourished into first a regular staple of the classroom then a collaborative project, I couldn't believe the impact that reading my words had on my peers.

Photo Credit: Anne Mulville Moore

The

Swax Report

By Meg Moore, Michaela Ahern, Gabby Cruz, Briana Richardson, and Colleen O'Sullivan

Table of Contents:

2008 Reflections

The History of SWAX

Roaring Brook Field Trip

Poetry Contest

Ask Swax

Letters from Swax

Photo Credit: Anne Mulville Moore

I never considered whether my work awarded me a special ranking at school—I was just doing my best in academics and was engaging in special projects like the *Swax Report* simply because they intrigued me. On my final day at Long Meadow, I was surprised to find just how much my hard work had earned me.

I can still picture the sight that crossed my eyes that morning. My yearlong classroom chore assigned by Ms. Kelly had been to deliver the lunch count to the cafeteria and the attendance record to the nurse's office each morning. Having become friends with the lunch ladies, Shirley and Connie—who spoiled me rotten with off-the-menu lunch options and little presents at holidays—and with the nurse, Mrs. Feeney, my route took longer than usual as they all wanted a moment to wish me well in middle school.

Myself with my pals Shirley and Connie.
Photo Credit: Anne Mulville Moore

Mrs. Feeney's visit to my soccer practice

I remember rolling back down the hallway next to my aide and seeing Ms. Kelly leaning against the wall next to her classroom. Her smile broadened when she saw me, and she shifted her weight back to her feet.

"Come on in, Megster," she called once we were within earshot. "I'm about to announce the winner of the reading award."

On the first day of school, Ms. Kelly had pointed out a small glass jar and a stack of paper slips on top of a file cabinet. The slips were to be filled out with the titles of the books we had just finished reading. This was not mandatory, but the student who had placed the most slips in the jar by the end of the year received a prize. With help from Mom and my aides, I had made out a form for every book I had read that year for class and for recreation. My peers, often dropping mine into the container with theirs, seemed to be submitting them just as much as I was, so I figured it could be anyone's prize.

"Okay, guys," our teacher said as she neared my desk with a gift bag in hand. "Why don't we all gather around Meg?"

My classmates migrated to the area, settling into vacant seats or standing around the desks.

"Alright," she began. "The recipient of the reading award is a student who has worked very hard this year—someone who has made many positive contributions to the class."

Everyone peered around at one another. That could have been any of us.

"Someone who is known for her love of the color purple."

A smile spread across my face and quickly turned into laughter as my friends began to chime in.

"The inventor of swax," said one of them.

"Admirer of purple monkeys!"

"The class clown, perhaps?"

With laughter vibrating her voice, Ms. Kelly placed the gift bag in front of me and exclaimed, "Congratulations, Meg Moore!" The class cheered as she hugged me and helped me open the prize—a small figurine of an angel sitting and reading a book. My friends and I slowly spun it around to admire its elegant angles as I marveled at the thought that such basic actions—devouring as many books as I could just like I always had and submitting the slips—had caught the light of recognition.

∽℮⌇

Hours later, my final Leopard's Pride sent me before all the eyes in the school.

LMES had a "Gotcha Award" system for students who had conducted good deeds or made exceptional effort in their academics. Faculty and staff members could submit a form detailing what the student had done to deserve recognition, and the principal announced the recipients in the daily morning announcements. The student received a certificate afterward. Before every Leopard's Pride, the names of all students who had earned Gotchas since the one prior were compiled and sorted by grade level. Just before the assembly concluded, a student co-host blindly pulled a name from each grade's envelope, called the selected students to the front of the stage, and helped Mr. Gusenberg to slide a special medallion over their heads. For any student, being awarded the medallion in front of the whole school was a huge deal, but to be the fifth grader selected for the last the class would ever be awarded was paramount.

"And the recipient of the last Fifth Grade Gotcha Award for the Class of 2008 is . . ." Mr. Gusenberg moved the microphone away from his own body and held it near the co-host's mouth as the boy reached into the envelope.

My name had been pulled a year prior, and the memory of it remained vivid. A sudden wave of excitement rushed over me as Mr. Gusenberg hung around my neck the seafoam-green, ribbon-shaped construction paper award that had a turquoise paper balloon on the front. The balloon's surface was marked in Sharpie with the month I received it—April. The whole cafeteria erupted into wild applause and cheers, followed by days of congratulatory sentiments from staff and students. My family was ecstatic when I arrived home with it. Mom even hung it in the living room, where visitors admired it for years.

⌒≻⧽⌒

Now just hours before graduating from the school, my peers and I looked around at one another, shifting anxiously in our seats. Several of us had been awarded Gotchas in the last month, including me.

Each week, my resource teacher, Mrs. Palios, came into my classroom to provide extra guidance as I worked through the day's math lesson. Watching me work, she stopped me and explained the steps again if she saw me begin to take a wrong turn in the equations. My memories of those sessions were largely filled with laughter, as we always managed to invent jokes from the subject of the word problems or the technological glitches that occurred while I wrote out the problems on my computer.

"What's going on back there, you two?" Ms. Kelly always laughed as she noticed the class turning to see why we were in hysterics. "Mrs. Palios, are you causing trouble again?"

What my teachers remembered, though, is the effort I exhibited in trying to succeed in my most challenging school subject. That spring, Mrs. Palios had watched as I made a mistake while solving an equation using the forgiving method of division. Before she could ask me to rethink my steps, I noticed my error and corrected it on the spot. She whispered words of praise to me right then and surprised me with a Gotcha the next morning.

424

Just when the anticipation in the cafeteria was beginning to approach an almost intolerable level, a young voice flooded the room.

"Meg Moore!"

My mind froze with disbelief, but as if on autopilot, my fingers were already operating my chair, bringing my seat up from the floor and driving me toward the stage. I could feel a grin stretch across my face as I weaved through the sea of screaming students, high-fiving them all the way. Reaching the perimeter of teachers sitting in their folding chairs, I noticed Ms. Kelly beaming at me while she cheered and applauded. I slowed briefly to smile at her before I turned to travel down the clear path to the stage.

"That was the Gotcha I gave you for working so hard in math a few weeks ago," Mrs. Palios whispered into my ear, meeting me halfway to the stage to hug me. "I'm so proud of you! We're all so proud of you!"

Photo Credit: Anne Mulville Moore

It was as if my smile had become my natural resting face by the time I joined the line of recipients in front of the stage. I applauded as the others were given their awards, still stunned that my name had been the one fished out of all those slips of paper. To my left, I saw Mom standing by the wall, operating our camera with a grin and an astonished expression that must have matched mine.

"Congratulations, Meg," Mr. Gusenberg exclaimed as he placed the Gotcha Award—a metal campaign button medallion that hung from a red cloth ribbon and displayed a triumphant-looking cartoon leopard under the school's name—around my neck and shook my hand.

I instantly knew this was the best way to conclude my career at Long Meadow.

One last task called my attention at the school—to give back to my home away from home. As Junior Girl Scouts, my troop and I were eligible to work on and earn our Bronze Award—the highest award Scouts our age could earn and the third-highest award in Girl Scouting. For our project, my friends and I decided to redo the then-overgrown gardens. We arrived early in the first morning of summer vacation with our parents and set to work weeding the dried brown stalks. Mom transferred me from my chair into a cross-legged position on the ground, where I was able to work alongside everybody else, using both a shovel and my hands to remove the plants from the soil.

After leaving midday and putzing around a nursery together, we returned to plant newly purchased butterfly bushes and other shrubs.

"Can you imagine what this will look like when everything blooms in the spring?" my friend asked as we gazed at the garden upon its completion. "I can't wait to . . ."

"Don't worry. We'll get to see it," I reassured her, the words falling from my mouth as I picked up on the realization that had crossed her mind and caused her to trail off. "We can come back to see it."

The thought of such a visit brought a smile to both our faces.

I didn't realize then how many bitter-cold days were to come before I would see the warm weather.

Epilogue

As an individual with a disability, I have experienced so much during my young life. I have learned what it means to be accepted. I have learned to endure and overcome the pain of discrimination. Many groups of people ask for my perspective on the best way to treat disabled people. The answer I always provide is quite simple and originated from many moments in my life. One of those moments occurred toward the end of my time at Long Meadow, on the fifth-grade class trip to the Boston Museum of Science.

❧

"Okay, Mego," Mom said, parking the car in the school lot. "How about I let you out here and you can go to the classroom and check in while I park and get the bags?"

"'Kay!"

"Don't let them leave without me," she smirked as she secured me into my chair a few minutes later.

"I guess I won't . . . hmm . . . ," I breathed, quickly surrendering to the laughter that mirrored hers as I began to turn toward the door. "Bye."

"Bye."

"*Bye, Mom!*" I belted, turning halfway back around and giving her an overly dramatic wave. "*Bye!*"

Her laughter was still ringing out as I followed another student into the building.

As I crossed the blue-tiled floor of the cafeteria, my mind flashed back to the scene of Brian stepping off the bus four years prior, a broad smile stretched across his fair-skinned, freckled face as he began to describe his epic trip. It was finally my turn to embark on this famous highlight-of-fifth-grade adventure, and I hoped to see many of the same exhibits, particularly those with live animals, that he had. It was hard to know whether they would be the same, but I was certain that some aspects of the visit would closely resemble his, because I had donned an outfit almost identical to the one he had worn.

Clusters of people were strewn across Ms. Kelly's classroom, thickening as more kids and parent chaperones arrived. I found my friends chatting a few feet from the door. The conversation ceased mid-sentence as they turned to take in my appearance.

"Hey," I said, the greeting popping out of my mouth as I slid into an open space in the group while they gaped at me.

"Uh—hey!" Colleen was the first to defrost. "We're going to Boston, and you chose to wear *that*? Really, Mego? Are you *trying* to get attacked?"

"I told you I'd wear it, didn't I?" I laughed as the Dyna, on a tray before me, read my words. "And besides, my brother did it, and he made it back fine. Plus, I wear this to Shriners all the time."

"The Shriners you go to is in *Springfield*, Massachusetts, Meg! This is *Boston* we're talking about here: the heart of—"

"Exactly!"

"You're insa—"

She, along with everyone else filling the room with conversations, was cut off by a sharp "*Meg Moore!*" The parents who had been surrounding Ms. Kelly parted, letting her stride forward. The entire room eyed her as she stood with her hands on her hips and *that* look directed at me. It was as though the chaperones and my peers were watching a checkers match, peering from my curious, slightly smiling face to hers, inquisitively waiting for the next set of moves.

"Just so we're clear, if you get mugged today because you woke up today and chose to wear *that* shirt," she began, gesturing to my white button-down jersey with the navy pinstripes running down

431

its length and that navy-blue emblem sitting boldly over my heart. "That's your own doing."

I could hear a few snickers ripple through the otherwise silent room while all eyes followed my fingers as they reached down to my tray and danced across the screen of my Dyna.

"Good morning, Ms. Kelly," my device projected. "How are you today?"

The room burst into laughter as, shaking her head, Ms. Kelly cracked up and suggested that I find a bodyguard.

Photo Credit: Anne Mulville Moore

That was my claim to fame for the trip—not only was I openly and very proudly traipsing through Boston in a New York Yankees jersey but, as all my female friends who were fellow Yankees fans had forgotten to don their gear that morning, I was the sole girl in the fifth grade sporting the attire, even sitting in the center of a few dozen boys dressed in jerseys as Mom snapped a picture. Passersby could not resist commenting as my friends and I followed Mom from exhibit to exhibit and as we watched and even participated in demonstrations involving super magnets and more. By the end of the day, we had heard everything from "Let's go Sox!" to "You've got a lot of guts wearing that around here, kid."

Photo Credit: Anne Mulville Moore

Years after returning home, these encounters replayed in my mind, and a key highlight, aside from the jokes and laughter, stood out to me. My exchanges, compared with the ones had by the boys who also wore Yankees apparel, were equal. People addressed me in the same manner they did the others. They did not hesitate to approach me with a joke. They did not see a "poor little girl in a wheelchair," as some do. All they saw was me—a girl who was making a comical statement. That is how I always wanted to be treated and how it always should be.

433

Acknowledgments

I am blessed to have an abundance of loved ones who have supported me through the journey of producing this book. The number of supporters far exceeds what this page contains.

Thank you to my mother, Anne Mulville Moore, for the countless interviews she partook in about my early life, for reading and critiquing the full manuscript of this book, for gathering photos, and for her overall support during the writing and publication processes.

Thank you to the Fairfield University Department of English and to the faculty of Fairfield University's Master of Fine Arts in Creative Writing Program; to my mentors, Michael C. White, Sonya Huber, Carol Ann Davis, Dinty W. Moore, and Adriana Pàramo; along with so many workshop instructors—Eugenia Kim, Susan Muaddi Darraj, Lynn Strong, Phil Klay, and Baron Wormser. I could never have produced a book of this quality if I didn't have your support, pushing me to become a writer who is stronger than I ever knew was possible. Thank you for always believing in my work and in me.

Thank you to the Fairfield University administration, Jesuit Community, and Campus Ministry for their support of my education, faith, community service, writing, and career endeavors.

Thank you to Mrs. Rose Marie Ahern for inspiring me to write this book, to Mr. Richard Gusenburg for his incredible support of my educational and writing ventures, to Dr. Susan Shaw and Mrs. Debra Caleca for always being there to celebrate my greatest achievements with my family and me, to Mr. David Luhman, my high school creative writing teacher who mentored me as I wrote the first real draft of this book, and to the entire Region 15 and Long Meadow Elementary School faculty and staff for their amazing support.

Thank you to Robert Berchem and Bryan LeClerc for guiding me as I developed this book in college and graduate school and pursued publication afterward. Words cannot describe how much I appreciate having phenomenal fellow Fairfield University alumni to support me.

Thank you to Craig "Doc" Kazin and Russ Mitchell for assisting in marketing and obtaining endorsements for this book.

Finally, a huge thank-you to the Woodhall Press team, David LeGere, Christopher Madden, Matthew Winkler, Miranda Heyman, Colin Hosten, our cover and layout artists, and our interns. Working with you as an editor and marketing coordinator has been amazing, but becoming an author with such a fantastic, dedicated, and diligent team behind me is paramount. Thank you for all that you do!

About the Author

Margaret Anne Mary Moore is a summer 2022 graduate of Fairfield University's Master of Fine Arts in Creative Writing Program, where she earned a degree in creative nonfiction and poetry. A 2020 magna cum laude graduate, she holds a bachelor's degree in English/creative writing with a minor in psychology from Fairfield University. Margaret is an editor and the marketing coordinator at Woodhall Press and also works as an ambassador for PRC-Saltillo. She has been featured on NBC Connecticut and WFSB News and delivers presentations at national and international writing conferences. Her writing has appeared or is forthcoming in *America Magazine, Brevity*'s Nonfiction Blog, *Kairos: A Journal of Rhetoric, Technology, Pedagogy,* and *Independent Catholic News* among other publications. Margaret lives in Middlebury, Connecticut.